National Trust
Complete Traditional Recipe Book

National Trust
Complete
Traditional
Recipe Book

Sarah Edington

For John

First published in the United Kingdom in 2006
Revised and expanded edition first published in 2010
by National Trust Books, an imprint of Pavilion Books Company Ltd
1 Gower Street
London
WC1E 6HD
www.pavilionbooks.com

This edition published in 2014 for WHSmith

ISBN 9781909881297

A CIP catalogue record for this book is available from the British Library.

10 9 8 7 6 5 4 3 2 1

Printed and bound by Mission Productions Ltd, Hong Kong
Reproduction by 1010 Printing International Ltd, China

Photography: Tara Fisher
Home economist: Jane Suthering

This book can be ordered direct from the publisher at the website www.pavilionbooks.com, or try your local bookshop. Also available at National Trust shops and www.nationaltrustbooks.co.uk.

Contents

Introduction

Welcome to the *National Trust Complete Traditional Recipe Book*. This book is a celebration of British cooking, complete in the sense that it contains recipes across the whole spectrum of traditional British food – from soups to drinks, via fish, meat and vegetable dishes, together with sweet and savoury sauces. Those high spots of British cooking, puddings and teatime recipes, are also well represented, with more than 50 recipes for hot and cold puddings, and more than another 50 recipes for breads, tea breads, cakes, scones and biscuits. We have not forgotten recipes for preserves, drinks and even confectionery. The recipes are mostly modern versions of traditional recipes from all over England, plus some recipes from other parts of the United Kingdom. They reflect two strands of cooking – the 'posh', and the more homely. Recipes from the more prosperous kitchens were those most likely to be written down, but we also know the basic ingredients for pottage, the ancestor of soup – vegetables for the less well-off, fish or meat for the rich – and there are modern recipes for pottage, and for soup, here. Much baking, especially on a griddle, was done in the poorest homes with only a simple hearth, as well as in the well-equipped kitchens of the grander households. So you will find griddle recipes for Welsh Cakes, Drop Scones and the delightfully named 'Singin' Hinnies'. Some recipes are elaborate and take time, but some are very simple. A number of these recipes have hardly changed in hundreds of years, while others are modern versions of the original. At the top of each recipe I have provided a short explanation of why I have chosen it, how it got its name or its history.

The original sources for this book are four books of recipes that I collected between 1986 and 1992, from cooks in restaurants attached to National Trust properties all over England, Northern Ireland and Wales. I was inspired by what I found on that journey: across the length and breadth of the United Kingdom, cooks were preserving culinary traditions. Not only that, but they were using the excellent ingredients that we take for granted in this country, they were cooking classic recipes and they were making them their own. Not every recipe given to me was suitable for this book. Some recipes, like lasagne for instance, are traditional to other cultures and have been adopted by ours. Some recipes were repetitious: I had no less than seven recipes for Apple Cake, and had to choose just two. Some recipes, particularly those for special-occasion food with expensive ingredients, were not in my original books, because the cooks I had spoken to had needed to keep to a strict budget. These recipes, and others that deserved inclusion, have been gleaned from a rich variety of sources. I have delved, fruitfully, into other cookbooks published by the National Trust, and I have myself cooked professionally for twenty years for other peoples' weddings, birthdays and special events. Other cooks gave me their recipes and I have devoured – it seems an appropriate word – a huge number of cookbooks, published over the last 200 years or so. Inspiration has come from all quarters. Some omissions are, I admit, subjective. I remember, with something approaching horror, the brawn I was forced to eat as a child; the smell of the pig's head cooking, and the result – gristly pieces of pig, some still with bristles on it, suspended in opaque jelly. So there is no recipe for brawn in this book, nor is there much for offal. Lovers of milk puddings can pick holes in this book, too, because there is no sago, no semolina and no tapioca. The preserve recipes here make up a small shelf only, and there are many more puddings and teatime recipes than I could include. I collected most of the recipes here over a period of 18 years. I did not ask their authors whether they invented them, or whether they wrote down recipes their grandmothers, mothers or friends had given to them. I was simply interested in whether they tasted good. I found – to paraphrase Mark Twain's telegram after reading his own obituary in *The Times* – that 'reports of the death of British Cooking are greatly exaggerated – it is alive and well.'

Cooking on the AGA

The AGA is manufactured from cast iron at the Coalbrookdale Foundry in Shropshire and works on the principle of stored heat, which is replenished automatically. With an AGA, there are no knobs or dials to turn up or down, as each part of the AGA is at a pre-set heat, so you cook by placing food in the appropriate oven. It is in fact a very easy way of cooking. Cast-iron ovens have long been acclaimed for their cooking excellence, as heat is radiated on to the food, which retains its natural succulence. The all-round heat is kinder to food.

An AGA can have two, three or four ovens, depending upon the model. The Roasting Oven is the hot oven for bread, pastries, roasting, scones, grilling and anything that requires a high heat, situated at the top of the oven. The Baking Oven is set at a moderate heat and is used for cakes, biscuits, medium roasting and potato-topped pies; the Simmering Oven is set at a low heat for casseroles, stocks, milk pudding, steamed root vegetables, slow-cooked roasts and steamed puddings. It is often used as a continuation oven: food is heated up first before being placed here. The Warming Oven is used for warming plates and serving dishes, keeping cooked food hot and drying out meringues and apple slices. There are two large hotplates: the hot one is the Boiling Plate, used for quick cooking and toast, while the Simmering Plate is used for more gentle cooking, such as making sauces. Some foods, such as drop scones or toasted sandwiches, can be cooked directly on this plate.

In 1922 Dr Gustav Dalen, a Swedish physicist and Nobel Prize winner, invented and patented the AGA, which took its name from his Aktiebolaget Gas Accumulator Company. He designed it so that 80% of the cooking takes place in the ovens rather than on the hotplates. Once you have taken that on board, you will never lose heat again – you cook in the AGA, not on it. AGA owners need to think of the Roasting Oven floor as an extension to the hotplate and use it to fry things such as onions and bacon. The AGA uses stored heat to cook, so my big tip is to keep the lids down and cook as much as possible in the ovens, which has many advantages: it reduces the need for cleaning, minimises cooking smells in the kitchen, reduces 'cooking stress' as radiant heat gives you more leeway, and there is less need for so much checking.

One of the myths about AGA cooking is that it is only good for stews and slow cooking. While it is brilliant for slow cooking, it is also fast for pizzas and perfect for quick cooking such as frying scallops directly on the Simmering Plate. The runners in the ovens are counted from the top down. If you have a three- or four-oven AGA, then use the Baking Oven when a recipe calls for things to be baked at 180°C. However, there are some exceptions to this rule, such as rich fruit cakes, which need long, slow cooking and are better baked in the Simmering Oven.

When you use the AGA to make preserves, do it when it is at its hottest. Soften the fruit in the Simmering Oven and use the Boiling Plate for a good rolling boil to achieve an excellent set.

Just keep your lids shut and your ovens hot, and there is nothing that an AGA cannot cook.

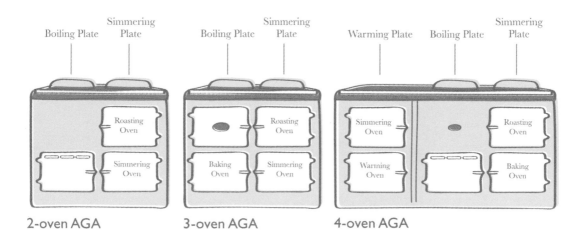

2-oven AGA   3-oven AGA   4-oven AGA

Soups

'Soup of the evening – beautiful soup' sang the Mock Turtle, in Lewis Carroll's Alice in Wonderland. And soup is fine for every other time of day, as well. Since man or, more probably, woman discovered that food cooked in water tasted good, everyone has eaten soup.

But it wasn't always called soup here. In Britain, in the Middle Ages, soup was called pottage, and was a staple part of everyone's diet. Made from meat or fish (or just vegetables, for the poor), cooked in water or broth that was thickened with oatmeal or bread, it was both filling and nutritious – the food of life. Then, as now, it was difficult to tell where pottages stopped and stews began, and the three recipes described as pottage in this book were certainly intended as main courses.

There are soups in this chapter that are direct descendants of pottage. Scotch Broth is one – it is a complete meal of meat, vegetables, barley and parsley. Sometimes the broth contained potatoes or dumplings as well, to fill up the hungry. Others closely related are Vegetable Barley Broth and Cock-a-Leekie Soup, while Chicken Noodle Soup is a more modern descendant. Cook any of these recipes and you need look no further for your nutritional needs. Some vegetable pottages can be found in the chapter on Vegetables and Side Dishes.

The description 'soup' came into use in the 16th century, at about the same time as the dish began to change, becoming thinner and less homely. At the same time, the pottages that were now called stews or ragoos became more solid, more elaborate, and joined the main courses. A soup was now considered as an appetiser, or opening course, for a large meal. It was the 'removed course' – the empty bowls being taken away before the main eating began, as they are today. Golden Cider Soup and Asparagus Soup are these kinds of soups – both use ingredients local to their origin, and are elegant enough for the grandest table.

Soups are often made to use up a glut of ingredients. Derbyshire Carrot Soup results from the arrival, at certain times of year, of quantities of fine-flavoured, locally grown carrots. I make Game Soup when I am lucky enough to have been given some game, and after we have eaten it roasted or casseroled and still have some leftover meat. Other soups in this chapter also use up leftovers, though not in the gloomy, 'better use them up' sense. Pea and Ham Soup and Butterbean and Ham Soup both require chopped ham. Elsewhere in this book you will find a recipe for Gammon Poached in Cider with Clove and Mustard Glaze (see page 106), and a gammon is nearly always too big for one meal. Cold ham is all part of the pleasure, but save some to make these soups, using the wonderful cider-flavoured stock that you have left after cooking the ham. Stilton and Onion Soup is perfect for early January, when the Stilton cheese bought for Christmas is still fine, but everyone has seen it too often.

Some medieval soups were thickened and flavoured with almonds. The almond soups here are Celery and Almond, where almond is the predominant flavour, and Cauliflower and Almond, where it is used more as a thickener. The use of herbs in soups also stretches back across the centuries. Dame Alice Soup is based on a very old recipe. It is named after Dame Alice Whitgreave, who sheltered the young Charles II while he was on the run after the Royalist defeat at Worcester in 1651. Celery seeds are an essential ingredient of this soup, and the recipe also uses bay leaves, fresh thyme and parsley. Green peas team up naturally with mint in Green Pea and Mint Soup, while aromatic rosemary is in both Rosemary Soup and Tomato and Rosemary Soup, where it perfectly complements the flavour of tomato.

Mulligatawny Soup is a tasty curiosity, with Indian roots. There is no tradition of a 'soup course' in Indian cookery, and Indian meals are taken as ours were before the 19th century, with all the dishes placed on the table at once, so that guests may pick and choose what they want. Mulligatawny is a derivation of the Tamil words *milagu-tannir*, meaning 'pepper water', a soup that developed into a more hearty dish, to please the British palate. It is slightly Indian and slightly British, like that other stalwart of Anglo-Indian cuisine, Kedgeree (see page 58).

I love the idea of wild food, and collecting and eating my own food is one of my greatest pleasures. The cliffs near my Devon home have crops of delicious mushrooms which we have collected over many years. When we tire of mushrooms on toast, or with bacon, we make the Mushroom Soup recipe in this book. Mushrooms are at their best in the early autumn, but the beautiful green Nettle and Watercress Soup must be made in the spring when the nettle tops are young. Nettle tops can't be bought, but asparagus can – even so, the Asparagus Soup is still best made in May when the English season, so tantalisingly short, is in full swing. I think the taste of home-grown asparagus can't be improved on – and, of course, the price is more reasonable.

There are two recipes for stock in this chapter (pages 15 and 33). Additionally, homemade chicken stock is an essential for Chicken Noodle Soup. Many other soup recipes specify vegetable stock as an ingredient. Of course you can use instant stock but there may be occasions where you want to control, for example, exactly how much salt is in your stock – and the recipes here let you do that.

Soup is a dish that is easy to prepare, almost impossible to spoil, and often uses inexpensive ingredients – and it brings the cook compliments out of all proportion to the effort and cost involved.

Nettle and Watercress Soup

Make this soup in the spring or early summer and use only the young new shoots of the nettles, which incidentally have the fiercest sting. Use rubber gloves to collect them. Once cooked, the sting disappears. If you have a stream that grows watercress nearby as well, you nearly have food for free in this green soup, high in iron and vitamins A and C.

Serves 4

175g (6oz) nettle tops
25g (1oz) butter
1 medium onion,
   finely chopped
1 litre (1¾ pints)
   vegetable stock
1 bunch of watercress
300ml (½ pint) creamy milk
Pinch of chilli pepper
Salt and pepper to taste
Rind and juice of
   half a lemon

For garnish
Single cream
Paprika

Pick only young, tender nettle tops and wash well. Cook over a low heat just in the water they hold on their leaves until they are tender. Drain in a colander. Melt the butter in a large pan over a low heat. Add the onion and cook gently until it is soft but not brown. Pour in the vegetable stock. Add the cooked nettle tops and stir so they are well mixed in. Roughly chop the watercress and add to the pan. Bring to the boil and simmer for 5 minutes. Liquidise the soup, which should be a rich, dark green purée. Season with the chilli, salt and pepper and add the milk. Last of all, stir in the rind and juice of the lemon. Serve with a swirl of cream and a dusting of paprika.

AGA method

Cook as above using the Simmering Plate. Bring back to the boil on the Boiling Plate then transfer to the Simmering Plate for 5 minutes.

Vegetable Stock

Vegetable stock is an essential ingredient of many soup recipes. The perfectly acceptable shortcut is to use instant vegetable stock, in either liquid, cube or granule form, but there may be occasions when a homemade vegetable stock is preferred, for instance when preparing fresh food for babies or when cooking for someone with a food intolerance, or just when you want to use the real thing.

2 large leeks
2 large carrots
2 large onions
1 celery head
2.5 litres (4 pints) water
1 teaspoon salt
8 peppercorns

Peel as necessary and chop all the vegetables. Put in a pan, add water, salt and peppercorns. Bring to the boil and simmer uncovered for 20 minutes. Allow to stand until cool, then strain and use as necessary.

This stock will keep well in the fridge for at least two weeks. You can also freeze it.

AGA method

Cook as above on the Boiling Plate then transfer to the Simmering Oven for 25–35 minutes.

Vegetable Barley Broth

Barley is the oldest cultivated cereal in Europe and the Near East. It was supplanted by wheat, which makes better bread, but has retained its importance in soups, stews and barley water (see page 404). This is a main-course soup from Northumberland – traditional fare to keep out the cold winds from the North Sea. Northumbrians say 'You should be able to stand your spoon up in it.'

Serves 6

1.2 litres (2 pints) strong
    vegetable stock
25g (1oz) pearl barley
25g (1oz) red lentils
1 carrot, peeled and grated
1 onion, peeled and finely
    chopped
1 leek, finely chopped
½ medium turnip, peeled
    and grated
1 celery stick, finely chopped
½ red pepper, finely
    chopped
Salt and pepper to taste

For garnish
Chopped parsley
Grated hard cheese

Put everything in a large pan, bring the mixture to the boil, then cover the pan and simmer for at least an hour. Season to taste. Everything should be well cooked and the flavour of the mixed vegetables brought out. Serve piping hot, sprinkled with chopped parsley and grated cheese, allowing a large bowl per person. The Leek and Onion Scones on page 315 go very well with this sustaining soup.

AGA method

Heat the large pan on the Boiling Plate and boil for 3 minutes. Transfer to the Simmering Oven for 1½–2 hours. Check after 1 hour and continue as above.

Rosemary Soup

Rosemary soup is breathtakingly simple but gives a subtle, sophisticated, creamy soup fit for any dinner party. Make it with the young rosemary leaves of early summer, which are especially fragrant. You can vary the amount of rosemary according to taste. I love rosemary and use four sprigs for a strong flavour. I am in good company. In the 16th century, Sir Thomas More wrote, 'I lett it runne all over my garden walls, not onelie because my bees love it but because it is the herb sacred to remembrance and therefore friendship.'

Serves 6

600ml (1 pint) milk
7.5cm (3in) rosemary sprig
25g (1oz) butter, chopped
25g (1oz) Cheddar cheese, chopped
A little extra rosemary for garnish

For the vegetable purée
1 medium onion, finely chopped
1 tablespoon sunflower oil
450g (1lb) potatoes, peeled and chopped
600ml (1 pint) vegetable stock

In a pan bring the milk up to the boil with the rosemary. Turn off the heat, cover the pan and allow the milk to stand for at least an hour to infuse. While the milk is infusing, make the vegetable purée as follows. Sauté the onion gently in the oil in a large pan until it is soft but not coloured. Add the potatoes and the vegetable stock. Bring the mixture to the boil, reduce the heat and simmer until the potato is cooked. Purée the mixture.

After an hour, discard the rosemary and add the milk to the vegetable purée (see above). Reheat gently to just below boiling. Mix in the butter and cheese and serve immediately with a little chopped rosemary added to each soup bowl.

AGA method

Bring the milk and rosemary to the boil on the Boiling Plate, cover and stand at the back of the AGA for an hour to infuse. Heat up a frying pan on the Roasting Oven floor, then soften the onions with the oil on the Roasting Oven floor for about 5–8 minutes. Add the potatoes and vegetable stock, bring to the boil on the Boiling Plate, then place in the Simmering Oven for 20–25 minutes. Continue as above.

Cauliflower and Almond Soup

The almonds in this soup not only add to the subtle blend of flavours, they also help to give the soup its rich, creamy texture. Ground almonds or hazelnuts were often used in medieval cookery to thicken sauces and soups, so this recipe may have a long history.

Serves 4–6

75g (3oz) butter
1 medium onion, peeled
    and chopped
1 medium cauliflower,
    divided into florets
110g (4oz) flaked almonds
¼ teaspoon nutmeg
¼ teaspoon turmeric
850ml (1½ pints)
    vegetable stock
Salt and pepper to taste

Melt the butter in a large pan. Sauté the onion until soft but not coloured, then add the cauliflower, almonds (retain a few almonds to garnish when serving), nutmeg and turmeric. Stir well so that all the ingredients are thoroughly combined and cook gently for 5 minutes. Add the vegetable stock, bring to the boil, cover the pan, reduce the heat and simmer until the cauliflower is cooked. Blend the soup until it is smooth, then season with salt and pepper to taste. Reheat if necessary and serve with a scattering of toasted almonds on the top.

AGA method

Heat up a large frying pan on the Roasting Oven floor. Add the butter and cook the onions until soft but not coloured on the Roasting Oven floor for 5–8 minutes. Move the pan to the Simmering Plate, add the cauliflower and other ingredients as above, and cook for 5 minutes.

Add the stock, bring to the boil on the Boiling Plate then move to the Simmering Oven for 15–20 minutes or until the cauliflower is cooked. Finish as above.

Dame Alice Soup

This is based on a very old recipe and is named after Dame Alice Whitgreave. She was the mother of Thomas Whitgreave, known as 'the preserver', who sheltered the future Charles II in Moseley Old Hall, Staffordshire, in 1651. The young prince was on the run with a price on his head after his disastrous defeat at the Battle of Worcester. Did she cook him a soup like this? We shall never know. We do know that Charles escaped to France disguised as a serving man to Jane Lane, a neighbour, and you can still read his letter of thanks at Moseley Old Hall.

Serves 4–6

1 small onion, peeled and
    chopped
2 small carrots, peeled and
    chopped
50g (2oz) butter
1 bay leaf
1 teaspoon celery seeds
    (these are essential)
1 teaspoon fresh thyme
1 teaspoon fresh parsley
6 peppercorns
50g (2oz) plain flour
600ml (1 pint)
    vegetable stock
250ml (9fl oz)
    full cream milk
½ teaspoon Marmite
Salt and pepper to taste

Fry the chopped onion and carrots in the butter in a large pan for a minute or two. Add the bay leaf, celery seeds, thyme, parsley and peppercorns, and continue to cook to bring out the flavours of the herbs. Stir in the flour, add the stock and bring to the boil, stirring frequently. Cover the pan and simmer gently for 15 minutes. Pour in the milk, season with salt and pepper and stir in the Marmite. Bring almost to the boil and serve.

AGA method

Cook as above on the Simmering Plate. When the stock is boiling, transfer the saucepan to the Simmering Oven to simmer for 15 minutes. Pour in the milk and continue as for the recipe above, using the hotplates.

Leek Soup with Cream

The delicate flavour and texture of leeks makes for particularly good soup. There's no waste here either – you can use the whole of the leek, including the green tops. Competitions are held in Northumbria to see who can grow the largest leek. However, you are better off with younger, slender leeks for this soup.

Serves 4

1 large onion, peeled and
     chopped
700g (1½lb) leeks, peeled
     and chopped
50g (2oz) butter
25g (1oz) plain flour
425ml (¾ pint) chicken or
     vegetable stock
425g (¾ pint) milk
Salt and pepper to taste

For garnish
1 tablespoon cream per
     serving
Chopped parsley

Wash any grit off the leeks and sauté with the onion gently in the butter until soft but not coloured. Add the flour and stir well, then add the stock and milk, cover the pan and simmer until the vegetables are cooked. Taste and season with salt and pepper. This soup can either be liquidised at this point or served as it is. Either way it is nicest with a spoonful of cream added at the last minute and a scattering of chopped parsley.

AGA method

Cook the leeks and onions in the butter on the Simmering Plate, then add the flour and liquids. Bring to the boil, cover and transfer to the Simmering Oven for about 15–20 minutes.

Stilton and Onion Soup

Stilton is a protected cheese, its manufacture limited to an area on the borders of Leicestershire, Rutland and Derbyshire. Its creamy yet salty flavour combines perfectly with the sweet flavour of the onion. It is also extremely good chilled, and makes an excellent starter for a summer party.

Serves 4–6

2 large onions, peeled and
    finely chopped
50g (2oz) butter
1 level tablespoon cornflour
600ml (1 pint) milk
850ml (1½ pints) chicken
    stock
225g (8oz) crumbled Stilton
    cheese
Salt and pepper to taste

Soften the onions in the butter over a gentle heat. Add the cornflour and stir for a minute or two. Gradually pour in the milk, stirring all the time, and bring to the boil. Add the stock and simmer for 5 minutes. Remove the pan from the heat and immediately add the cheese, allowing it to melt without boiling. Liquidise the soup until it is smooth. Season to taste and serve hot with crusty bread.

AGA method

Cook as above using the Simmering Plate.

Green Pea and Mint Soup

This soup, with its beautiful colour and lovely delicate flavour, is unbelievably simple to make.

Serves 4

600g (1¼lb) frozen peas
1 tablespoon fresh mint
850ml (1½ pints) chicken
    stock
1 medium onion, chopped
50g (2oz) butter

For garnish
Double cream
A few fresh mint leaves

Place the peas, mint, chicken stock and onion in a large pan. Bring to the boil, cover the pan and simmer gently for 20 minutes. Liquidise in a blender or food processor with the butter. Serve either hot or cold with a swirl of cream and a few fresh mint leaves.

AGA method

Bring to the boil on the Boiling Plate then transfer to the Simmering Oven for 20 minutes. Liquidise and serve as above.

Derbyshire Carrot Soup

The name of this soup refers to the excellent carrots grown in Derbyshire rather than a particular regional soup.

Serves 4

25g (1oz) butter
450g (1lb) carrots, grated
1 onion, peeled and
    chopped
1 celery stick, finely chopped
750ml (1¼ pints)
    vegetable stock
2 tablespoons double cream
½ teaspoon sugar
Salt and pepper to taste
Chopped parsley, for garnish

Melt the butter in a large pan and stir in the carrots, onion and celery. Cook for 15 minutes, stirring frequently, over a low heat without allowing the vegetables to colour. Pour in the vegetable stock. Bring to the boil, cover the pan and simmer for a further 15 minutes. Add the cream and sugar and season to taste with salt and pepper. Serve with a sprinkling of chopped parsley.

AGA method

Heat up a large frying pan on the Roasting Oven floor and melt the butter. Stir in the carrots, onions and celery and cook on the Roasting Oven floor for 10–15 minutes or until the vegetables are soft but not coloured. Transfer to a saucepan. Add the stock and bring to the boil on the Boiling Plate, then move to the Simmering Oven and cook for a further 20–30 minutes. Continue as above.

Country Vegetable Soup

This is a modern version of an old idea. The variety and amounts of vegetables are not set in stone – they have been chosen here for their colour as well as their flavour. If you do not like peppers or sweetcorn, just substitute something else. You need to end up with 700g (just over 1½lb) of vegetables, not including the potatoes, which are there to thicken the broth.

Serves 4

25g (1oz) butter
2 red peppers, chopped
110g (4oz) peas (fresh or
    frozen)
110g (4oz) carrots, peeled
    and diced
110g (4oz) swede, peeled
    and diced
110g (4oz) sweetcorn
    (fresh or frozen)
450g (1lb) potatoes
Milk to taste
Salt and pepper to taste

For garnish
Freshly chopped parsley
A few spring-onion tops,
    chopped

Melt the butter and sauté all the vegetables gently, except the potatoes, until cooked. Peel the potatoes and barely cover them with water. Cover the pan and boil until soft. Drain, reserving the cooking liquid, and mash until creamy. Stir the mashed potato and the potato cooking liquid into the pan containing the cooked vegetables and stir together. Add milk until you get your desired texture. Season with salt and pepper, reheat and serve piping hot, sprinkled with parsley and a few chopped spring-onion tops.

AGA method

Heat up a large frying pan on the Roasting Oven floor and sauté the vegetables in the butter on the Roasting Oven floor until cooked. Cook the potatoes on the Boiling Plate and continue to cook for 8 minutes until soft. Continue as above.

Golden Cider Soup

This recipe was given to me by the cook at Montacute in Somerset, a glorious, golden house set in lush countryside of orchards and green fields, so use Somerset cider for preference. The cider gives this simple recipe a wonderful, luxurious flavour. I have served this soup hot and cold – it is equally delicious either way. I think it is best very smooth – I know pushing a soup through a sieve is tedious, but in this recipe the result is rewarding.

Serves 6

50g (2oz) butter
225g (8oz) carrots, diced
225g (8oz) potatoes, diced
2 garlic cloves, crushed
400g tin chopped tomatoes
450ml (¾ pint) medium or
    sweet cider
450ml (¾ pint)
    vegetable stock
Salt and freshly ground black
    pepper to taste

For garnish
Crème fraîche
Basil leaves

Melt the butter in a large saucepan and sweat the diced carrots and potatoes for 5 minutes. Add the crushed garlic, tin of tomatoes, cider and vegetable stock and bring to the boil. Cover and simmer until the vegetables are tender. Season with salt and pepper. Pour into a food processor and blend until very smooth. Then press the mixture through a sieve before returning it to the pan and reheating before serving. Garnish each bowl with a spoonful of crème fraîche and a couple of basil leaves.

AGA method

Melt the butter in a large saucepan on the Simmering Plate and sweat off the carrots and potatoes for 5 minutes. Transfer the saucepan to the Boiling Plate and add the remaining ingredients. Bring to the boil, then move to the Simmering Oven for 20–25 minutes or until the vegetables are tender. Continue as above.

Celery and Almond Soup

A rich soup with a delicate flavour.

Serves 6

1 large onion, chopped
50g (2oz) butter
1 small celery head
1 large potato
2 vegetable stock cubes
   dissolved in 125ml
   (4fl oz) boiling water
1.2 litres (2 pints) milk
110g (4oz) ground almonds
Few drops of almond
   essence
Salt and pepper to taste
Handful of chopped parsley
   and chives for garnish

In a pan large enough to hold all the ingredients, cook the chopped onion gently in butter until soft but not coloured. Chop the celery into chunks and cube the potato and add to the onion. Pour in the vegetable stock and milk, cover the pan and simmer until the vegetables are soft (20–25 minutes). Remove from the heat and liquidise in a blender or food processor; add the ground almonds and a few drops of almond essence and blend for a further few seconds to make a smooth soup. Season to taste with salt and pepper. Return to the heat and serve piping hot with chopped parsley and chives stirred through the soup so that it is a pretty green and white colour.

AGA method

Melt the butter in a large saucepan on the Simmering Plate and cook the onion until soft. Add the celery and potato. Move the pan to the Boiling Plate and add the stock and milk. Bring to a gentle boil for 1–2 minutes, then move to the Simmering Oven for 25–30 minutes. Continue as above.

Asparagus Soup

Although asparagus is available all the year round now, English asparagus is a luxury food. For a few blissful weeks from mid-April to mid-June, we can buy home-grown spears and the price comes down. If you are lucky enough to be out and about in the countryside, look out for the sign 'Fresh Asparagus for Sale', and stop and buy some. If you tire of fresh steamed green spears with vinaigrette or melted butter, this soup has a beautiful colour and the authentic individual taste.

Serves 4

1 bundle fresh asparagus
   (about 450g/1lb)
110g (4oz) butter
1 small onion, peeled and
   chopped
425ml (¾ pint)
   vegetable stock
25g (1oz) plain flour
425ml (¾ pint) extra-strong
   vegetable stock (double
   strength)
Salt and freshly ground black
   pepper to taste
300ml (½ pint) double
   cream

Remove the asparagus tips and reserve for garnishing. Cut off the tough ends, scrape the stems clean and cut these into 2–5cm (1–2in) pieces. Melt the butter, add the asparagus pieces and chopped onion and cook until barely tender, stirring regularly. Add the ordinary vegetable stock, cover the pan and simmer until the stalks are cooked and soft. Whisk in the flour. When it is smoothly blended, add the double-strength stock and continue stirring until the soup comes to the boil. Pour into a food processor and blend until smooth. Season to taste.

Steam or simmer the asparagus tips very gently in water until they are cooked but still crunchy.

Return the soup to the pan and just before serving reheat. Pour into individual bowls, swirl in some double cream to give a marbled effect and scatter the asparagus tips on top.

AGA method

Cook this soup as above, using the Boiling Plate and Simmering Plate.

Carrot, Coriander and Orange Soup

Coriander and orange have an affinity with each other, and just sharpen the taste of the carrots without drowning it. We have been growing carrots in Britain since the Dutch set up market gardens here in the reign of Elizabeth I. The first carrots were pale yellow or purple – the orange carrot we now take for granted was cultivated later.

Serves 6

450g (1lb) carrots
1 large onion
50g (2oz) butter
1.5 litres (2½ pints)
    vegetable stock
½ teaspoon crushed
    coriander
2 tablespoons ground rice
Zest and juice of 2 oranges
Salt and pepper to taste

Slice the carrots and onions thinly and sweat with the butter in a large pan with the lid on until soft. Pour in the stock and crushed coriander, bring to the boil, cover the pan and simmer for 15 minutes. Add the ground rice and orange juice and zest and continue to simmer for a further 30 minutes. Liquidise in a blender or food processor, return to the pan and season to taste.

AGA method

Sweat the carrots and onions in a large pan on the Simmering Plate until soft. Move the pan to the Boiling Plate and add the stock and coriander. Bring to the boil, cover with a lid then transfer to the Simmering Oven for 20–25 minutes.

Add the ground rice, orange juice and zest and continue to cook in the Simmering Oven for another 35–40 minutes. Continue as above.

Parsnip, Paprika and Mustard Soup

Parsnips are one of the few vegetables native to Britain. In the Middle Ages, before sugar was regularly available, they were often used in sweet dishes. During the Tudor period, they were a substitute food for the poor when the grain harvests failed. Now their subtly sweet flavour is again appreciated in fine cooking. This soup has both a fine colour and a smoky, interesting flavour.

Serves 6

450g (1lb) parsnips
1 medium leek
1 tablespoon oil
25g (1oz) butter
1 heaped teaspoon paprika
   (use smoked paprika if
   possible)
1.25 litres (2 pints)
   vegetable stock
1 tablespoon Dijon mustard
1 teaspoon sugar
Salt and pepper to taste

Peel and dice the parsnips, wash and dice the leek. Heat the oil and butter together in a pan large enough to take all the ingredients. Sauté the diced leek and parsnips for 5 minutes. Add the paprika, stir well to coat the vegetables and cook for a couple of minutes more. Add the vegetable stock. Bring to the boil, cover the pan and simmer until the vegetables are soft. This takes approximately 20 minutes. Liquidise the mixture; return to the pan and stir in the mustard and sugar. Adjust the seasoning, reheat until very hot and serve immediately with warm buttered bread rolls.

AGA method

Heat the oil and butter in a large pan and sauté the leeks and parsnips on the Boiling Plate for 3–5 minutes. Add the paprika and stock and bring to the boil for 3 minutes. Move the pan to the Simmering Oven for 30–35 minutes or until the vegetables are soft. Finish as above.

Game Soup

For this recipe I am assuming that you have some leftover game. Perhaps you have roasted a couple of pheasants and are left with the carcasses, or you may have made a recipe that required saddle of rabbit and have the rest of the beast on your hands.

Serves 4–6

For the stock
1kg (2¼lb) game carcasses
   or bones (pheasant,
   rabbit, grouse or hare)
1 small onion
1 celery stick
1 small carrot
1 bay leaf
1 black peppercorn
1.8 litres (3 pints) water
Salt to taste

For the soup
25g (1oz) butter
1 tablespoon olive oil
1 small onion, peeled and
   chopped
1 carrot, peeled and
   finely diced
1 celery stick, peeled and
   finely diced
850ml (1½ pints) stock,
   made as above
225g (8oz) game of any kind
   (pheasant, grouse, hare or
   guinea fowl) diced into
   small pieces
1 small glass sherry
1 teaspoon redcurrant jelly
Grated zest and juice of
   ½ lemon

To make the stock, put all the ingredients in a pan and cover them with the water. Bring to the boil, then turn the heat down, cover the pan and simmer for at least 1½ hours. Season with salt and strain.

For the soup, melt the butter and oil in a large pan and sauté the onion, carrot and celery until softened and beginning to brown. Add the stock and the chopped game. Bring to the boil, cover, turn the heat down and simmer for 10 minutes (if you want a thicker soup, take half of the liquid out, purée it and return it to the pan). Add the sherry, redcurrant jelly and the lemon zest and juice. Heat the soup until just below boiling and serve.

AGA method

For the stock: roast off the game carcasses or bones until brown in the Roasting Oven (about 45 minutes). Then put them into a stockpot or large pot and cover with cold water. Add the onion, celery, carrot, bay leaf, a black peppercorn and the water. Bring to the boil on the Boiling Plate and boil rapidly for 5–10 minutes. Cover with a lid and transfer to the Simmering Oven for 3 hours. Skim off the fat and strain through a sieve. Add salt to taste.

For the soup: heat up a large pan on the Roasting Oven floor. Melt the butter and oil and sauté the onion, carrot and celery in the pan until soft and beginning to brown. Add the stock and the chopped game, bring to the boil on the Boiling Plate, then transfer to the Simmering Oven for 15 minutes and continue as above.

Mushroom Soup

Any kind of mushroom is fine for this soup but the best, of course, are ones you have picked yourself. There is something intensely satisfying about eating food for free, even if the soup it makes does look like a muddy puddle. Please take care when picking mushrooms.

Serves 4

50g (2oz) butter
1 tablespoon olive oil
1 large onion, peeled and
    chopped
3 garlic cloves, peeled and
    chopped
1 potato, peeled and diced
600g (1¼lb) mushrooms,
    chopped
1 litre (1¾ pints)
    vegetable stock
1 small glass medium or
    cream sherry
Grated zest and juice of
    1 lemon
Salt to taste
Crème fraîche, to serve

Melt the butter with the oil in a large pan. Put in the onion, garlic and potato, and fry gently for 5 minutes. Stir in the mushrooms and then add the stock and sherry. Season with salt to taste. Bring to the boil, then cover the pan and simmer until everything is cooked. This will probably take about 20 minutes. Purée the mixture. Don't worry if it isn't very smooth; a little texture is good. Add the lemon zest and juice and reheat until piping hot. Serve with a bowl of crème fraîche for people to stir in as desired.

AGA method

Fry the onion, garlic and potato on the Simmering Plate for 5 minutes. Add the mushrooms, stock and sherry, and season to taste. Bring to the boil on the Boiling Plate, then transfer to the Simmering Oven for 30–35 minutes. Continue as above.

Chicken Noodle Soup

Chicken Noodle Soup has a bad reputation thanks to the pale imitations you can buy in supermarkets. Made properly, it is sustaining, soothing and tasty in equal proportions. If you haven't got time to make your own stock, use chicken stock cubes made up according to the packet instructions.

Serves 4

2 tablespoons olive oil
1 large onion, peeled and
   chopped
2 garlic cloves, peeled and
   chopped
1 leek, peeled, sliced and
   washed
1 large carrot, peeled and
   finely chopped
2 litres (3½ pints)
   chicken stock
450g (1lb) cooked chicken
   pieces
1 nest of egg noodles
A handful of chopped
   parsley, for garnish

Heat the olive oil in a large pan and add the onion, garlic, leek and carrot. Fry for about 5 minutes. Add the stock and simmer the mixture for about 20 minutes, until the vegetables are cooked. Add the chicken and the noodles, and simmer for a further 5 minutes. Just before you serve the soup, stir in the parsley. Serve piping hot.

AGA method

Fry the onions, garlic, leek and carrot on the Boiling Plate for about 5 minutes. Add the stock and bring to the boil, then transfer to the Simmering Oven for 25–30 minutes, until the vegetables are cooked. Add the chicken and noodles and continue as above on the Simmering Plate.

Tomato and Rosemary Soup

This soup is simple and economical, and is good made with tinned tomatoes. Make it with fresh tomatoes and it is very special.

Serves 6

225g (8oz) chopped onions
3 teaspoons chopped fresh
    rosemary
3 400g tins of tomatoes
    (or the equivalent weight
    in fresh tomatoes)
2 teaspoons tomato purée
25g (1oz) sugar
900ml (1½ pints)
    chicken stock
1 level tablespoon cornflour
300ml (½ pint) single cream
Salt and pepper to taste
Chopped parsley, for garnish

Place the chopped onions, rosemary, tomatoes, tomato purée, sugar and stock in a large pan. Reserve a little of the stock to cream the cornflour. Add the blended cornflour to the pan, cover it and simmer all the ingredients for approximately 20 minutes. Remove from the heat and liquidise. Adjust the seasoning. Reheat and stir in the cream just before serving. Serve very hot with a garnish of chopped parsley.

AGA method

Cook this soup as above, using the Boiling Plate and Simmering Plate.

Butter Bean and Ham Soup

This is the perfect soup to make after you have poached the gammon on page 106. If you haven't got the full two litres of ham stock, extend it with vegetable stock to the right amount. You need to begin this recipe the day before you want to serve it.

Serves 6

225g (8oz) butter beans
25g (1oz) butter
1 onion, peeled and sliced
1 carrot, peeled and
    chopped
2 litres (3½ pints) ham stock

For garnish
50g (2oz) diced ham
1 tablespoon chopped
    parsley

Soak the butter beans overnight. In a pan large enough to take all the ingredients, melt the butter, then gently fry the onion and carrot for 5 minutes. Add the butter beans and the stock. Bring to the boil, cover the pan, then simmer until the butter beans are cooked, which will take up to an hour. Take off the heat, liquidise the mixture and adjust the seasoning if you wish. Add the diced ham and the parsley and serve piping hot.

AGA method

Soak the butter beans as above. Fry off the onion and carrot as above on the Boiling Plate. Add the beans and stock and bring to the boil for 3 minutes. Cover the pan and move to the Simmering Oven for 2–3 hours or until the beans are cooked. Check them after 1½ hours. Continue as above.

Mulligatawny Soup

Mulligatawny Soup originated in Kerala, southern India, during the rule of the Raj. The name is an anglicised version of the Tamil words *milagu-tannir*, meaning 'pepper-water'. It was very popular in Queen Victoria's reign, different recipes being introduced by British families returning from the sub-continent. If you make your own curry paste, the result will be even more interesting.

Serves 6

50g (2oz) butter
1 large onion, peeled and
  chopped
2 carrots, peeled and
  chopped
1 cooking apple, peeled and
  chopped
1 tablespoon sultanas
1 tablespoon sweetish pickle
  (mango is particularly
  good)
Pinch of cayenne
1 teaspoon curry paste
  (mild or hot according to
  taste)
1 teaspoon sugar
850ml (1½ pints) vegetable
  stock
Salt and pepper to taste

Melt the butter in a largish pan and sauté the onion and carrots. Add the apple, sultanas and pickle. Cook gently with the lid on until the carrots are tender. Put the mixture in a food processor and process briefly – the mixture should be chunky, not a smooth purée. Return to the pan. Stir in the cayenne, curry paste, sugar and stock and reheat, stirring all the time. Season the soup. Serve very hot.

AGA method

Sauté the onion and carrots in a large pan on the Roasting Oven floor. Add the apple, sultanas and pickle and cook gently on the Simmering Plate. Cover with a lid and cook until the carrots are tender. Finish as above.

Pea and Ham Soup

This soup is made in the same way as the Rosemary Soup on page 17. It requires a similar vegetable purée. The soup should be very thick, but if you prefer it less so, thin it down with more stock. It is a winter soup, perfect on Boxing Day after a cold, invigorating walk, made with the stock from the Christmas ham. Note: you need to start this recipe a day in advance.

Serves 2–3

110g (4oz) dried split peas
600ml (1 pint) chicken or
    ham stock
Vegetable purée (see
    Rosemary Soup recipe,
    page 17)
Salt and pepper

For garnish
50g (2oz) smoked ham,
    diced
Chopped parsley

Soak the peas overnight. Drain and cook in the chicken or ham stock. Liquidise and combine with the purée base (see above). The soup should be very thick but if you prefer a slightly thinner soup, dilute with a little more stock. Bring to the boil. Season to taste, then add the diced ham and a little chopped parsley. Serve very hot.

AGA method

Puree the base as for Rosemary Soup, page 17. Soak the peas overnight. Drain and cook in the stock according to the directions on the packet using the AGA hotplates. If the directions say to simmer for longer than 10 minutes, move the peas to the Simmering Oven and approximately double the cooking time given. Season to taste, then add the diced ham and a sprinkling of chopped parsley.

Cock-a-Leekie Soup

A famous old Scottish recipe, this is the alternative to Scotch Broth on Burns Night or St Andrew's Day. *Kettner's Book of the Table* **describes this as the modern version of Malachi, a 14th-century recipe that featured a 'Ma', the old name for a fowl or chicken. Modern cookery writers have questioned the addition of prunes, but I think they give the dish a distinctive flavour.**

Serves 4

Leg and wing joints of
   1 chicken, plus the carcass
700g (1½lb) leeks, chopped
   and washed
3 bacon rashers, chopped
1 mixed bunch of parsley
   and thyme
1 bay leaf
1.2 litres (2 pints) water
110g (4oz) stoned prunes
Salt and pepper to taste

Put the chicken leg and wing joints, and the carcass, in a large pan, together with all but two of the leeks, the bacon and the herbs. Cover with the water. Bring to the boil, turn down the heat, cover the pan and simmer for at least 1 hour, until the chicken is tender. Season to taste, then strain off the liquid, picking out the chicken meat and cutting it into pieces to serve. Put the broth and the chicken pieces back in the pan together with the stoned prunes and the remaining leeks. Simmer very gently for 15 minutes and serve piping hot.

AGA method

Put the chicken leg and wing joints and carcass into a large pan, together with all but two of the leeks, the bacon and the herbs. Cover with water. Bring to the boil on the Boiling Plate then move to the Simmering Oven for 1½–2 hours, until the chicken is tender. Continue as above, using the Simmering Plate for the final cooking.

Scotch Broth

'At dinner, Dr Johnson ate several plates of Scotch Broth, with barley and peas in it and seemed very fond of the dish. I said, "You never ate it before?" Johnson replied, "No, sir, but I don't care how soon I eat it again." '

James Boswell, *Diaries*, 1786

This soup can be a meal in itself. Originally mutton would have been used but lamb shanks are more readily available today.

Serves 4

2 lamb shanks, chopped
1.5 litres (2½ pints) water
25g (1oz) pearl barley
   (usually available at
   health-food shops)
1 large onion, peeled and
   finely chopped
2 small turnips, peeled and
   finely chopped
3 carrots, peeled and finely
   chopped
2 leeks, trimmed, chopped
   and washed
Grated zest and juice of
   ½ lemon
At least 2 tablespoons finely
   chopped parsley
1 teaspoon salt
Black pepper to taste

Ask your butcher to chop the lamb shanks into chunks for you. Put the meat in a large pan and cover with the water. Bring to the boil, add the pearl barley and simmer for 20–30 minutes.

Add all the vegetables to the pan with the salt and black pepper to taste. Cover and simmer for 1½ hours. Lift out the meat, extract the bones and stir the meat back into the soup. Check the seasoning, stir in the lemon and parsley and serve very hot.

AGA method

Put the meat into a large pan and cover with water. Bring to the boil on the Boiling Plate, add the pearl barley, bring back to the boil, and then move to the Simmering Oven for 30–40 minutes. Add the rest of the vegetables to the pan with salt and black pepper to taste. Bring back to the boil on the Boiling Plate, cover, and then transfer to the Simmering Oven for 2–2½ hours. Continue as above.

Fish Dishes

Fish tastes good, and is good for you – we are exhorted to eat at least two portions of oily fish a week. And Britain is a maritime nation, where it is geographically impossible to be more than a hundred miles from the sea. So, why is this chapter so short, compared to those for meat dishes or vegetables? There are several reasons, one being the good reason that you don't need a complicated recipe to cook very fresh fish. By and large, those people who lived by the sea and had access to fish that was 'straight from the boat' did not bother to write down their recipes.

The best place to obtain very fresh fish is as near to the sea as possible. Buy it from stalls by the harbour, in fishing ports like Whitby, Brixham or Aberdeen. Buy it, as I have done, from a fisherman with a box of plaice or lemon sole, standing by his boat on the beach at Dungeness in Kent, or from a boatman selling cod on a quay in Ireland. Fish this fresh needs only covering in seasoned flour, brushing with butter, and then grilling, frying or roasting in a hot oven until it is cooked – 15 minutes for steaks, fillets or small flat fish, or 30–40 minutes for a larger fish. The test for 'doneness' is when the flesh falls away from the bone, and is white or cream-coloured rather than opaque. For similar reasons I have no recipes here for shellfish – except Potted Shrimps and Crab. We eat oysters uncooked. We eat whelks, cockles, winkles, queens and mussels boiled, and eaten plain or with vinegar. Lobsters and crabs are best simply boiled, as soon as they come out of the sea – serve them with Mayonnaise or Green Sauce (see page 166).

In the Middle Ages, England was still part of the Roman Catholic Church and Fridays and saints' days were nominated 'fast days', when meat could not be eaten. People ate far more fish than we do today – huge shoals of herring were caught and, in winter, fresh sea fish was transported inland. 'Stockfish' (dried cod), and pickled or salted herrings were also important staples. Meanwhile, both the aristocracy and the monasteries caught carp and pike from their own 'stew ponds', and there are accounts of fish traps and weirs on many rivers.

At the beginning of the 19th century, poor people in the cities survived mainly on a bland diet of bread and potatoes. But the advent of the railways brought with it a wider distribution of food – the availability of fresh fish, often fried in beef dripping (and later with its inseparable companion, deep-fried potato chips) was greeted with understandable enthusiasm. In fact the one fish dish that probably every British person has eaten at one time or another is battered cod, or haddock, with chips.

Today, most of us buy our fish from a supermarket, partly because we are lucky if we have a fishmonger within easy reach. We probably have no idea when our fish was actually caught – how fresh it is – although we are at least told these days if it has been deep-frozen. Fish is also expensive in comparison to other foods. And, finally, we get so many mixed messages from the media – about over-fishing, pollution, sustainability, farmed or wild fish – that we can find ourselves confused. My advice is to buy from a fishmonger if you have one locally, because he or she knows the stock, and what fish is freshest and best – or cheapest – on any particular day. Sometimes, for instance, mackerel and herring are cheap. On those days, use the recipes here for potting and pickling fish. If you have to buy fish at a supermarket, choose fish from the counter rather than the pre-packed fish in the cabinet. Not only can you choose exactly how much you want – and the thickness and shape – but it is likely to be fresher.

Fish is wonderfully simple to cook with. Look at the recipe for Poached Salmon – it is absolutely foolproof. A cooked salmon can be central to several meals, rather in the way you would treat a joint of meat. Eat it warm first – a poached salmon, huge and impressive on a platter, makes any meal into a celebration. Then eat it cold the next day, and afterwards make fishcakes out of what is left. When you count up the meals one salmon has provided, you will find it is not that expensive at all.

The Salmon Pie is another dish that is perfect for a special occasion – it looks spectacular and tastes even better. Kedgeree, an Indian dish that was brought here in the days of the British Empire, was a favourite breakfast dish for the Victorians. In our modern lifestyle, with no time for huge breakfasts, it makes an excellent supper dish. Cullen Skink is officially a smoked haddock soup, but as one of those soups that is a meal in itself, it fits well in this chapter.

Some recipes reflect the regionality of fish. Stargazey Pie uses Cornwall's most famous fish, the pilchard. Not only a staple of the Cornish diet, huge quantities of pilchard were caught with seine nets 'between harvest and all hallowtide' and exported – at first salted and smoked, later canned. Incidentally, the complaint that all our prime fish ends up elsewhere is a continuing one.

So keep eating fresh fish. Not only will you keep the local fishmongers in business, but you ensure that fishermen have an income. And what could be better than eating fish? You can enjoy eating it with family and friends, and it is good for everyone's health. Perhaps fish is best summed up by Andrew Boorde, physician and writer, in his *Compendyous Regyment or Dyetary of Health*, of 1542: 'Of all nacyons and countres, England is bests served of Fysshe, not onely of al maner of see-fysshe, but also of fresshe-water fysshe, and al maner of sortes of salte-fysshe.'

Potted Crab

'Potting' – preserving cooked fish or meat in fat – is a very old process. Even cheese can be potted. This recipe comes from south Devon where crabs abound – the taste is superb.

Serves 4

2 tablespoons dry or
    medium sherry
Juice and zest of 1 orange
    (reserve 1 teaspoon of
    the zest to use in the
    clarified butter)
150g (5oz) softened butter
225g (8oz) dressed crab
    (white and dark meat)
¼ teaspoon ground ginger
Salt and pepper to taste
50g (2oz) butter
2 tablespoons water

Bring the sherry, orange zest and juice to the boil and boil hard until reduced to 1 tablespoon of liquid. Remove from the heat, cool and beat with the softened butter until creamy. Combine with the crab meat and ginger. Add salt and pepper to taste. Mix well and spoon into ramekins. Seal with orange clarified butter made as follows.

Bring the reserved orange zest, the butter and water slowly to the boil. Remove from heat, allow to cool slightly and gently spoon over the ramekins.

Chill in the fridge for at least a couple of hours. Serve with hot toast or melba toast. Potted crab keeps well for two or three days in the fridge.

AGA method

Cook as above on the Boiling Plate.

Cullen Skink

Cullen is a village in north-east Scotland. Skink means 'essence' in Gaelic. All the villages on the north-eastern coast had their own particular stews and soups, but this one seems to be the most famous – perhaps it's the intriguing name. I have put this in the fish dishes rather than the soups as it's a meal in itself. Crusty bread is all the accompaniment it needs.

Serves 6

450g (1lb) smoked haddock
  or cod
1 medium onion, peeled and
  finely chopped
600ml (1 pint) full cream
  milk
600ml (1 pint) fish stock
225g (8oz) cooked potato,
  cubed
1 small tin sweetcorn,
  approximately 225g (8oz)
Salt and pepper to taste

For garnish
Paprika
Chopped parsley

Steam or poach the fish for 5 minutes. Remove from the water with a slotted spoon. Discard the skin and any bones. Divide the fish into chunks with a fork. Use the water to make up the fish stock.

Peel and finely chop the onion and place in a large pan with the milk and stock. Simmer until tender (about 10–15 minutes), then add the potatoes and sweetcorn. Reheat until just below boiling, add the fish and season to taste. Serve immediately, garnishing the soup bowls with a dusting of paprika and a little chopped parsley.

AGA method

Cook as above on the Boiling Plate and Simmering Plate.

Salmon Fishcakes

This is an excellent way to use up leftover fish if you have poached a whole salmon (see page 60). The contrast between the crisp outside and the pink, cream and green inside of the cake is particularly appetising.

Serves 4

225g (8oz) salmon fillet
450g (1lb) potatoes, cooked,
    mashed and cooled
2 tablespoons onion or
    spring onion, finely
    chopped
2 tablespoons parsley, finely
    chopped
Grated zest and juice of
    ½ lemon
1 egg, well beaten
2 tablespoons plain flour
25g (1oz) butter
2 tablespoons olive or
    sunflower oil
Salt and pepper to taste
Lemon wedges

Steam the salmon until cooked (approximately 10 minutes). Put in a mixing bowl and flake, removing any bones. Allow to cool. Then add the mashed potato, onion, parsley and lemon. Use the rest of the lemon for the lemon-wedge garnish. Stir in the beaten egg and season to taste. The mixture is quite soft, but if you wet your hands before forming the cakes it will not stick quite so much. Spread the flour on a plate and as you make each cake (the mixture will provide eight, two per person), roll it in flour mixed with a little extra seasoning. Heat the butter and oil in a large frying pan and fry the cakes on each side until crisp and golden. Serve immediately with a wedge of lemon. The fishcakes are delicious with either Green Sauce (see page 166) or Tartare Sauce (see page 160).

AGA method

Steam the fish on the Boiling Plate. Assemble the fishcakes as above. Heat the butter in a frying pan on the Roasting Oven floor and, either on the Roasting Oven floor or the hotplates, fry the cakes on each side until crisp and golden.

Pickled Salmon (Gravadlax)

Pickling in salt was one method used not only for fish but also for meat to keep it through the lean winter months. This recipe is practical but also delicious, particularly if you use fresh dill. The salty, aromatic fish makes a perfect appetiser. Very good for entertaining, too – the work, such as it is, has been done days before it is needed.

Serves 4

450g (1lb) fresh salmon fillet, skinned
Coarse-grain mustard
1 packet fresh dill, finely chopped (dried dill can be used)
Rock salt
Freshly ground pepper to taste
Lemon wedges

Ask the fishmonger for a cut from the thick end of the fillet, and allow approximately 50g (2oz) of salmon per serving. Start this dish at least three days before you wish to serve it.

Cut a piece of clingfilm large enough to wrap the salmon in. Scatter a thick layer of rock salt on the clingfilm. Spread both sides of the salmon first with coarse-grain mustard, then with the dill, to cover the fish completely. Wrap the salmon in the clingfilm, then wrap the parcel in foil and chill for at least 3 days, turning from time to time. You can leave it to pickle for 7 days. It is not necessary to unwrap the fish.

To serve, remove the foil and clingfilm, slice the salmon thinly, garnish with lemon wedges and serve with brown bread and butter, a little green frisée and some Dill Mayonnaise (see page 160).

Pickled Herring

For centuries, huge shoals of herring have been caught around our shores, particularly on the east coast of Britain. In 1902–3, 500 million fish were caught by Yarmouth boats alone. Preserving this bounty by salting, smoking and pickling has occupied us for generations. Of course you can buy pickled herring in jars in delicatessens and supermarkets, but there is a certain pleasure in preserving your own fish – particularly if you have bought them on the quayside, as you can in the autumn in ports such as Whitby, Great Yarmouth or King's Lynn.

Serves 6

6 herring fillets
600ml (1 pint) water
50g (2oz) salt
50g (2oz) caster sugar

For the marinade

300ml (½ pint) white wine
   vinegar or cider vinegar
3 bay leaves
1 tablespoon pickling spices,
   including chilli
¼ teaspoon black
   peppercorns
1 tablespoon sugar
3 gherkins
1 mild sweet onion (Spanish
   or red), very thinly sliced

If the herring fillets are large, cut them in half lengthwise. Bring the water to the boil, take it off the heat and mix in the salt and sugar. Stir until they have dissolved. Let the mixture stand until it is cool. Roll up the herring fillets and lay them in a shallow dish, just large enough to take them. Pour over the brine and leave the fish for 3–4 hours.

Meanwhile, make the marinade. Bring the vinegar, bay leaves, pickling spices, peppercorns and sugar to the boil. Remove from the heat and leave to cool. Drain the brine from the fish. Dry the fillets with kitchen paper and re-roll each one round a piece of gherkin and a slice of onion. Arrange them back in the dish, tuck slices of gherkin and onion round the fish and pour over the marinade with the spices. Cover and leave for at least 4 days before eating. Serve with brown bread and butter.

AGA method

Use the AGA Boiling Plate to boil the water and to make the marinade.

Soused Mackerel

Brought up by the sea, I was taught that a mackerel went straight from the sea into the frying pan. The catch was unpredictable and often we caught more than we could eat immediately. The extras were soused as below and were a great treat for tea the next day (a friend of mine had another good idea, though, and disposed of his share in return for lifts as he hitchhiked back to London after a fishing weekend).

Serves 4

6 mackerel fillets
1 mild sweet onion (Spanish or red) or 2–3 shallots, peeled and sliced
3 bay leaves
1 marjoram sprig
1 parsley sprig
½ teaspoon black peppercorns
4 whole cloves
200ml (7fl oz) cider
200ml (7fl oz) cider vinegar
Water, to cover
Salt and pepper to taste

Preheat oven to 140°C, 275°F, gas mark 1. Cut each mackerel fillet in half lengthwise. Roll each piece up from the tail and lay the rolls in an ovenproof dish just large enough to take the fish. Make sure they are all facing the same way, so that the colours match. Scatter the onion slices over the fish and tuck the bay leaves and sprigs of marjoram and parsley around it. Scatter the peppercorns and cloves over the dish and season with salt and pepper. Pour over the cider and cider vinegar, and add sufficient water to cover the fish. Cover the dish with foil and cook for 1 hour in the oven. Leave the dish to cool before serving with brown bread and butter.

AGA method

Prepare the mackerel fillets as above. Put the ovenproof dish into the Roasting Oven for 5 minutes, then transfer to the Simmering Oven for an hour. Leave to cool and serve as above.

Potted Trout

The deep, cold lakes of the Lake District used to be home to thousands of char (a freshwater relative of trout and salmon). In the eighteenth century, char from the Lake District, cooked and potted with spices and butter, was often sent as a delicacy to other parts of the country. Sadly, the char were overfished and are now rare, but trout responds well to the same treatment.

Serves 4–6

2 dried bay leaves, crumbled

½ teaspoonful ground mace

¼ teaspoon freshly grated nutmeg

1 teaspoon ground white pepper

2 teaspoons salt

450g (1lb) fresh trout, heads and tails removed, skinned and filleted

125g (4½oz) butter, cut into small pieces

Preheat the oven to 180°C, 350°F, gas mark 4. Mix the bay leaves, mace, nutmeg, pepper and salt together in a small bowl. Rub the mixture all over the filleted trout, then fold the fillets in half lengthways and lay in a baking dish just big enough to hold them. Cover with foil and bake in the hot oven for 20–25 minutes. Remove from the oven and pour off and discard any liquid that has accumulated around them during cooking. Leave to cool.

Cut the cooked trout up into small bite-sized pieces and layer in a round dish, about 15cm (6in) in diameter. Clarify the butter by putting it in a pan and melting it gently over a low heat. Skim any scum from the surface and pour the butter off into a bowl, leaving behind the milky solids at the bottom of the pan. Allow to cool a little, then pour it over the fish. Cover the dish and chill in the refrigerator until needed. To serve the potted trout, cut into wedges and lift out of the dish. Serve with a green salad and thin slices of wholemeal bread. Use within 3 days.

AGA method

Prepare the trout as above and place the baking dish in the Roasting Oven, on the fourth set of runners. Cook for 15–20 minutes, or cook in the Baking Oven (on three- or four-oven models) for 20–25 minutes. Continue as above, using the Simmering Oven to clarify the butter.

Potted Shrimps

Shrimps have a delicate flavour and are best eaten as soon as possible after they are caught. Potting enables us to enjoy them for a day or two longer. If you can't find brown shrimps, you can use this method to pot crab, prawns or flaked cooked salmon. The flavour of the seafood is very important; the fish really needs to be fresh, not frozen then defrosted.

Serves 6

200g (8oz) butter
350g (12oz) brown shrimps, peeled
¼ teaspoon or one stick mace
¼ teaspoon freshly grated nutmeg
¼ teaspoon cayenne pepper
1 lemon, cut into 6 wedges, for garnish

First clarify 100g (4oz) of the butter. Cut it into small pieces and melt it gently over a low heat. Skim off any scum from the surface and pour off the clarified butter into a bowl. Leave behind the milky solids at the bottom of the pan. The clarified butter is now ready to use.

Heat the remaining 100g (4oz) butter in a pan (large enough to hold the shrimps) until it has melted. Add the peeled shrimps, spices and cayenne pepper and heat through, stirring gently all the time. Do not let the mixture boil. Take out the mace and divide the mixture between six small ramekins. Spoon clarified butter over each one. Chill until ready to serve.

To serve, unmould each pot on to a plate, garnish with a wedge of lemon and eat with hot, thin brown toast.

AGA method

To clarify the butter, gently melt it in a saucepan at the back of the AGA or on the Warming Plate (on a four-oven model). All the impurities will settle on the bottom of the saucepan. Pour off the golden butter into a bowl and discard the white bits (the impurities). The butter is then ready to use. You can store clarified butter in the fridge for up to a month. Continue to make the potted shrimps on the Simmering Plate as above.

Florence Nightingale's Kedgeree

British-Indian cuisine was very chic in Victorian Britain, as was naming dishes after well-known people. Charles Francatelli, chef to Queen Victoria, named his version of this then-new dish Kedgeree (the English version of the Indian *Khichiri*) after Florence Nightingale, heroine of the Crimean War. This dish would have been served at breakfast in the 19th century. Today, it is a good supper or party dish. I have kept pretty well to Signor Francatelli's original recipe (as interpreted by Sara Paston-Williams) but when I cook this for buffet parties, I add cooked prawns, salmon chunks and peas, and colour the rice with turmeric.

Serves 4–6

450g (1lb) smoked haddock, cooked
4 eggs, hard-boiled
1 tablespoon Parmesan cheese, grated
110g (4oz) butter
175g (6oz) long-grain rice, cooked
Salt and freshly ground black pepper to taste
Freshly grated nutmeg
2 tablespoons fresh chives, chopped
2 tablespoons fresh parsley, chopped

For garnish
Small triangles of fried bread (optional)
Lemon wedges

Remove the skin and bones from the fish and flake coarsely. Chop the whites of the hard-boiled eggs and add to the fish. Press the yolks through a sieve and mix with the cheese. Melt the butter in a saucepan and toss the rice in it over a gentle heat until well coated and heated through. Mix in the fish and egg whites and gently continue to toss until the whole mixture is hot. Season with salt, pepper and nutmeg, chopped chives and 1 tablespoon of the parsley, then pile on to an ovenproof plate. Scatter the egg yolk and cheese mixture on top and place under a gentle grill for a few minutes until the cheese begins to colour. Arrange the triangles of fried bread around the rice and sprinkle with the remaining parsley. Serve immediately, with a lemon wedge for each serving.

AGA method

Melt the butter on the Simmering Plate and continue to cook as above. To melt the cheese, slide the grid shelf on to the first set of runners in the Roasting Oven, put the ovenproof dish on to the grid shelf, and cook until the cheese melts (about 5 minutes). Serve as above.

Poached Salmon

Salmon is sold as steaks and fillets, but if you want to cook a whole salmon, by far the best and easiest way is to poach it in a court-bouillon. If you are going to serve the salmon cold, you can twist the fish into an S-bend and cook it in, for instance, a preserving pan. Alternatively, if you buy your salmon from a fishmonger, they may allow you to borrow or hire a salmon kettle. Follow the instructions below for a foolproof method for poaching a salmon to be served either cool, at room temperature or chilled.

Serves at least 10

1 whole salmon,
    approximately 4kg (8½lb)
Water, to cover

For the court-bouillon
½ teaspoon black
    peppercorns
2 lemons, chopped into
    chunks
1 tablespoon salt
3 shallots, peeled and cut
    into quarters
1 carrot, roughly chopped
1 celery stick, sliced
300ml (10fl oz) white wine
    vinegar
300ml (10fl oz) white wine
A few sprigs of thyme,
    parsley and fennel or dill
A few parsley sprigs, for
    garnish

If you are using a salmon kettle, lay the fish on its side on the perforated tray. If you haven't got a salmon kettle, grease or oil a large pan, then twist the fish into an S-bend and jam it upright in the pan, mouth on one side, tail on the other. Don't worry if it is right up against the edge of the pan: this will hold it in place while it cooks. Add all the ingredients for the court-bouillon to the kettle or pan. Then add water until the fish is just covered. Cover and bring the bouillon up to the boil. As soon as you are sure that it is boiling, turn off the heat and leave the fish to cool completely. This may take a couple of hours. Carefully lift the fish out of the pan on to a large plate. By this time it should be set in its S-bend, if you are cooking it in a pan.

Poached salmon needs the minimum of garnish – carefully remove the skin and fill the mouth and the eye sockets with parsley. Serve with lemon wedges for squeezing, Mayonnaise (see page 160) and warm new potatoes. Celebration food indeed!

AGA method

Poach the salmon in a fish kettle or other large roasting tin or large pan, bring to the boil on the Boiling Plate, and continue as above.

Fish and Cider Casserole

I am very happy with this casserole since it uses coley, and at the time of writing, stocks of this fish round the British coast are at a sustainable level. Coley makes a good substitute for cod and haddock, which are both under threat of over-fishing. I was given this recipe by the cooks at Fountains Abbey, North Yorkshire, the spectacular ruins of a great Cistercian monastery where the monks led lives of rigorous simplicity and only the sick ate 'the meat of quadrupeds'. Fish must have been a welcome treat when it appeared on the frugal daily menu.

Serves 6

700g (1½lb) coley fillets
300ml (½ pint) vegetable
    stock
1 onion, peeled and sliced
50g (2oz) butter
50g (2oz) plain flour
300ml (½ pint) cider
2 teaspoons anchovy
    essence
1 tablespoon lemon juice
Salt and pepper to taste

For the topping
225g (8oz) cooked potatoes,
    peeled and sliced
225g (8oz) apples, peeled
    and sliced
25g (1oz) butter

Preheat the oven to 150°C, 300°F, gas mark 2. Poach the coley in the stock until cooked, approximately 10 minutes. Set aside while you make the sauce. Sauté the onion in the butter until cooked but not coloured. Stir in the flour and cook gently for a further 5 minutes. Stir in the cider, anchovy essence and lemon juice. Then use as much of the stock as you wish to make the sauce thick, but not too thick. Season as desired. Divide the coley fillets into six portions and place in a gratin dish. Pour over the cider sauce, coating the fish evenly. Cover with foil and place it in the oven to keep warm while you prepare the topping.

At this point, preheat the grill. Melt the extra 25g (1oz) of butter in a frying pan and gently fry the cooked potato and the apple slices for a few minutes. Arrange them on the top of the dish to cover the fish mixture completely. Then pop the dish under the grill for 5 minutes to brown the top before serving.

AGA method

Poach the coley and make the sauce on the AGA hotplates. Assemble the dish and keep it warm in the Simmering Oven. Cook the topping of potatoes and apples on the Simmering Plate, arrange on top of the fish dish, then slide the dish on to the first set of runners in the Roasting Oven and bake for 5–8 minutes to brown.

Salmon in Pastry

Pastry was often served as a covering for a whole fish, or part of one, to protect it from drying out or scorching when cooked in the fierce heat of a brick oven. Like foil, it also helps to preserve the flavours of any seasonings or stuffing. The one used here is based on a seventeenth-century recipe. It is best to use the tail end of a salmon, as it is least likely to contain lots of small bones.

Serves 4

40g (1½ oz) butter, softened
zest of ½ lemon,
     finely grated
zest of ½ orange,
     finely grated
2.5–4cm (1–1½in) cube
     fresh ginger root, peeled
     and finely grated
½ teaspoon black
     peppercorns, coarsely
     ground
½ teaspoon finely grated
     nutmeg
1 piece of skinned salmon
     fillet, approximately 600g
     (1¼lb)
½ teaspoon salt
50g (2oz) raisins
Plain flour, for dusting
225g (½lb) frozen puff
     pastry, thawed
1 beaten egg, to seal and
     glaze

Preheat the oven to 220°C, 425°F, gas mark 7. Blend the butter, lemon and orange zest, ginger, ground peppercorns and nutmeg together in a small bowl. Take the piece of salmon and cut it in half lengthwise. Season each half with the salt, then spread the prepared butter mixture over the top of one piece and scatter the raisins on top. Cover with the other piece of salmon.

On a lightly floured work surface, roll out the pastry into an oblong slightly longer than the salmon and twice as wide, to a thickness of approximately 2.5mm (⅛in). Put the stuffed salmon on top and roll the pastry around it, so that the fish is completely enclosed. Trim off and reserve any surplus pastry to make a neat parcel. Brush the edges of the pastry with some of the beaten egg and press firmly together to seal. Turn the parcel so that the join in the pastry is underneath and use the pastry trimmings to decorate the top. Brush over the remaining beaten egg to glaze, then lay the parcel on a sheet of baking paper on a baking tray and cook in the hot oven for 15 minutes. Lower the heat to 180°C, 350°F, gas mark 4 and cook for a further 15 minutes. Serve hot, warm or cold.

AGA method

Prepare the salmon in pastry ready to go into the oven. Slide the grid shelf on to the floor of the Roasting Oven and place the salmon tray on top. Cook for 15 minutes then slide the cold plain shelf directly above the tray and bake for a further 15–20 minutes.

Stargazey Pie

Stargazey Pie is Cornwall's most famous dish, but you don't see it on many menus today. Made traditionally, it is all about visual effect: the heads of the fish are outside the pastry.

Serves 4–6

For the shortcrust pastry
250g (8oz) plain flour
1 teaspoon salt
75g (3oz) butter
75g (3oz) vegetable
    shortening or lard
Approximately 4
    tablespoons cold water

For the filling
110g (4oz) white
    breadcrumbs
50ml (2fl oz) milk
1 tablespoon chopped
    parsley
1 onion, peeled and finely
    chopped
Juice and grated zest of
    1 lemon
8 pilchards or 8 small herring
    or 8 large sardines (ask
    your fishmonger to clean
    and bone the fish, but
    leave the heads in place)
2 hard-boiled eggs, chopped
50g (2oz) bacon, chopped
150ml (¼ pint) cider
1 beaten egg, to seal and
    glaze
Salt and pepper to taste

With pastry, it is important to keep everything as cold as possible and to handle the dough as little as possible. Sift the flour with the salt into a bowl. Add the butter and shortening and cut with a knife until it is all small pieces. Then rub with your fingertips until the mixture forms fine crumbs. You can do this part of the recipe with a food processor.

Make a well in the centre of the mixture and add water. Mix with a knife to form crumbs. Then work together to form a ball. Wrap it tightly in clingfilm and chill in the fridge for about 30 minutes. Knead the dough after it has chilled. Flour the work surface and work the dough with your hands until it is smooth. This should only take a minute or two. It is now ready to be rolled out.

Preheat the oven to 220°C, 425°F, gas mark 7. First, grease the pie dish. (You will need a shallow, round pie dish, large enough to fit the fish tail-to-tail in the centre, with their heads resting on the rim.) Divide the pastry into two pieces. Roll out the first piece to line the dish, and prick the base. Leave it to rest while you make the stuffing.

Soak the breadcrumbs in the milk for about 5 minutes. Squeeze them out and mix with the parsley, chopped onion and juice and zest of the lemon. Stuff the fish with some of this mixture – you should have about a third left over. Lay the stuffed fish in the dish, heads on the rim, tails at the centre. Mix the remainder of the stuffing with the chopped egg and bacon, and use this mixture to fill in the gaps round the fish. Pour over the cider, season with pepper and a little salt (beware of adding too much as the bacon will taste salty).

Roll out the second piece of pastry to cover the pie. Brush the rim with beaten egg to give a good seal, but leave each head sticking out. Make a hole in the centre to let out the steam and brush the top with beaten egg. Bake for 10 minutes in the oven, then reduce the heat to 180°C, 350°F, gas mark 4 and bake for a further 40 minutes. Stargazey Pie is best served at room temperature.

AGA method

Make the pastry and line the round pie dish as above. Assemble the pie filling and when the pie is covered with the remaining pastry, brush with the beaten egg and leave a hole for the steam to escape. Place the dish on the floor of the Roasting Oven and cook for 10 minutes, then slide the cold plain shelf on the set of runners directly above, though allowing room for air movement. Bake for 30–35 minutes, checking after the first 20 minutes.

Haddock and Prawn Cobbler

My recipe for Haddock and Prawn Cobbler came from the National Trust York Tea Room. York abounds with tea rooms, but this is one of the best, butting up against the Minster and serving hot dishes throughout the day as well as scones, teacakes, cakes and biscuits. I assumed cobbler was an old Yorkshire word meaning 'dish with a scone topping'. Imagine my surprise when *The Oxford Companion to Food* told me it is from New England However, I'm not going to leave it out, since it is a variation on the British pie and is too tasty to miss.

Serves 6

700g (1½lb) haddock fillet, skinned and cut into 5cm (2in) chunks
50g (2oz) butter
50g (2oz) plain flour
2 teaspoons mustard powder
600ml (1 pint) milk
4 teaspoons wine vinegar
2 hard-boiled eggs, peeled and chopped
50g (2oz) prawns

For the topping
175g (6oz) wholemeal flour
1 tablespoon baking powder
Pinch of thyme
40g (1½oz) butter
1 egg, beaten
2 tablespoons milk

Serves 6

Preheat the oven to 180°C, 350°F, gas mark 4. Cook the haddock in boiling water. This will take approximately 10 minutes. Allow to cool. Make a white sauce with the butter, flour and mustard powder, using the milk and wine vinegar as liquid. Don't worry if the sauce curdles; just give it a quick whisk. Lay the cooked haddock in a 20 x 23cm (8 x 9in) china gratin dish, approximately 6.5cm (2½in) deep. Sprinkle over the prawns and chopped hard-boiled eggs and cover with the white sauce. Put aside while you make the topping.

Sift together flour, baking powder and thyme into a large bowl. Rub in the butter, then make up into a dough using the egg and milk. Roll out into a sheet approximately 1cm (½in) thick and cut into 5cm (2in) rounds. Arrange on the top of the fish mixture. Brush with milk and bake for approximately 20 minutes, until well risen and brown. Serve with green vegetables or a green salad.

AGA method

Cook the haddock and white sauce on the AGA hotplates. Make the cobbler topping and arrange on the top of the fish mixture. Brush with milk, then bake in the Roasting Oven, on the fourth set of runners, for 20 minutes. If the top browns too much, slide in the cold plain shelf.

Trout with Almonds

Michael Smith attributes this dish to Oxford University, but doesn't say which college. He fries the trout in oil; I prefer to reduce the fat content a little by oven-baking the trout. The result is rich and delicate at the same time. Boiled new potatoes served with the fish, and a green salad afterwards are all it needs.

Serves 4

4 trout, heads removed and cleaned
2 tablespoons plain flour, seasoned with salt and pepper
1 tablespoon olive oil
50g (2oz) butter
50g (2oz) flaked almonds
Grated zest and juice of 1 lemon

Preheat the oven to 200°C, 400°F, gas mark 6. Coat the trout with flour seasoned with pepper and salt to taste. Place them in a large roasting tin lined with baking paper (this prevents the trout from sticking to the tin, making it much easier to clean). Bake for 15 minutes, then turn off the oven and leave the trout to rest while you make the sauce. Put four serving plates in the oven to warm up.

To make the sauce, melt the olive oil and butter in a small frying pan. Shake in the almonds and sauté them until they are brown. Watch and stir the pan constantly as they can go from golden to burnt very quickly. Take the pan off the heat and stir in the lemon zest and juice. To serve, place each trout on a warmed plate and pour over the almonds and sauce.

AGA method

Assemble the trout as above, then place the tin on to the fourth set of runners in the Roasting Oven and bake for 10–15 minutes. Remove the trout and set aside to rest. Make the sauce on the Simmering Plate.

Pickled Herring and Fruit Pie

This unusual Norfolk recipe was researched and written up by Sara Paston-Williams. The mixture of fish and fruit may seem odd to our modern taste, but it is a great favourite at the Elizabethan banquets held from time to time at Oxburgh Hall in Norfolk.

Serves 6

For the pastry
350g (12oz) plain flour
Salt and black pepper
    to taste
75g (3oz) butter
75g (3oz) lard
Cold water to mix

For the filling
450g (1lb) pickled herring
    or rollmops
1 large cooking pear, peeled,
    cored and sliced
25g (1oz) raisins
25g (1oz) currants
50g (2oz) dates, pitted and
    minced
¼ teaspoon ground
    cinnamon
2 tablespoons dry white
    wine
25g (1oz) butter, cut into
    small pieces
Beaten egg, or milk, to glaze
1 teaspoon sugar
Pinch of salt

Preheat the oven to 220°C, 425°F, gas mark 7. To make the pastry, sieve the flour and salt together into a bowl. Add a sprinkling of pepper, then rub in the butter and lard until the mixture resembles fine breadcrumbs. Mix with enough cold water to make a firm dough. Knead lightly until smooth. Divide into two portions, about two-thirds and one-third. Roll out the two portions and then chill them for about 10 minutes.

Grease a deep 20cm (8in) flan tin and line it with the larger portion of pastry. Bake blind for 10 minutes. Leave to cool. Reduce the temperature of the oven to 190°C, 375°F, gas mark 5.

Meanwhile, prepare the filling. Unroll the herring if necessary. Remove any onions and reserve. Rinse the herring in cold water and drain. Plunge them into 1.8 litres (3 pints) boiling water in a pan, cook for 1 minute, remove and drain well. Cut into chunks.

Mix the pear, dried fruit, salt, cinnamon and wine together in a bowl and add the herring. Transfer the filling into the pastry-lined flan tin, using a slotted spoon to drain off any excess liquid. Dot the mixture with the butter and cover with the remaining pastry. Decorate the top with any pastry trimmings, then brush with the egg or milk. Make a slit in the top to allow the steam to escape and sprinkle with the sugar. Bake for 1 hour, or until golden brown.

AGA method

Make the pastry as above. There is no need to blind bake in an AGA. Boil the water in which to plunge the herring on the Boiling Plate and continue as above. Mix the pear, dried fruit, salt, cinnamon and wine together in a bowl and add the herring. Put the filling into the pastry-lined flan tin as above, then cover with the remaining pastry.

Decorate the top with any leftover pastry, make a slit, and brush with the egg. Place the tin on the floor of the Roasting Oven with the cold plain shelf on the set of runners directly above, but still allowing room for air movement. Bake for 25 minutes, check and remove the cold plain shelf to brown the top of the pastry, then continue to bake for another 15–20 minutes. If the top browns too much, slide the cold plain shelf back in, or cover with a sheet of foil.

Fish and Chips

Homemade fish and chips, made with best-quality ingredients, are special indeed. If you come from the north you will want vinegar and mushy peas with your fish and chips. Green peas and Tartare Sauce (see page 160) taste good too.

Serves 4

For the fish
4 thick cod or haddock
    fillets, skinned
Flour
Salt and pepper to taste
Best-quality beef dripping or
    lard or sunflower oil for
    frying

For the batter
110g (4oz) plain flour
½ teaspoon salt
1 tablespoon olive oil
1 egg, separated
About 150ml (¼ pint) beer
    or water

For the chips
900g (2lb) potatoes,
    preferably Maris Piper, cut
    into even-sized chips
Lard or oil for deep-frying
Salt and pepper to taste

Note: all the ingredients should be at room temperature. Sieve the flour for the batter with the salt into a bowl, make a well in the centre and gradually beat in the olive oil, egg yolk and beer or water to make a smooth batter that will coat the back of a wooden spoon. Let it rest at room temperature for about 30 minutes.

Heat the fat in a deep-fat fryer with a basket to 180°C, 350°F. Test the lard or oil with a square of bread. It should cook crisp and golden immediately.

Dust the fish fillets with seasoned flour. Whip the egg white until stiff and fold it gently into the batter. Dip the flour-covered fillets in the batter and fry immediately until crisp and golden. Drain on kitchen paper. Don't overload the pan. Better to do the frying in batches and keep the drained cooked fillets warm in the oven while you finish the rest.

Dry the chips well on kitchen paper. Fry them in batches for about 10 minutes until soft, making sure not to overload the fryer. Drain on kitchen paper.

Increase the heat to 190°C, 375°F. Salt the chips and return in batches to the fryer for a few minutes until crisp and golden. Drain on kitchen paper again and add salt and pepper. They are now ready to serve with the fish.

AGA method

Use the AGA hotplates to fry the fish and chips.

Hobbler's Seafood Pie

This recipe was given to me by the Sail Loft restaurant at St Michael's Mount, a magical island off the coast of Cornwall. It is unusual in that it uses raw fish, which seems to intensify the flavour. At the Sail Loft, this pie is made with any fish the boats land on the Mount, so generally there are leftovers after filleting for the stock. However, if you buy fish from the supermarket it will probably be easier to use a vegetable stock cube.

Serves 4

350g (12oz) white fish
   (the Sail Loft uses ling for
   preference, but coley, cod
   or haddock may be easier
   to find)
110g (4oz) peeled prawns
1 tablespoon chopped
   parsley
50g (2oz) butter
50g (2oz) flour
300ml (½ pint) creamy milk
300ml (½ pint) fish stock
450g (1lb) mashed potato

Preheat the oven to 180°C, 350°F, gas mark 4. Cut the fish into large chunks and lay it on the bottom of a pie dish. Scatter over the prawns and the parsley. Make up a thick white sauce using the butter, flour, milk and fish stock and pour over the fish. Cover the fish and sauce with mashed potato, fluffing the top with a fork. Bake uncovered in the oven for approximately 30 minutes, until the top is crisp and brown.

AGA method

Assemble the pie as above and make the sauce on the Simmering Plate. Bake the pie in the Roasting Oven, on the third set of runners, for 25–30 minutes or until the top is crispy and it is piping hot.

Herring Fried in Oatmeal

Herring or trout fried in oatmeal have always been popular for breakfast, high tea or supper, especially in Scotland. If possible, use a food processor to produce a mixture of coarse, medium and finely blended oatmeal for use in this recipe. Plain boiled new potatoes or granary bread are the best accompaniments.

Serves 4

4 large herring, heads, tails
   and backbones removed,
   scaled and cleaned
3–4 tablespoons milk
110g (4oz) oatmeal
110g (4oz) unsalted butter
Salt and pepper to taste
2 lemons, cut into wedges,
   to serve

Ask your fishmonger to prepare the herring. Sprinkle salt and pepper over the inside of the fish. Return them to their original shape. Dip the herring in the milk. Put the oatmeal in a shallow dish, season with salt and pepper and press the fish firmly into it so that they are coated evenly.

Heat the butter until it is bubbling in a large, heavy-based frying pan. Fry the herring for 5 minutes or so on each side. Lift the fish on to the plates, pour over any butter from the pan and serve with lemon wedges to squeeze over them.

AGA method

Prepare the fish as above. Heat up the butter in a frying pan on the Roasting Oven floor and fry the fish there or on the Boiling Plate for 3–5 minutes on each side. Serve as above.

Cheese and Anchovy Straws

The idea for these came from an important eighteenth-century cookery book, *The Experienced English Housekeeper* (1769), written by Elizabeth Raffald, who for a time was housekeeper at Arley Hall in Cheshire.

Makes 16

Plain flour, for dusting
225g (8oz) puff pastry
25g (1oz) anchovy fillets, drained of oil or washed free from preserving salt
1 egg, separated
100g (3½ oz) Cheshire cheese, grated
1 tablespoon chopped parsley

Preheat the oven to 220°C, 425°F, gas mark 7. Dust a work surface with the flour and roll out the pastry into an oblong about 5mm (¼in) thick. Cut in half to give two equal-sized oblongs.

Mash the anchovy fillets to a soft paste with a little of the egg yolk in a small bowl (do not make the mixture too runny). In another bowl, mix the cheese, parsley and some of the egg white to make a firm paste (again, you may not need all of the egg). Spread the anchovy paste over one of the oblongs of pastry, right up to the edges. Stack the other pastry oblong on top. Carefully spread the cheese paste evenly over this, again taking it right up to the edges. Cut the pastry sandwich with a sharp knife to give 16 equal-sized fingers. Carefully transfer them to a baking tray, covered with a sheet of baking paper, leaving plenty of space around each one (use two baking trays, if necessary).

Bake in the hot oven for 5 minutes, then check to see that the straws are cooking evenly and not scorching – shuffle them around on the baking tray, if necessary. Return to the oven until they are golden; this may take 15–20 minutes, but check frequently. Eat fresh from the oven with drinks, or serve as an accompaniment to soup.

AGA method

Prepare the cheese straws ready to go into the oven. Slide the oven grid shelf on to the floor of the Roasting Oven and place the baking tray on top. Bake for 8–10 minutes or until golden.

Omelette Arnold Bennett

This recipe is said to have originated at the Savoy Hotel and was a favourite of the writer Arnold Bennett (1867–1931). An excellent brunch or supper dish, its origins in a restaurant are reflected in the preparation, which needs several items all to be put together at the very last minute, including a small quantity of cheese sauce.

Serves 2

Approximately 350g (¾lb) smoked haddock
4 eggs
15–20g (½ –¾oz) butter
Approximately 2 tablespoons cheese sauce (see page 195), made with full-cream milk
2 tablespoons double cream, whipped until stiff
25g (1oz) strong Cheddar cheese, finely grated
Freshly ground black pepper

Preheat the oven to 200°C, 400°F, gas mark 6. Put the smoked haddock in a shallow ovenproof dish, cover with boiling water and cook in the hot oven for 10–15 minutes, or until the fish is just cooked through. Drain off the water, and remove and discard all of the skin and bones. Flake the fish into small pieces. Beat the eggs with a little black pepper in a bowl, then stir in the fish.

When ready to cook the omelette, light the grill and have heated serving plates ready. Heat the butter in a large omelette or frying pan. Once the foam has subsided, pour in the egg mixture, shaking the pan so that it spreads evenly. Cook gently for 3–4 minutes, until the base has set. Mix the cheese sauce and whipped cream together and spread this mixture over the cooking omelette. Scatter over the grated Cheddar cheese, then put the pan under the hot grill. Cook until the cheese has melted and is beginning to brown, but don't overcook – it is better if the omelette remains slightly soft in the centre. Quickly divide into two and slide each portion on to a heated serving plate. Serve at once.

AGA method

Prepare the smoked haddock for poaching, then cook in the Roasting Oven, on the fourth set of runners, for 10 minutes. Make the omelette using the AGA hotplates, in an ovenproof omelette pan or frying pan, and place at the top of the Roasting Oven to melt the cheese for a couple of minutes.

Meat, Poultry and Game Dishes

Aberdeen Angus, Galloways, Devons, Lincoln Reds, Sussex Old Herefords and Welsh Blacks – our beef breeds have been the envy of the world. British lamb, fed on sweet green pasture, is equally prized, with Cheviot, Herdwick, Romney, Southdown and any amount of crossbreeds. We raise splendid pork, and both chickens and ducks thrive in the mild climate. There are rabbits in the countryside, and a thriving market in game. You could say that Britain is a paradise for meat eaters.

In the 18th century the British were known throughout Europe, and particularly by the French, as 'Rosbifs' – a rather scathing tribute to what was, then, our national dish. Indeed, some would say it still is. Throughout the centuries, as today, roasting has been the preferred method for cooking the choicest cuts of meat. But, of course, we have other great traditional dishes and it is these that are celebrated here.

British cooking traditions have been built round the good quality of the meat, where there was never any need to disguise the taste. Spicing, herbs, ale, cider or wine are all there to enhance the goodness and flavour of the meat itself, and even casseroles are for the cuts of meat that need longer cooking to become tender, rather than to taste better. None of these recipes is complicated; Boiled Beef and Carrots may need to simmer for several hours, but it makes no demands upon the cook – and neither do Irish Stew, Oxtail Stew or Steak and Kidney Pie.

I have tried to provide at least one recipe for every beast or fowl (the old words seem appropriate) that the British not only eat today, but have eaten over the last six hundred years. That includes turkey, which had a fixed price in the London markets by the 1550s, when it was already talked of as a Christmas food – although it wasn't until the 20th century that it supplanted goose as the traditional bird. Some of the dishes are modern adaptations that stick as closely as possible to the old recipes – as in the versions of Chicken in Hocchee and Venison Casseroled with Apricots.

'Take chykens and scald them, take parsel and sawge … take garlic and grapes, and stoppe the chikens ful, and seeth them in good broth.' This old recipe for Chicken in Hocchee, a medieval or Tudor recipe for chicken breasts stuffed with grapes, garlic, fresh parsley and sage, and then poached in stock and wine, is still very much to modern tastes. Many of the old recipes are for game or poultry. Game parks, enclosed areas where game was hunted for sport by the aristocracy, had actually been part of the English countryside since the time of the Romans. These are recipes from the rich man's table, written down as a reminder to the household cooks. Medieval and Tudor cooks did not have hard and fast rules about the use of fruit in savoury recipes, and it is interesting to notice how often the game and poultry recipes include fruit, sometimes instead of vegetables.

Certain recipes have regional roots. Recipes for lamb dishes, such as Irish Stew, come from upland areas, where sheep were the main beasts raised for market. Lancashire Hotpot – lamb or mutton cooked in a deep pot with a layer of potatoes on the top – has a long tradition, but not just in Lancashire. There are 'hot pots' right across northern England, with slightly different names, and slightly different ingredients and side dishes. 'Tatie Pot' is made in Cumbria, from lamb, black pudding and vegetables, but with the addition of beef as well. 'Tater 'Ash' is the Cheshire name for a similar dish, where it is eaten with Piccalilli rather than the usual Red Cabbage. Interestingly, I was given a recipe for Hodgepodge, the ancestor of today's Hotpot, in Northumberland.

There are no less than ten pies in this chapter. Pies have always been a great favourite with the British, eaten hot, like Steak and Kidney Pie or Chicken Thyme Pie, or cold, like Pork Pie or Bacon and Egg Pie. There are two squab pies here. In old recipes 'squab' meant a young pigeon, but in Cornwall and Devon it often refers to mutton or lamb. Both of the recipes here have local apples as one ingredient. But Lanhydrock Squab Pie (page 95), from Cornwall, uses lamb as a filling and the other pie, from the rich pastureland at the other end of Devon – more suitable for raising pigs – uses pork. Medieval Britain loved joke pies – you only have to think of the old nursery rhyme, 'Sing a song of sixpence, a pocket full of rye/Four and twenty blackbirds baked in a pie'. Huge celebratory pies were cooked on special occasions; Denby Dale, a small village in Yorkshire's West Riding, still cooks a huge pie for special festivals, each pie bigger than the last. In 1988, the pie cooked to mark the double centenary of the first Denby Dale pie weighed over 9 tons (over 9,000 kg). Our pies are more manageable, with pies suitable for every meal, for picnics, and even portable pies – since pasties are a meal-for-one in a pie, originally made for the tin miners in Cornwall to take to work.

Until the agricultural Enclosure Acts, at the end of the 18th century, every cottage had its patch of land, and people could keep a pig without a licence. A pig would eat anything, and could be fed on scraps, so most people could afford one, and pork was readily available. When a pig was killed, generally in the autumn, those parts of the animal that were not immediately eaten were preserved for the leaner months ahead. Sausages and sausage meat were made, hams and bacon were smoked, tripe was soaked in brine and trotters were salted. There are recipes here for sausage dishes, for bacon and gammon and for Haslet and Faggots. If you don't want to tackle the last two yourself, find a good butcher and, with any luck, you'll find them ready-made.

British meat cooking has always relied on the good quality of its ingredients. If you have the time, hunt out a good meat supplier. Apart from the butcher, who will be only too happy to provide you with advice, there is now a network of farmers' markets across the country, where you will find specialist butchers and game dealers. Some National Trust farmers sell direct to the customer – you can find out more about these on pages 414–417. If the supermarket is all that is available to you, take time to choose, and look for organic or free-range meat and poultry. It may cost more but it will taste much better.

Chicken and Ham Pie

This is a good recipe to make during periods when you are catering for a crowd, such as Christmas, when there may be a gammon to cut into and some cold chicken (or turkey) in the fridge. The addition of the forcemeat balls is an old idea – the cheaper stuffing extends the expensive chicken and ham.

Serves 6

225g (8oz) cooked chicken
    meat
225g (8oz) cooked ham
175g (6oz) fresh
    breadcrumbs
½ small onion, peeled and
    finely chopped
1 celery stick, finely chopped
1 teaspoon mixed herbs
Zest of 1 lemon
1 egg
Salt and pepper to taste

For the sauce
50g (2oz) butter
50g (2oz) plain flour
300ml (½ pint) chicken, ham
    or vegetable stock
300ml (½ pint) creamy milk
1 tablespoon chopped
    parsley

For the shortcrust pastry
225g (8oz) plain flour
110g (4oz) margarine or
    lard
1 egg yolk mixed with a little
    milk to glaze
50g (2oz) sesame seeds

Preheat the oven to 190°C, 375°F, gas mark 5. Cut the chicken and ham into chunks. Mix together the breadcrumbs, chopped onion and celery, herbs, lemon zest and salt and pepper to taste. Use the egg to bind into a dryish stuffing. Form the stuffing into balls the size of a large marble. Fill a deep pie dish with the chicken, ham and stuffing balls.

Make a white sauce with the butter, flour, stock and milk and stir in the parsley. Season with salt and pepper and pour over the pie filling.

Make the pastry with the flour and margarine, roll it out and cover the dish, using any trimmings as decoration. Make a hole in the centre to let out the steam. Brush with egg and milk glaze and cover with a layer of sesame seeds. Bake for 30–40 minutes, until golden brown.

AGA method

Prepare the pie filling as above and make the white sauce using the Simmering Plate. Assemble the dish and brush with the egg glaze and sesame seeds. Cook in the Roasting Oven, on the oven grid shelf set on the floor of the oven, for 25–30 minutes. If the pie is colouring too quickly, slide the cold plain shelf directly above it.

Roast Duck with Sage and Onion Stuffing and Apple Sauce

This classic British recipe can be cooked all year round, but it is at its best in late spring, when you can eat fresh garden peas with it – the perfect vegetable accompaniment.

Serves 4

1 duck, approximately 2kg
    (4½lb), with giblets
2 bay leaves
2 apples
1 onion, peeled
3 garlic cloves, peeled
2 teaspoons salt

For the stuffing balls

50g (2oz) butter
1 small onion, finely chopped
2 celery sticks, chopped
25g (1oz) flaked almonds
1 duck's liver, finely chopped
Grated zest and juice of
    1 large orange
1 apple (Cox's Orange Pippin
    or Braeburn), chopped
150g (5oz) fresh white
    breadcrumbs
5 sage leaves, finely shredded
A large handful of fresh
    parsley, chopped
1 large egg, well beaten
Salt and pepper to taste

For the gravy

2 tablespoons tawny port

Preheat the oven to 200°C, 400°F, gas mark 6. If necessary, remove the giblets from the duck and separate out the liver to use in the stuffing. Put the giblets in a small pan with a couple of bay leaves, cover them with water, put the lid on and leave them to simmer while the duck is cooking.

Roughly chop the apples, onion and garlic cloves. There is no need to peel or core the apples. Mix the apples, onion and garlic together and use to stuff the carcass. Prick the skin of the duck all over. Rub it with the salt and place it, breast down, on a trivet in a large roasting tin. Roast in the oven for 30 minutes, then reduce the heat to 180°C, 350°F, Gas Mark 4 and turn the duck the right way up for the rest of the roasting time. It should take approximately 1½ hours.

Make the stuffing balls as follows. Melt the butter in a medium-sized pan. Fry the onion and celery for about 5 minutes or until slightly softened but not coloured. Add the almonds and the liver for the last minute or so – watch them carefully and give them a good stir. Take the pan off the heat and stir in the orange zest and juice, chopped apple, breadcrumbs, sage leaves and parsley. Mix well, season with salt and pepper to taste and bind together with the beaten egg. Either press the mixture into a buttered ovenproof dish or make it into patties the size of a golf ball. Put these on a baking tray lined with baking parchment. Put the dish or the patties in the oven for the last 30 minutes of the duck's cooking time. The top of the mixture or the patties should be golden brown.

When the duck is cooked, turn the oven off. Put the duck on a serving dish, cover it with foil and put it back in the oven to rest for 10–15 minutes before carving it. Make a thin gravy to serve with the duck by pouring off the excess fat from the roasting pan, leaving about 2 tablespoons behind. Drain off the stock from the giblets. Give a good scrape to the bottom of the roasting pan and add the stock from the giblets along with the tawny port. Boil vigorously for a minute or two and season with salt and pepper.

Serve the duck with the stuffing balls, the gravy and Apple Sauce (see page 164). Potatoes roasted with the bird, braised red cabbage and crisp, steamed green vegetables are good accompaniments.

AGA method

Prepare the duck and giblets as above. To make the giblet stock, bring to the boil on the Boiling Plate, then place in the Simmering Oven while the duck is cooking.

Put the duck into the Roasting Oven, on the third or fourth set of runners, depending on the size of the bird, and roast for 1½ hours. Turn the duck the right way up after 30 minutes. Check after one hour. If it is browning too much, slide in the cold plain shelf above.

Prepare the stuffing balls as above, on the hotplates. Once the patties are made, heat up a shallow baking tin lined with Bake-O-Glide silicone liner on the floor of the Roasting Oven. When it is very hot, add the patties and continue to cook them there for the final 30 minutes of the duck's cooking time, turning them over after 15 minutes. If you are cooking the stuffing balls in an ovenproof dish, slide the dish on to a baking tray and, if possible, hang from the last set of runners in the Roasting Oven. Alternatively, cook in the Baking Oven (on three- or four-oven models). You may have to move the duck up a little. Continue to cook as above, making the gravy on the AGA hotplates.

Chicken in Hocchee

This is a modern adaptation of a medieval or Tudor recipe: 'Take chykens and scald them, take parsel and sawge, without any other erbes, take garlec and grapes, and stoppe the chikens ful, and seeth them in good broth, so that they may esly be boyled thereine. Messe them and cast thereto powdor-douce [a mixture of mild spices].'

Serves 4

4 chicken breasts
110g (4oz) green grapes
2 tablespoons mixed
    chopped fresh parsley
    and sage
1 garlic clove
250ml (½ pint) chicken
    stock
1 small glass white wine
½ teaspoon caster sugar
½ teaspoon ground
    cinnamon

For garnish
Chopped parsley
A few grapes

Slice the chicken breasts in half so you can stuff them. Pip the grapes, if necessary, reserving a few for garnishing. Mix the rest with the garlic and the herbs and stuff the chicken breasts with the mixture. Pin each breast into a neat parcel with a cocktail stick and place in a dish that just holds them. Add the stock and wine and cover the dish with foil. Simmer until tender (about 45 minutes). Remove the breasts and place on a warm serving dish. Sprinkle with the sugar and cinnamon mixed together, the chopped parsley and the grapes. Serve with the cooking juices as a light gravy.

AGA method

Prepare the chicken as above. Put the ovenproof dish, covered with foil, on to the fourth set of runners in the Roasting Oven and cook for 30–40 minutes. Remove the breasts and continue as above.

Chicken Thyme Pie

Certain herbs have particular affinities. Thyme and chicken makes a good partnership. It rescues this chicken pie from lack of flavour while still leaving it the kind of easy, non-complicated recipe that conservative eaters like.

Serves 4

450g (1lb) shortcrust pastry (see page 64)

1 tablespoon oil

25g (1oz) butter

1 large onion, peeled and sliced

6 large celery sticks, chopped

4 chicken breasts (1 per person), cut into thick slices

Either 6 stems of fresh thyme or a small teaspoon of dried thyme

Salt and pepper to taste

300ml (½ pint) chicken stock (make it with a stock cube if you have none fresh)

300ml (½ pint) thick white sauce made with 50g (2oz) butter, 50g (2oz) flour and 300ml (½ pint) milk (see page 159)

Preheat the oven to 180°C, 350°F, gas mark 4. Melt the oil and butter and sauté the onion and celery until soft. Take out the vegetables and lay them in a pie dish. Sauté the sliced chicken in the same pan (add a little more oil if you need it) until nice and brown. Add the browned chicken to the dish. Scatter the fresh or dried thyme over the chicken. Make the white sauce (see page 159 for method) and then stir it in to make a good thick mixture with the chicken. Cover the pie dish with the pastry and decorate with any oddments. Make a hole in the centre to let out the steam and glaze with milk. Put the pie in the oven and cook for about 30–40 minutes until golden brown.

AGA method

Melt the oil and butter in a sauté pan and soften the onion and celery until soft on the Roasting Oven floor. Lay the vegetables in a pie dish, then sauté the chicken pieces in the same pan, using more oil if needed, on the AGA hotplates until browned. Add to the dish. Make the sauce on the Simmering Plate, then assemble the dish and cook in the Roasting Oven, on the fourth set of runners and with the cold plain shelf directly above, for 40–45 minutes. If the pie is not colouring, remove the cold plain shelf for the final 10 minutes. Alternatively, cook in the centre of the Baking Oven (on three- or four-oven models) for 30–40 minutes.

Devilled Fowl

There are wet devils (sauces) and dry devils (marinades). I have chosen a recipe for a dry devil because this is traditional in our family. My mother always bought a huge turkey at Christmas time. We only ever had turkey during the festive season: hot on Christmas Day; cold on Boxing Day; the various joints, legs and thighs devilled with whatever chutney came to hand, the day after. She fricasseed the last small cuts from the bird the next day, and finally the carcass was made into soup.

You can 'devil' any meat. The idea is to liven up something that is either rather bland or has perhaps lost a little flavour in the keeping. I have called this recipe Devilled Fowl as I think poultry responds best to this treatment. Nigel Slater suggested this marinade in *Real Fast Food*. I have just added the option of including chilli if you haven't got tabasco sauce in your cupboard. This recipe is also good cooked on the barbecue.

Serves 2

2 cold chicken or turkey
    joints

For the marinade
1 tablespoon Dijon mustard
2 garlic cloves, finely
    chopped
2 tablespoons fruity chutney
    (apple, mango, plum –
    whatever is in the
    cupboard)
1 tablespoon Worcester
    sauce
1 teaspoon minced chilli or
    a good shake of tabasco
    sauce (according to taste)

Preheat the grill to high. Mix the ingredients for the marinade into a paste. Slash the skin and flesh of the chicken or turkey with a sharp knife and spread the spicy mixture over the flesh and into the slashes. You can leave the meat to rest and soak up the marinade for a couple of hours, but this is optional. Grill, turning once, at about 10cm (4in) from the element, till sizzling and hot throughout. This should take approximately 10 minutes. Serve with a green salad.

AGA method

You will need a ridged grill pan for this dish. Prepare the chicken or turkey joints as above. Put the ridged grill pan on to the floor of the Roasting Oven and heat it until it is smoking hot. Move the pan to the Simmering Plate – if it starts to lose heat, transfer it to the Boiling Plate and cook the meat for 3–4 minutes on each side or until it is cooked all the way through.

Casseroled Pigeon with Herbs and Spices

This recipe was researched by Sara Paston-Williams, who found a recipe for 'Peiouns ystewed' in *The Forme of Cury*, our oldest English cookery book. It is a series of 'receipts' which were used at the coronation of Richard II and was written in about 1390. Pigeons were then raised for the pot, but only by the Lord of the Manor – he didn't want other people's pigeons eating his corn so only he had a licence.

Serves 4

4 oven-ready pigeons

12 large garlic cloves

4 teaspoons chopped fresh thyme

2 tablespoons chopped fresh parsley

Dripping or lard for frying

300ml (½ pint) chicken stock

Juice of ½ lemon

Large pinch of ground ginger

Pinch of saffron strands

½ teaspoon ground cinnamon

Salt and freshly ground black pepper to taste

4 slices wholemeal toast

Fresh herbs for garnish

Preheat the oven to 180°C, 350°F, gas mark 4. Stuff each pigeon with 3 garlic cloves, 1 teaspoon chopped fresh thyme and ½ tablespoon chopped fresh parsley. Season with a little salt and freshly milled black pepper, then brown the pigeons all over in a little dripping or lard in a heavy flame-proof casserole which is just big enough to take them. Pour over the stock, then add the lemon juice, ginger, saffron and cinnamon. Cover with a lid, place in the preheated oven and cook for 1–1½ hours or until very tender. Taste the gravy and adjust the seasoning as necessary. Serve each person with a pigeon arranged on a slice of wholemeal toast with a little gravy poured over. Garnish with fresh herbs.

AGA method

Prepare the pigeon as above. Place the covered casserole on the fourth set of runners in the Roasting Oven and cook for 45 minutes, then transfer to the Simmering Oven for another 1–1½ hours or until the pigeon is very tender. Alternatively, cook in the centre of the Baking Oven (on three- and four-oven models) for 1–1½ hours. Adjust the seasoning and serve as above.

Lanhydrock Squab Pie

Squabs were pigeons, but as these were scarce and generally eaten by the rich (see opposite), lamb has been substituted in this poor man's version. The apples and onions were used to make up for the lack of meat. In latter years the cream etc. has been added to make the dish more special.

Serves 6 plus

700g (1½lb) stewing lamb
  or cooked diced lamb
450g (1lb) onions, sliced
450g (1lb) cooking apples,
  peeled and sliced
Mixed herbs
125ml (4fl oz) vegetable
  stock (using a stock cube)
350g (12oz) shortcrust or
  puff pastry
300ml (½ pint) double
  cream or clotted cream
Salt and pepper to taste

Preheat the oven to 200°C, 400°F, gas mark 6. Arrange the meat, onions and apples in alternate layers in a pie dish. Sprinkle with mixed herbs (or just rosemary) and pour the stock over everything. Cover with the pastry and cook in the oven until the pastry is done – approximately 30 minutes. Turn the oven temperature down to 160°C, 325°F, gas mark 3, and cook for a further hour. If the pastry starts to brown too much, cover it with foil. If the meat is pre-cooked, you may need a little less time. Remove from the oven and gently lift off the pastry top. Stir in the cream and adjust the seasoning. Replace the pastry lid and reheat for a further few minutes until ready to serve.

AGA method

Prepare the pie as above and cook on the fourth set of runners in the Roasting Oven for 30 minutes. If the pastry is browning too much, protect it with the cold plain shelf. Move the pie to the Simmering Oven and continue to cook for a further 1½–2 hours.

Chicken Liver Paste

Chicken livers enjoyed a vogue as an ingredient in Edwardian cookery. Sometimes served whole, sometimes as pastes, they were used in rich 'savouries', little mouthfuls served on croutons of fried bread that were thought to cleanse the palate at the end of a rich meal. This recipe is adapted from one given in *Cookery for Every Household*, written by Florence Jack in the early twentieth century. It is nicest eaten while still warm, but remains very good chilled.

Serves 4

225g (8oz) chicken livers
60g (2½oz) butter
2–3 tablespoons Madeira
½ garlic clove, crushed
4 sprigs fresh thyme, leaves only
Salt and freshly ground black pepper
Hot toast, to serve

Carefully check that the gall bladders (small dark green sacs) have been removed from the livers and cut off and discard any if necessary. Also cut out any greenish stained patches. Divide each liver into four or five pieces.

Melt the butter in a small frying pan and cook the livers very gently for 4–5 minutes, or until they are just cooked through. Towards the end of the cooking time, add the Madeira, garlic and thyme leaves. As soon as the livers are done, tip the mixture into a blender and process until very smooth. Season to taste with salt and pepper. Divide the mixture between four ramekins and serve, accompanied by slices of hot toast.

AGA method

Use the AGA Simmering Plate to make the paste (or the Boiling Plate if you need a higher heat).

Chicken or Rabbit Fricassee

Fricassee is a French word which has come to mean white meat served in a savoury white sauce. This is Sara Paston-Williams's reconstruction of an 18th-century recipe.

Serves 4–6

4–6 chicken or rabbit joints
chicken stock or water, to
    cover
2 medium onions, sliced
1 bouquet garni
50g (2oz) mushrooms
15g (½oz) butter
Salt and black pepper to
    taste

For the sauce

40g (1½oz) butter
2 tablespoons plain flour
1–2 egg yolks
150ml (¼pt) single cream
Squeeze of lemon juice
Slices of lemon, for garnish

Put the chicken or rabbit joints in a shallow pan, cover with stock or water and add the sliced onions and bouquet garni. Season well. Cover and simmer for about 40 minutes, or until very tender. Drain off the cooking liquor into a measuring jug, cover the pan again and keep hot. The stock should measure 600ml (1 pint); if it is more, turn into a saucepan and reduce.

To prepare the sauce, melt the butter in a separate pan, stir in the flour, cook for a few seconds, without letting the butter brown, then pour on the stock and stir in well. Cook over a gentle heat, stirring all the time until thick. Boil briskly for 3–4 minutes, and then draw aside. At the same time, sauté the mushrooms in butter in another pan. To finish the sauce, mix the yolks with the cream in a bowl, add a little of the hot sauce, then pour the mixture slowly back into the rest of the sauce. Check the seasoning again and add the lemon juice and mushrooms. Pour the sauce over the joints, shaking the pan gently to mix all together. Cover and keep hot for 15 minutes before serving, so that the flavour of the sauce can penetrate the meat. Garnish with lemon slices.

AGA method

Simmer the stock in the Simmering Oven. Put the chicken or rabbit joints in the stock, bring to the boil on the Boiling Plate, and boil for 5 minutes. Cover, transfer to the Simmering Oven, and poach for 45 minutes, or until tender. Make the sauce and sauté the mushrooms as above, using the hotplates. Continue as above, keeping the dish warm in the Simmering Oven or Warming Oven, if you have one.

Coronation Chicken

The original recipe for this dish was devised by the Cordon Bleu Cookery School in London, for the coronation of Queen Elizabeth II. For a truly special summer meal, it is worth roasting a top-quality chicken to make this. Adding yoghurt to the sauce reduces the fat content and makes it lighter.

Serves 6

1 chicken, about 1.5–1.8kg (3½–4lb) weight, cooked and cooled
1 tablespoon sunflower oil
1 small onion, very finely chopped
1cm (½in) cube fresh ginger root, peeled and grated
1 tablespoonful curry powder (use an old-fashioned Madras type)
2 heaped tablespoons mango chutney (chop up any large pieces of fruit)
150ml (¼ pint) mayonnaise (see page 160)
110g (4oz) plain yoghurt (use full-fat or Greek-style, if a richer result is desired)
Approximately 50g (2oz) flaked almonds
Salt and pepper to taste
Fresh parsley or coriander herb, to garnish

Skin, joint and bone the chicken into neat serving pieces and arrange on a platter. Keep cool while you prepare the sauce.

Heat the oil in a small frying pan. Add the onion and ginger and cook over a low heat for 5–10 minutes or until the onion is soft and transparent. Stir in the curry powder and continue to cook gently for 1–2 minutes. Scrape the mixture into a bowl, stir in the mango chutney and set aside to cool. Once cool, stir in the mayonnaise and yoghurt, then add a little water to thin the sauce to a coating consistency. Taste and correct the seasoning. Spoon this sauce over the chicken. Toast the almonds gently in a low oven until golden brown. Allow them to cool, then scatter over the top of the chicken and garnish with parsley or coriander. Keep in a cool place or the refrigerator until ready to serve.

AGA method

Use the AGA hotplates to make the sauce, according to the required temperature for each stage.

Christmas Dinner with all the Trimmings

Although the concept of what a proper Christmas-Day dinner is has varied greatly over the centuries, the present-day ideal of roast turkey and 'trimmings' (the various vegetables and bits and pieces that traditionally go with it) did not show signs of developing until the nineteenth century, but it is now a well-established favourite.

Serves 6–8

1 fresh turkey, approximately 4.5–5.5kg (10–12lb)
75–100g (3–3½oz) butter, softened
Salt and black pepper

For the stuffing
150g (5½oz) stale breadcrumbs
A large handful of fresh thyme or marjoram, leaves only
1 tablespoon finely chopped parsley
Zest of ½ lemon, grated
75g (3oz) beef suet or butter, broken into small pieces
1 teaspoon salt
Pinch of black pepper
1–2 eggs, beaten

For the gravy
1 tablespoon olive oil
Approximately 110g (4oz) bacon, gammon or ham (uncooked), cut into 1cm (½in) cubes
1 shallot, peeled and chopped
A 7.5cm (3in) piece of leek, chopped
1 stick of celery, chopped
1 carrot, chopped
1 slice of turnip, chopped
A few mushroom stalks, if available
Giblets from the turkey
1 tablespoon of finely chopped parsley
450ml (¾ pint) chicken or veal stock, or water
1–2 tablespoons arrowroot

For the roast potatoes
Approximately 1.5 kg (3½ lbs) potatoes, peeled and cut into suitable-sized pieces

Approximately 75g (3oz) fat for roasting (beef or pork dripping, but lard is a good alternative if these are not available)
Salt

For the garnish
Approximately 450g (1lb) chipolata sausages
12 small rashers streaky bacon

For the brussels sprouts with chestnuts
700-800g (1½–1¾lb) Brussels sprouts
Approximately 110g (4oz) bacon, cut in thick strips
A little of the giblet stock (used for the gravy)
125–150g (4½–5½oz) peeled chestnuts
Salt and black pepper

Continued over page

Preheat the oven to 170°C, 325°C, gas mark 3. Remove the giblets from the turkey and set on one side to use for the gravy. Mix all ingredients for the stuffing together, adding the eggs last in stages until the consistency is soft but not too wet. Stuff into the neck end of the turkey, then draw the skin flap down to cover the stuffing and secure it in place with a skewer. Spread the softened butter over the stuffed turkey and season well with salt and pepper.

Calculate the roasting time for the turkey, based on 30 minutes per 500g. Place it on one side in a large roasting tin and cook in the hot oven for about 45 minutes, basting every 15 minutes. Turn the bird on to the other side, baste well and cook for another 45 minutes. Finally, turn it on to its back, baste again, place a piece of foil over the breast to protect it from drying out and continue to cook, basting every 30 minutes or so, until the turkey is cooked. About 15 minutes before the end of the cooking time, remove the foil from the turkey, baste again, and allow the skin to brown. When the bird is fully cooked, the juices that run out of the thigh when pierced with a skewer should be clear. If not, cook for another 15 minutes or so and test again. Remove the cooked turkey to a warm platter, cover loosely with foil and allow to rest for at least 20 minutes, preferably up to an hour. Set the roasting tin with any cooking juices on one side.

While the turkey is cooking, make a giblet stock for the gravy. Heat the olive oil in a fairly large saucepan and add the bacon. Fry gently until it loses its translucency, then add the vegetables, and giblets, turn the heat up and cook briskly, stirring, until they begin to brown. Add the parsley and pour in the stock or water, bring to the boil, lower the heat and simmer gently for about 1 hour. Strain, discarding the debris, and skim off any fat. Cool and chill until needed.

Put the potatoes for roasting in a large pan, just cover with cold water and bring to the boil. Cook for 5 minutes, or until just beginning to soften. Tip them out into a colander and drain well. Once the turkey is cooked and is resting, turn the oven up to 200°C, 400°F, gas mark 6. Put the fat for the potatoes in a large roasting tin and place in the oven to melt and get very hot. Take it out and add the potatoes (wear oven gloves and an apron in case the fat spits – it should be hot enough to sizzle). Turn the potatoes so that they are coated in the hot fat, add a scattering of salt, then roast the potatoes in the hot oven for 40–50 minutes. In a gas oven, put the potatoes at the top. Turn once or twice during the roasting time, adding a light sprinkling of salt each time.

Once the potatoes are in the oven, wrap each sausage in a bacon rasher, spearing it with a cocktail stick to keep the bacon in place. Put into a small ovenproof dish and put in the oven to cook with the potatoes for 30–40 minutes. Turn once or twice during cooking.

To make the gravy, remove and discard any fat from the reserved cooking juices in the roasting tin and add most of the prepared giblet stock. Bring to the boil over a high heat, scraping round the roasting tin to collect any browned bits from the sides. Mix some arrowroot (2 heaped teaspoons per 450 ml/¾ pint liquid) with a little cold water and stir into the liquid in the tin. Heat gently, stirring, until the gravy has just boiled and thickened slightly. Set aside and reheat when needed.

Trim the sprouts, peeling off the outer leaves and cutting a cross in the base of any large ones. Put them in a saucepan, cover with boiling water and cook for about 7–10 minutes, or until just tender. Drain. Take a large frying pan and cook the bacon pieces gently until they start to crisp up. Add the sprouts and turn them around in the bacon fat (if the amount of fat seems excessive, drain a little off). Add just enough of the remaining giblet stock to moisten the mixture. Then put in the chestnuts and stir gently to heat them through. Try not to break them up too much. Taste, add a little salt, if necessary, and a liberal sprinkling of black pepper.

Present the turkey surrounded by the sausage and bacon rolls and the potatoes, if there is room for them on the serving platter. Hand round the freshly cooked sprouts and hot gravy separately.

AGA method

Cook the turkey in the Roasting Oven as above. A 4.5–5.5kg (10–12lb) bird should take about 2–2½ hours. Alternatively, if you have a three- or four-oven AGA, cook for 1 hour in the Roasting Oven then around 2½ hours in the Baking Oven.

To make the giblet stock for the gravy, prepare the giblets as above and bring to the boil on the Simmering Plate. Cover and move to the Simmering Oven and cook for 1½ hours. Continue as above.

To roast the potatoes, use the Boiling Plate to cook for 5 minutes. Drain and continue as above using the Roasting Oven, on the third set of runners, or place the tin directly on to the Roasting Oven floor.

To make the bacon-wrapped sausages, prepare the bacon and sausages as above and cook in the Roasting Oven, on the third set of runners, for 30 minutes, or cook in the Baking Oven (on three- or four-oven models), on the second set of runners.

Make the gravy and cook the sprouts using the AGA hotplates.

Haslet

Haslet is a meatloaf that can be eaten hot or cold. Local bakers in Derbyshire serve Haslet cold as a sandwich filling. Recipes for haslet can be found in several English counties: I have come across a similar recipe from Hampshire. The name comes from the Old French *Hastelet*, which means 'entrails' or 'innards', but here it seems to refer to the finely chopped mixture.

Serves 4

450g (1lb) minced shoulder of pork – not sausage meat
150g (5oz) brown or white breadcrumbs
2 teaspoons finely chopped fresh sage
1 teaspoon mace
110g (4oz) onion, finely chopped
Salt and pepper to taste

Preheat the oven to 180°C, 350°F, gas mark 4. Either line a 450g (1lb) loaf tin with baking paper or grease it well. Soak the breadcrumbs in a little water, then add to the rest of the ingredients in a mixing bowl and mix well together. Season to taste and pack into the tin. Bake uncovered for 1 hour. Serve hot or cold.

AGA method

Assemble as above. Cook the haslet in the Roasting Oven, on the fourth set of runners, for 40–45 minutes. If it is browning too much, slide in the cold plain shelf just above it. Alternatively, cook in the centre of the Baking Oven (on three- or four-oven models) for 1 hour.

Pork and Apricot Trelissick Pipkin

The pipkin in this recipe refers to the casserole dish, traditionally a pot that is glazed on the inside and coarse red earthenware on the outside. Old recipes for pork often have fruit in them, the acidity of the fruit contrasting with the rich meat.

Serves 4

3 onions, peeled and
  chopped
700g (1½lb) diced pork
50g (2oz) dripping or
  4 tablespoons sunflower
  or olive oil
25g (1oz) plain flour
2 teaspoons tomato purée
850ml (1½ pints) chicken or
  vegetable stock
75g (3oz) dried apricots
½ teaspoon mixed herbs
Salt and pepper to taste

Preheat the oven to 190°C, 375°F, gas mark 5. Fry the onions and pork in the dripping or oil, taking care not to burn them. Stir in the flour, then add the tomato purée and stock. Place in a casserole dish with the apricots, mixed herbs, salt and pepper. Cover and cook in the oven for 1½ hours or until tender.

AGA method

Using the Simmering Plate, gently fry the onions and pork in the dripping or oil. Stir in the flour and add the tomato purée and stock. Pour into a casserole dish and add the remaining ingredients. Cook in the Roasting Oven for 20 minutes then transfer to the Simmering Oven for 1½ hours or until tender.

Gammon Poached in Cider with Clove and Mustard Glaze

'With a roly-poly gammon and spinach, "hey-ho" says Anthony Rowley', in the song 'A Frog He Would A-Wooing Go'. This combined method of beginning by poaching and finishing with a blast in a hot oven seems to work perfectly with large or small joints of gammon or bacon. Use the wonderful stock the ham produces to help with the parsley sauce.

Serves 6

1.8kg (4lb) piece of gammon
450ml (15fl oz) cider
Small quantity of onion, carrot and celery for stock
Peppercorns or freshly ground pepper

For the glaze

2 tablespoons Dijon mustard
2 tablespoons soft brown sugar
A few whole cloves

Place the gammon joint in a pan. Pour in the cider and add sufficient water to cover. Add the onion, carrot and celery plus a few whole peppercorns. Cover the pan and bring the liquid slowly to the boil, reduce the heat and simmer, very gently, for approximately 1 hour 40 minutes.

Strain off and reserve the stock. Turn the oven on to full heat. Line a roasting tin with baking paper and place the joint in it. Slice off the skin, leaving a layer of fat on the joint. Smear the fat with the mustard and sugar and score with a sharp knife as if you were laying out a noughts-and-crosses game. Stud the pattern with cloves. Pour in a little of the ham stock to stop the joint sticking and return it to the fully heated oven. Roast for 30 minutes, then turn off the oven and leave the joint to rest for at least 10 minutes. The ham is delicious sliced thickly and served with Parsley Sauce (see page 159).

AGA method

For this recipe, it is important that your cooking pan will fit into the AGA ovens. Prepare the gammon joint in the poaching liquor, bring to the boil on the Boiling Plate, then move to the Simmering Oven and simmer for 2–3 hours. Remove the joint from the oven and prepare it for roasting. Roast in the middle of the Roasting Oven for 25–35 minutes.

Toad in the Hole

The *Oxford Dictionary of Food* gives the earliest reference to a Toad in the Hole as 'The dish called toad in the hole, meat boiled in a crust' in 1787. In 1861, Mrs Beeton has steak and kidney cooking in the batter, so neither version was quite the same as today's dish. Never mind – the combination of sausages and crisp, hot batter is irresistible. The cherry tomatoes are my own touch.

Serves 4

2–3 tablespoons sunflower
    oil or approximately 25g
    (1oz) hard vegetable fat
    such as Trex
6 large sausages
2–3 cherry tomatoes per
    portion

For the batter
110g (4oz) plain flour
½ teaspoon salt
2 large eggs, well beaten
300ml (½ pint) milk, full
    cream or semi-skimmed

Sieve the flour and salt into a mixing bowl and make a batter by stirring in the eggs, and making a smooth paste with a little of the milk. Next, beat in the rest of the milk until the mixture resembles unwhipped double cream. At this point leave it to stand for at least 30 minutes, preferably 1 hour. Preheat the oven to 220°C/425°F/Gas Mark 7.

You can use either a 20 x 16cm (8 x 6in) roasting tin or individual round tins. Add the fat or oil to the roasting tin (or, if using individual tins, put a knob of fat or a little oil in each) and heat in the oven until the fat smokes. Chop each sausage into four and arrange the chunks in the roasting tin or use three chunks per round tin. Intersperse the sausage pieces with cherry tomatoes. Put in the oven for 5 minutes, then pour on the batter and cook for a further 15 minutes. Check to see if the Toad is cooked. The small tins may well be ready at this point, but a large Toad in the Hole will probably require a little longer.

AGA method

This dish is best made when the AGA is at its hottest. Heat the roasting tin or individual tins in the Roasting Oven for 5 minutes. Add the fat or oil to the tin, arrange the sausages and tomatoes on top, and cook for 5 minutes on the Roasting Oven floor. Remove the tin and pour over the batter, then hang the tin on the third set of runners in the Roasting Oven and cook for 15–20 minutes or until it has puffed up and is golden.

Sausage and Apple Plait

A grander version of the sausage roll, this recipe makes good portable picnic fare when cold.

Serves 4

450g (1lb) frozen puff pastry
450g (1lb) sausage meat
1 medium onion, finely
    chopped
1 leek, chopped
1 eating apple, peeled and
    chopped
1 tablespoon fresh herbs –
    a mixture of sage, thyme
    leaves and parsley, all
chopped finely, is perfect
1 tablespoon tomato purée
2 teaspoons Worcester
    sauce
1 egg yolk mixed with a little
    milk to glaze

Preheat the oven to 210°C, 425°F, gas mark 7. Roll the pastry fairly thin, into an oblong approximately 20 x 30cm (8 x 12in). Mix the sausage meat with the chopped onion, leek, apple, herbs, tomato purée and Worcester sauce. Form it roughly into a sausage and lay it on the pastry, leaving a border of at least 5cm on each side. Brush the edges of the pastry with the egg and milk mixture, than make downward diagonal cuts along the length of each side. Weave the resulting strips of pastry into a plait on top of the sausage filling. Seal the ends. Brush with beaten egg, lay it on a piece of baking paper on a baking tin (this makes it easier to move later) and bake for 30 minutes. Serve hot, warm or cold.

AGA method

Assemble the sausage and apple plait as above. Lay the sausage plait on to a shallow baking tin lined with Bake-O-Glide silicone liner and cook on the oven grid shelf set on the Roasting Oven floor for 20–30 minutes. If it is browning too quickly, protect it by sliding in the cold plain shelf directly above it.

West Country Honeyed Pork Stew

The combination of pork and beans is a winner. Before the Industrial Revolution, everyone had a pig. It was the one animal you did not need to have a licence for. Pigs were the garbage collectors before local councils got lumbered with the job. The pig was not a pet; its time was up at Christmas or some other celebration, and every part of the pig was eaten.

Serves 4

1 tablespoon vegetable oil
450g (1lb) shoulder of pork, diced
50g (2oz) butter beans
1 medium onion stuck with cloves
1 teaspoon mixed herbs
1 tablespoon clear honey
600ml (1 pint) chicken stock
250ml (9fl oz) apple juice
3 medium carrots, peeled and cut into 3cm (1in) sticks
2 celery sticks, chopped
2 leeks, washed and chopped
2 tablespoons Worcester sauce
1 tablespoon tomato purée
Salt and pepper to taste

You will need to start this recipe the day before you cook it by soaking the butter beans.

Heat the vegetable oil in an ovenproof casserole and sauté the pork until nicely browned. Drain the beans and add to the pork together with the onion and mixed herbs. Turn everything for a minute or two in the oil. Then add honey, stock and apple juice. Bring to the boil, reduce the heat, cover the pan and simmer for approximately 1 hour, until the beans are just becoming tender. Add carrots, celery, leeks, Worcester sauce and tomato purée. Simmer for a further 30 minutes, or until the meat is tender and the vegetables are cooked. Season to taste.

AGA method

Brown the pork in the casserole on the AGA hotplates. Drain the pre-soaked beans and stir into the casserole along with the onion and mixed herbs. Add the honey, stock and apple juice, then bring to a rapid boil on the Boiling Plate for 2–3 minutes. Cover with a lid, then transfer to the Simmering Oven for 1½ hours, until the beans start to become tender. Place the casserole back on to the Boiling Plate and add the carrots, celery, leeks, Worcester sauce and tomato purée. Bring to the boil again, then return to the Simmering Oven for another hour or until the meat and vegetables are tender.

Bacon and Egg Pie

This pie is best made on a shallow enamel or ceramic ovenproof pie plate. It is a great picnic dish as it is easy to transport on its plate. You won't need knives and forks as it is quite solid when cool.

Serves 4–6

450g (1lb) shortcrust pastry
   (see page 64)
Milk, to seal and glaze

For the filling

225g (8oz) chopped bacon
   or lardons
3 tablespoons chopped
   parsley
6 eggs
Salt and pepper

Preheat the oven to 170°C, 325°F, gas mark 3. Divide the pastry in half. Roll out the first piece to fit a buttered pie plate. Prick the base. Fill the middle of the plate with the bacon or lardons and chopped parsley. Leave the rim clear for sealing. Season to taste; you probably won't need salt. Make six round indentations in the bacon mixture and crack an egg into each one. Roll out the second piece of pastry to form the lid. Brush the rim of the pie with milk and lay the lid carefully over the top, pressing firmly on the rim to seal it. Trim the lid to fit and use the trimmings to decorate the top of the pie. Make a hole in the middle to let the steam out and glaze the pie with milk. Bake for approximately 1 hour. Serve at room temperature.

AGA method

Assemble the pie as above. Place the grid shelf on the floor of the Roasting Oven. Cook the pie on the grid shelf, with the cold plain shelf directly above, for 25–35 minutes or until golden brown. Alternatively, cook in the Baking Oven (on three- and four-oven models) on the oven grid shelf set on the oven floor, for 45–55 minutes.

Pork Pie

Laura Mason in *The National Trust Farmhouse Cookbook* writes: 'In the past pork pies showed local variations in recipe and method and a good pie was a source of pride to a housewife or local butcher. Melton Mowbray in Leicestershire still produces a distinctive pie, and this recipe incorporates elements of that tradition – anchovy essence as a flavouring, and fresh meat instead of brined. The pastry recipe, from Derbyshire, is unusual in the combination of fats. Lard is the usual choice, and can be used for the total weight of fat in this recipe if desired. The method for the jellied stock was worked out by Jane Grigson as a better alternative to the gelatine-fortified stock now used by many makers. The stock can be made in advance, but the pastry should be as fresh as possible.'

Makes 1 large pie, which will serve 10

For the stock

2 pig's trotters, bones, skin or trimmings from the pie meat
1 bay leaf
2–3 sprigs thyme
4 peppercorns
1 onion, stuck with cloves
3 litres (5¼ pints) water

For the filling

1kg (2¼lb) pork, a quarter of which should be fatty, the rest lean; I use a mixture of shoulder and belly
1 teaspoon salt
1 teaspoon anchovy essence
6–8 sage leaves, chopped
Pepper to taste

Place the stock ingredients in a large pan and bring to the boil. Skim well and simmer, covered, for about 3 hours. Strain the liquid into a clean pan and discard the debris. Boil the stock to reduce it to around 500ml (18fl oz). Leave to cool and jellify.

Cut a quarter of the leanest pork into cubes 1cm (½in) across. Mince the rest coarsely – this is best done by hand with a sharp knife, as a mincer tends to compact the meat. Add the seasonings and turn well so they are evenly distributed throughout.

Put the flour in a large bowl and add the salt. Measure the water into a pan and add the fats. Heat the pan, stirring, until the water has come to the boil and all the fat has melted. Remove the pan from the heat and stir the mixture into the flour. Use a wooden spoon at first, then, as it cools slightly, knead to make sure it is all incorporated properly. Cover the bowl and keep it in a warm place. To raise the pie, take three-quarters of the pastry, still warm, and shape it into a disc. Put it in the cake tin and quickly raise it up the sides to the top, making it as even as possible and trying not to get the pastry too thick. The dough should be malleable – if it flops, it is too warm.

For the pastry

450g (1lb) plain flour
½ teaspoon salt
150ml (¼ pint) water
5og (2oz) lard
5og (2oz) butter
25g (1oz) suet
1 egg, beaten

An 18–19cm (7½in) round, sprung cake tin with a removable base

Once the pastry is raised, pack the filling into it. Roll out the remaining quarter to make a lid and brush the edges with beaten egg. Trim any excess and crimp the edges. Make a small hole in the middle and cover it with a pastry rose. Cut leaves from the trimmings and use them to decorate the top of the pie. Brush with beaten egg.

Bake at 200°C, 400°F, gas mark 6 for 30 minutes, then lower the heat to 170°C, 325°F, gas mark 3 and bake for another 1½ hours. Some gravy may bubble out of the pie, but don't worry too much about this – some recipes cite this as an indication that the pie is cooked.

At the end of the cooking time, remove the pie from the oven and allow to stand for 20 minutes. If the jellied stock has cooled off, reheat to boiling. Ease off the pastry rose and pour in as much hot stock as the pie will hold. Replace the rose and allow the pie to cool. Wait 24 hours before cutting.

AGA method

Bring the stock ingredients to the boil on the Boiling Plate for 8 minutes. Cover, then move to the Simmering Oven and cook for 4 hours. Strain the liquid into a clean pan and boil on the Boiling Plate to reduce the stock to 500ml (18fl oz). Leave to cool. Prepare the pork as above. Make the pastry using the AGA hotplates and 'raise' the pie as above. To cook the pie, slide the grid shelf on to the Roasting Oven floor and put the pie on to a shallow baking tray then on to the grid shelf. Slide the cold plain shelf directly above the pie and cook for 25–30 minutes. Move to the Simmering Oven and continue to cook for another 2–2½ hours. Heat the stock on the Simmering Plate and continue as above.

Pease Pudding and Ham

This well-loved combination hails from the north-east of England. Cooking the split peas in the liquid in which the ham is cooked is the traditional method.

Serves 6, plus leftover ham

1 piece unsmoked ham or
    gammon, approximately
    1.5kg (3½lb)
450g (1lb) yellow split peas,
    soaked overnight in cold
    water
1 bouquet garni (1 celery
    stalk, 1 bay leaf, 2 sprigs
    thyme, and a few
    peppercorns, wrapped in
    the green outer leaf of a
    leek and tied)
50g (2oz) butter
Salt and pepper to taste

Ask your butcher if you need to soak the ham or gammon overnight in cold water first to draw out some of the salt. If not, start by putting it in a large pan or flameproof casserole, large enough to hold both the ham and a bag containing the peas. Put the ham in the pan with the bouquet garni and cover with cold water. Bring to the boil.

Meanwhile, drape a pudding cloth over a bowl or colander, then tip the peas into it, allowing the water to drain away. Leaving some space for them to expand as they cook, tie the cloth so that the peas are completely enclosed. When the ham comes to the boil, skim the surface of the water and add the bag of peas. Lower the heat, cover and leave to simmer gently for 1½ hours.

Lift the ham out on to a warm serving dish. Check if the peas are soft by squeezing one through the cloth. If they seem a little underdone, cook them for a few minutes longer. Lift out the bag of peas and allow it to drain, then open it carefully and decant the peas into a food processor. Add the butter and one or two ladlefuls of cooking liquid and blend to a smooth purée. Taste and season with salt and pepper. Discard the bouquet garni and keep the remaining cooking liquid to use as a stock for preparing vegetable, pea or lentil soup. To serve, carve the ham into slices and hand the pease pudding around separately.

AGA Method

Prepare the ham as above. Bring to the boil on the Boiling Plate and boil for 10 minutes. Add the peas, and move to the Simmering Oven for 2–2½ hours. Continue as above.

Fidget Pie

Fidget – or Fitchett – Pie is made throughout the Midlands. I have found recipes for this dish in various cookbooks, including one in *Farmhouse Fare: Recipes from Country Housewives Collected by The Farmers' Weekly*, published in 1950. This seemed particularly appropriate since it was a popular dish with harvesters, as it could be eaten hot or cold. It always contains pork or gammon, apples and onions. I have chosen a recipe associated with Shropshire, where they add potatoes, which makes the pie very sustaining and perfect for hearty appetites. By the way, fidget is a local name for a polecat – the pie was supposed to smell very strong (like a polecat) when cooking!

Serves 4

450g (1lb) potatoes, peeled
   and thickly sliced
350g (12oz) lean gammon
2 large onions, sliced
2 large cooking apples,
   peeled and sliced
2 teaspoons sugar
4 sage leaves
300ml (½ pint) consommé
   or jellied fresh stock
225g (8oz) shortcrust pastry
   (see page 64)
Milk, to glaze
Salt and pepper to taste

Preheat the oven to 180°C, 350°F, gas mark 4. Put a layer of sliced potatoes in a 1.2 litre (2 pint) pie dish. Dice the gammon and put a layer on top of the potatoes, then cover this with onion and apple slices. Sprinkle with 1 teaspoon of the sugar. Shred the sage leaves and sprinkle half of them on top of the onion and apple. Repeat the layers until the dish is full, ending with a layer of gammon. Sprinkle the top layer with the rest of the sugar and sage. Pour just enough stock over the pie to cover the filling and season to taste. Roll out the pastry to make a fairly thick pie crust and cover the top of the dish. Brush the top with milk and bake for 20 minutes, then reduce the heat to 160°C, 325°F, gas mark 3 and bake for a further 45 minutes. If you think the pastry is getting too brown, cover it with foil for the last 15 minutes of the cooking time.

AGA method

Assemble the pie as above, slide the grid shelf on to the Roasting Oven floor, and put the pie on to the grid shelf. Cook for 15 minutes, then slide the cold plain shelf above the pie and cook for a further 10 minutes. Move to the Simmering Oven and continue to cook for another 1½ hours, until the meat is cooked.

Slow-roasted Belly Pork with Apples and Onions

This recipe was mentioned in the book *The English Housekeeper*, published around 1840.

Serves 4–6

2–3 tablespoons oil

6 small onions or banana shallots, peeled

1kg (2¼lb) potatoes, peeled and cut into large chunks

500ml (¾ pint) light chicken or pork stock

1 piece belly pork, approximately 1.5kg (3½lb), skin scored

A few fresh sage leaves, torn up

6 small apples, preferably a dry aromatic variety such as a russet, peeled, halved and cored

Salt and freshly ground black pepper

Preheat the oven to 220°C, 425°F, gas mark 7. Put a generous tablespoon of the oil in a large roasting tin, add the onions or shallots and potato and turn until they are well coated in the oil. Pour in about a quarter of the stock. Season with salt and black pepper.

Prepare the pork by drying the skin, then rubbing it with some of the remaining oil followed by a generous sprinkling of salt. Put a rack over the vegetables in the roasting tin and place the pork on it. Cook in the hot oven for 20 minutes, then reduce the heat to 150°C, 300°F, gas mark 2 and cook for another hour.

Remove from the oven, lift off the rack and add the sage leaves to the vegetables, stirring to ensure that they are well coated. Nestle the apple halves among the vegetables. Put the rack of pork back over the roasting tin and return to the oven to cook for a further hour. Again, remove from the oven and turn the heat up to 200°C, 400°F, gas mark 6. Carefully lift off the rack of pork and stir the vegetables around once more. Replace the rack and return to the oven for a further 20 minutes. Remove the pork and vegetables to a heated serving dish and use the remaining stock to deglaze the roasting tin, to make a thin gravy.

AGA method

Cook in the Roasting Oven for 40–45 minutes until the crackling is golden, then transfer to the Simmering Oven for 2 hours or more. Return the pork to the Roasting Oven for 20–30 minutes to finish.

Welsh Lamb and Leek Casserole

Two Welsh specialities combined in one dish. Welsh lamb is famous for its flavour – the purebred mountain lamb is smaller than its crossbred cousin but the taste is the best of all. The leek is the vegetable of Wales – tradition says that Welsh warriors wore leeks in their hats to show which side they were on in a victorious battle with the Saxons in the 7th century.

Serves 4

50g (2oz) butter
450g (1lb) neck of lamb, cut into large dice
450g (1lb) leeks, washed and chopped
1 eating apple, peeled, cored and sliced
2 tablespoons plain flour
1 teaspoon mixed herbs or 1 tablespoon fresh mixed herbs, finely chopped
600ml (1 pint) vegetable stock
Salt and pepper to taste
Chopped parsley, for garnish

Preheat the oven to 180°C, 350°F, gas mark 4. Melt a quarter or so of the butter in a frying pan. Brown the lamb and transfer to a large casserole. Add the leeks and apple slices to the same pan, fry gently for 5 minutes and add to the lamb. Melt the remaining butter in the pan, stir in the flour and cook gently for 2 minutes or so. Add the herbs and stock. Heat gently, stirring all the time, until the sauce thickens. Season to taste, then pour over the lamb. Cover and cook for approximately 2 hours until the lamb is tender. Sprinkle with chopped parsley and serve with potatoes or rice. It does not need further vegetables.

AGA method

Melt a quarter of the butter in a frying pan and brown the lamb on the AGA hotplates. Transfer the lamb to a casserole. Add the leeks and apple to the frying pan and gently cook for 5 minutes. Add to the casserole. Make the sauce in the frying pan as above and pour over the lamb. Bring to a rapid boil on the Boiling Plate for 2–3 minutes. Cover with a lid, then transfer to the Simmering Oven for 2–2½ hours, or until the lamb is tender. Serve as above.

Irish Stew

'Then hurrah for an Irish Stew/That will stick to your belly like glue.' Irish Stew is a dish that causes arguments. Should it have pearl barley in it or not? Are carrots and/or turnips allowed? The only consensus is that mutton (nowadays, lamb) is the dominant ingredient. This recipe was given to me in Northern Ireland. It makes use of the excellent raw ingredients available there, and tastes delicious. I rest my case!

Serves 4

1 tablespoon vegetable oil

450g (1lb) neck fillet of lamb, cut into chunks

1 large onion, peeled and sliced

2 medium carrots, peeled and cut into short lengths

1 celery stick (optional), chopped

450g (1lb) new potatoes, scrubbed

Approx 1 litre (1¼ pints) vegetable stock

225g (8oz) cooked potato, mashed

Salt and pepper to taste

Preheat the oven to 150°C, 300°F, gas mark 2. Heat the oil in a cast-iron casserole and fry the meat and the onion together until nicely browned. Take the casserole off the heat and add the carrots, celery and potatoes. Stir and add the vegetable stock to cover the meat and vegetables. Bring the casserole to the boil and then either simmer very slowly on the top of the cooker or stew gently in the oven until the meat is tender and the vegetables are cooked but still have a little crunch. Stir in the mashed potato to thicken the gravy and season to taste with salt and pepper.

AGA method

Heat the oil in a casserole on the Roasting Oven floor, and fry the meat and onions until brown. Add the carrots, celery, potatoes and stock to the casserole. Bring to a rapid boil on the Boiling Plate for 2–3 minutes. Cover with a lid then transfer to the Simmering Oven for 2–2½ hours, or until the lamb is tender. Continue as above with the mashed potato.

Shepherd's Pie

Shepherd's Pie probably originated in the north of England or Scotland, where there are large numbers of sheep. In company with its frugal rural traditions, it tastes best when made with leftover chopped or minced lamb. This is weekday fare after Sunday's roast. This well-loved recipe can also be made with beef mince, in which case it is known as Cottage Pie.

Serves 4

2 tablespoons olive or
    sunflower oil
1 large onion (approximately
    225g/8oz), finely chopped
225g (8oz) carrots, peeled
    and finely chopped
450g (1lb) minced lamb –
    leftover cooked lamb
    from a joint is particularly
    good
1 tablespoon plain flour
300ml (½ pint) beef or lamb
    stock
1 tablespoon tomato purée
2 teaspoons Worcester
    sauce
½ teaspoon dried mixed
    herbs
Salt and freshly ground black
    pepper to taste

For the topping

450g (1lb) potatoes, peeled
    and sliced
25g (1oz) butter
150ml (¼ pint) half cream

Preheat the oven to 190°C, 375°F, gas mark 5. Melt the oil in a saucepan and sauté the onion and carrots until the onion is soft but not coloured. Add the minced lamb and cook gently until the meat is browned. Stir in the flour and cook for 5 minutes. Gradually stir in the stock, tomato purée, Worcester sauce, herbs and seasoning and bring to the boil. Reduce the heat, cover the pan and simmer for 10 minutes. Turn into an ovenproof dish and allow to cool a little before topping with potato.

Boil the potatoes and drain. Mash them and beat in the butter, together with the cream. Season to taste with salt and pepper. Spread the potato with a fork over the meat. Fork up the top so that there are furrows which will become crisp and golden in cooking. Bake for 20–30 minutes, until the top is golden brown.

AGA method

Prepare the onion, carrots and meat as above, using the AGA hotplates. Boil the potatoes on the Boiling Plate for 4 minutes, then drain off all the water and transfer the covered saucepan to the Simmering Oven for 25 minutes. Remove from the oven and mash. Beat the mashed potatoes with the butter and cream and then spread over the meat. Move to the Roasting Oven for 30–35 minutes, until the top is golden brown.

Lancashire Hotpot

Every county in the North has its hotpot. There's even a vegetable version that was cooked when the family's breadwinner was laid off and money was scarce – called, logically, 'Fatherless Hotpot'. However, hotpot generally means meat and potatoes in a deep pot, stewed slowly in the oven until tender, with the lid removed at the end of the cooking time to crisp the potatoes. Extras are important: some swear by a layer of black pudding cut into chunks in the middle; others add chunks of stewing beef or lambs' kidneys. Both black pudding and kidney add flavour to the pot and thicken the gravy. Robust root vegetables also add flavour and pad out the (more expensive) meat.

Serves 6–8

900g (2lb) lamb, cut into
  chunks
2 tablespoons plain flour,
  seasoned with salt and
  pepper
25g (1oz) butter
1 tablespoon olive oil
1 onion, peeled and sliced
2 carrots, peeled and
  chopped
1 turnip, peeled and
  chopped
110g (4oz) black pudding,
  skinned and cut into
  chunks
2 bay leaves
1 bouquet garni
Approximately 600ml
  (1 pint) vegetable stock
6 large potatoes

Preheat the oven to 190°C, 375°F, gas mark 5. Dust each piece of meat with seasoned flour. Melt half the butter and the oil in a deep casserole and brown the meat. Take it out and put in the onion. Cook it until it begins to soften. Remove the onion and layer up the casserole as follows. Pack a layer of meat at the bottom. Then put in half the onion, carrot, turnip and black pudding. Next put in a second layer of meat and finish with another layer of vegetables and black pudding. Tuck in the bay leaves and bouquet garni.

Fill the casserole with vegetable stock to just below the top of the vegetables. Peel and slice the potatoes and overlap them in several layers on the top. Melt the rest of the butter and brush it over the potatoes. Bake for at least 3 hours, removing the lid for the last 30 minutes to brown the potatoes.

AGA method

Prepare the hotpot as above using the AGA hotplates. Cook the hotpot in the Roasting Oven for 30 minutes, then transfer to the Simmering Oven for 2½ hours. Move the hotpot to the Roasting Oven, lid off, for the final 20 minutes cooking.

Kebob'd Lamb

The earliest picture of grilled 'kebob'd' meat on a shish, or skewer, that I have seen is a part of the Bayeux Tapestry. The scene is a feast at Pevensey, just after the Norman army landed in Sussex. Cooks are preparing chunks of meat and small whole birds, and threading them on to skewers. To their left, William, Duke of Normandy sits down to dine while Bishop Odo says grace. The recipe below is for lamb and vegetable skewers (some of the best lamb in Britain is raised on Romney Marshes, very near Pevensey). Don't thread the pieces on to the skewers too tightly; you want the heat of the fire to penetrate the skewer. Ideally you need to begin this recipe the day before you want to serve it: the longer the lamb marinades, the better it will taste.

**Serves 6
(2 kebabs per person)**

900g (2lb) lamb (neck fillet
or leg)
1 onion, peeled
2 red peppers
18 cherry tomatoes
12 button mushrooms
12 fresh bay leaves, cut
in half

For the marinade
150ml (¼ pint) olive oil
150ml (¼ pint) red wine
2 garlic cloves, crushed
1 fresh rosemary sprig,
chopped
Salt and pepper to taste

Mix all the ingredients for the marinade in a bowl large enough to take the lamb and allow you to stir it. Cut the lamb into 2.5cm (1in) cubes and mix into the marinade, making sure that every piece is well coated. Cover the bowl, refrigerate and leave to stand overnight, if possible, giving it a stir from time to time.

When you are ready to make up the kebabs, cut the onion and peppers into pieces that are about the same size as the cubes of lamb. Oil 12 skewers and thread the meat and vegetables on alternately, interleaving them with the half bay leaves, until you have used up all the pieces. Cook on a barbecue, basting the kebabs with the marinade when you turn them. Serve with couscous or saffron-flavoured rice and a salad. Green Sauce (see page 166) made with mint and parsley is a delicious accompaniment.

AGA method

Prepare the lamb as above. Heat a ridged grill pan on the Roasting Oven floor until smoking hot, and use it to cook the lamb. Alternatively, grill at the top of the Roasting Oven, on the top set of runners, with the grill rack set in its highest position in the roasting tin.

Lamb Cutlets Reform

This special-occasion recipe was invented for the Reform Club by an Italian, Charles Francatelli, chef to Queen Victoria. The magic ingredient in the sauce is the redcurrant jelly. The tart sweetness is perfect with the lamb.

Serves 6

12 lamb cutlets
Olive oil, for brushing

For the sauce
1 carrot
1 small onion
1 gammon steak
25g (1oz) butter
150ml (5fl oz) white wine
    vinegar
600ml (1 pint) vegetable
    stock
150g (6oz) redcurrant jelly
4 cloves
Finely grated nutmeg, to
    taste
¼ teaspoon dried thyme
2 tablespoons arrowroot

For garnish
'Reform Chips' – matchsticks
    of chopped cooked
    carrots, gherkins, hard-
    boiled egg whites and
    ham
A handful of chopped
    parsley

Finely dice the carrot, onion and gammon. Melt the butter and fry the carrot, onion and gammon until golden brown. Add the white wine vinegar and boil the mixture so that the liquid reduces rapidly. When it is reduced by about one-third, add the vegetable stock, redcurrant jelly, cloves, nutmeg and thyme. Simmer very slowly for 30 minutes. Put the arrowroot in a small bowl, add 1 tablespoon of the sauce and stir until it is smooth. Then stir the mixture into the sauce and whisk or stir until smooth. The arrowroot should thicken the sauce without colouring it. Strain the sauce into a basin and stand it in a pan of boiling water to keep warm while you grill the cutlets (alternatively, you can make the sauce ahead of time and reheat it gently when you need it).

Preheat the grill to high. Alternatively, you can cook the cutlets in a heavy, ridged grill pan over a high heat. Brush the cutlets with oil and grill for approximately 3 minutes on each side. To serve, put a couple of tablespoons of sauce on a heated plate with two cutlets on the top and garnish with the Reform Chips and parsley. Accompany with steamed or boiled potatoes.

AGA method

Put a ridged grill pan on to the floor of the Roasting Oven while you make the sauce, using the AGA hotplates. Simmer the sauce in the Simmering Oven for 40–45 minutes. Finish the sauce, then keep warm at the back of the AGA, or in the Simmering or Warming Oven. Cook the cutlets in the smoking-hot grill pan on the Roasting Oven floor or on the Boiling Plate. Serve as above.

Lamb Casseroled in Ale with Prunes and Raisins

'Take a piece of Mutton, and cutte it in pieces, and wash it very cleane, and put it in a faire pot with ale…and season it with sinamon and Ginger Nutmeggs…so serve it on soppes and garnish it with fruite'. Thomas Dawson in *The Good Huswife's Jewel* in 1596. Below is Sara Paston-Williams's tasty adaptation of that old recipe.

Serves 4

25g (1oz) butter
1 tablespoon vegetable oil
4 lamb leg steaks,
    approximately 700g (1½lb)
1 large onion, finely sliced
600ml (1 pint) real ale
½ tablespoon fresh
    rosemary, chopped or ½
    teaspoon dried rosemary
½ tablespoon fresh thyme,
    chopped or ½ teaspoon
    dried thyme
2 tablespoons fresh parsley,
    chopped
½ teaspoon ground allspice
2–3 whole cloves
50g (2oz) raisins
25g (1oz) fresh white
    breadcrumbs
225g (8oz) prunes, stoned
4 slices wholemeal toast
Freshly ground black pepper
    and salt to taste
Orange slices, for garnish

Preheat the oven to 180°C, 350°F, gas mark 4. Heat the butter and oil in a heavy casserole dish and brown the lamb steaks quickly on both sides. Remove with a slotted spoon and set on one side. Reduce the heat and cook the onions in the remaining fat until soft. Replace the meat in the casserole and cover with ale. Add the herbs, spices and raisins, then season with salt and pepper. Cover tightly with a lid and place in a moderate oven for 30 minutes. Add the breadcrumbs and prunes and return to the oven for a further 30 minutes, or until the lamb is tender. Check the seasoning and adjust as necessary, then serve each lamb steak on a slice of toast. Pour over the gravy and garnish with slices of orange before serving.

AGA method

Brown the lamb steaks on each side in the casserole on the AGA hotplates. Remove with a slotted spoon and set aside. Soften the onion in the casserole, then put back the meat and cover with the ale. Add the herbs, spices and raisins, and season. Bring to a rapid boil on the Boiling Plate for 2–3 minutes. Cover with a lid, then transfer to the Roasting Oven for 20 minutes. Add the other ingredients as above and cook for a further 20–30 minutes, until the lamb is tender. Continue as above.

Oxtail Stew

Kettner's Book of the Table **suggests that our taste for oxtail was learnt from the Huguenots who settled in Bermondsey, south London. Bermondsey was full of tanneries. The leather workers were sold ox hides with their tails intact, which weren't needed in the process. The Huguenots made the tails into soup so good that its fame spread far and wide. The Oxtail Stew below is spicy and rich. It doesn't take long to prepare, but it needs hours of slow cooking.**

Serves 6

2 pieces of oxtail per person
Plain flour seasoned with salt
    and pepper
25g (1oz) butter
1 tablespoon olive oil
110g (4oz) bacon, cut into
    cubes
200ml (7fl oz) red wine
2 onions, stuck with cloves
2 garlic cloves
1 celery stick, chopped
1 large carrot, peeled and
    chopped
2 small turnips, quartered
1 bouquet garni
2 bay leaves
2 tablespoons tomato purée
600ml (1 pint) vegetable
    stock
2 large carrots, peeled and
    cut into chunks
3 leeks, trimmed, sliced and
    washed

Preheat the oven to 140°C, 275°F, gas mark 1. Dust the pieces of oxtail with seasoned flour. Melt the butter and oil. Fry the bacon cubes until they start to brown. Take them out with a slotted spoon and set aside while you brown the oxtail pieces all over. Pour in the wine, let it bubble. Then add the onions, garlic, celery, carrot, turnips, bouquet garni and bay leaves. Mix the tomato purée with the vegetable stock and add it to the casserole. Bring slowly to the boil, then cover the pan and put it in the preheated oven to stew gently for 2–3 hours. If you are going to serve the dish later, let it get cold at this point and skim the cold fat off the surface before you reheat it. Otherwise skim the fat off the hot casserole, add the carrots and leeks and return it to the oven for the final hour's cooking.

AGA method

Dust the oxtail pieces with seasoned flour. Brown the bacon in the casserole on one of the AGA hotplates. Remove with a slotted spoon and then brown the oxtail pieces. Add the red wine and bubble for a minute, then add everything except the leeks and carrots. Bring to a rapid boil on the Boiling Plate for 2–3 minutes. Cover with a lid, then transfer to the Simmering Oven for 3–3½ hours. Continue as above: either let it go cold and take the fat off, or skim the fat from the hot casserole, add the carrots and leeks, return to the boil on the Boiling Plate and transfer to the Simmering Oven for a further 1–1½ hours.

Beef and Guinness Casserole

This recipe uses two of Ireland's best-known products – beef and stout. Because they are so good and so complementary to each other there is no need for complex spices and herbs. The recipe is simple, the result delicious. You will find a recipe for Champ – the perfect vegetable accompaniment – on page 181.

Serves 4

1 tablespoon vegetable oil
450g (1lb) steak, cubed
225g (8oz) onions, chopped
425ml (¾ pint) Guinness
225g (8oz) carrots, peeled and cut into fine matchsticks
A little cornflour to thicken the sauce
Salt and pepper to taste

Preheat the oven to 150°C, 300°F, gas mark 2. Heat the oil in a cast-iron casserole and fry the steak and the onions until all are nicely browned. Pour over the Guinness – it should cover the meat and the onions, but if it does not, add a little water. Cover the pan and cook in a slow oven until the meat is just tender. At this point add the carrots and cook for a further 45 minutes. Thicken the gravy with a little cornflour – probably about 2 teaspoons creamed with a little water. Season with salt and pepper.

AGA method

Heat the oil in a casserole on the Roasting Oven floor and fry the steak and onions until brown. Add the Guinness and water if necessary. Bring to a rapid boil on the Boiling Plate for 2–3 minutes. Cover with a lid, then transfer to the Simmering Oven for about 1½ hours, or until tender. Add the carrots and continue to cook for another hour. Thicken the gravy, season and continue as above.

Beef Olives

Serves 6

675g (1¼lb) topside of beef,
　　cut in thin slices
2 teaspoons Dijon mustard
Salt and pepper to taste

For the stuffing
25g (1oz) butter
2 shallots, peeled and
　　chopped
2 garlic cloves, peeled and
　　chopped (optional)
110g (4oz) chopped bacon
　　or lardons
75g (3oz) white
　　breadcrumbs
2 tablespoons parsley
1 tablespoon other mixed
　　herbs (thyme, tarragon,
　　sage and marjoram are
　　all good)
1 egg

For the sauce
25g (1oz) butter
1 tablespoon olive oil
2 shallots, peeled and
　　chopped
2 garlic cloves, peeled and
　　chopped
450g (1lb) mixed root
　　vegetables
300ml (½ pint) vegetable
　　stock
150ml (¼ pint) red wine

Beef Olives are named presumably because of the shape of these rolls of best beef with a savoury stuffing.

Preheat the oven to 170°C, 325°F, gas mark 3. Put the slices of beef between pieces of clingfilm and beat them very thin. Then trim so that you have at least two pieces per person about 10cm (4in) square. Spread mustard on each slice and season them. Let them rest while you make the stuffing.

Melt the butter and fry the shallots and garlic gently for a couple of minutes, add the bacon and continue to cook for about 5 minutes. Remove from the heat, add the breadcrumbs, herbs and egg, season and combine all the ingredients. Put about a tablespoonful of stuffing on the mustard-covered side of each beef slice. Roll them up, tuck the ends over and tie them up with cotton like a parcel. Set them aside while you prepare the sauce.

Melt the butter and oil and fry the shallots and garlic gently for a few minutes. Add the rest of the vegetables, then turn them so that they are covered with the butter and oil. Spread across the bottom of a shallow ovenproof dish or casserole. Put the beef olives on the top in a single layer. Tip the stock and red wine into the pan that held the vegetables, bubble it up until it is boiling and pour the liquid over the meat. Cover the casserole and cook for 1 hour. Remove the lid, turn the beef olives over and continue cooking with the lid off until they are brown and tender. Snip the cotton off before you serve the beef.

AGA method

Prepare as above, using the AGA hotplates. Assemble the casserole then cook in the Roasting Oven for 45 minutes. Remove the lid and continue to cook in the Simmering Oven for another 45 minutes to an hour. Continue as above.

Beef and Ham Loaf

This recipe is very simple – it is the English equivalent of a French terrine. It tastes very good with new potatoes.

Serves 6

350g (12oz) best minced
    beef
350g (12oz) minced cooked
    ham
50g (2oz) fresh
    breadcrumbs
1 teaspoon mixed herbs
4 shredded sage leaves
2 eggs, beaten
Salt and pepper to taste

Preheat the oven to 180°C, 350°F, gas mark 4. Grease a loaf tin large enough to take all the ingredients, approximately 700g (1½lb). Put all the ingredients except the eggs in a large bowl and mix together evenly. Stir in the eggs and transfer the mixture to the loaf tin, pressing it in well and smoothing the top. Cover with a layer of greaseproof paper and layer of foil and stand the loaf tin in a roasting tin. Fill the roasting tin with water to come halfway up the loaf tin. Bake for 1 hour. Allow to cool and chill overnight. Unmould on to a serving dish and serve cold.

AGA method

Assemble the loaf and put a grid shelf on the Roasting Oven floor. Stand the loaf tin in the roasting tin and fill it halfway up with boiling water. Place the roasting tin on to the grid shelf and bake for 1–1½ hours. Alternatively, cook in the centre of the Baking Oven (on three- and four-oven models). Follow the cooling instructions above.

Lobscouse

Lobscouse denotes a stew of meat and root vegetables, cooked by simmering on top of the stove. It is made in parts of North Wales, Staffordshire, Cheshire and Lancashire (and is supposed to be the origin of the word 'scouse', used to describe someone from Liverpool). Similar dishes of the same name are also known around the Baltic coast, where they are part of a tradition of seafaring food.

Serves 6

1 piece brisket of beef, approximately 650–700g (1¼–1½lb)
1 bay leaf
1 large onion, chopped
Approximately 200g (7oz) carrots, peeled
½ small swede, peeled
5 large potatoes, peeled
Salt and black pepper to taste
Chopped parsley, to garnish

Follow your butcher's advice as to whether or not the meat needs to be soaked overnight in cold water to draw out some of the salt before using. When ready to make the stew, put the beef into a pan in which it fits snugly, cover with water, add the bay leaf and bring slowly to a simmer. Cover the pan and cook for about 1½–2 hours until tender.

Remove the beef from the pan and allow it to cool enough for you to handle it. Trim of any excess fat and cut the meat into 1cm (½in) cubes. Reserve the cooking broth, skimming off some of the fat if it seems excessive. Cut all the vegetables into approximately 1cm (½in) cubes.

Return the diced meat to the pan with the skimmed broth. Add the onions, carrots and swede, bring to a simmer and cook gently for 10–15 minutes, then add the potatoes and cook for another 20 minutes, or until the potatoes are starting to disintegrate and thicken the stew, especially if stirred. Taste and correct the seasoning, using plenty of black pepper. Serve piping hot in warm bowls, with a little chopped parsley sprinkled over each portion.

AGA method

Assemble the beef for simmering, then bring to the boil on the Boiling Plate and boil for 5 minutes. Cover and move to the Simmering Oven for 2½–3½ hours, or until tender. Finish the dish using the AGA hotplates and the Simmering Oven.

Boiled Beef and Carrots with Parsley Dumplings

'Boiled beef and carrots,' sang music-hall star Harry Champion, 'Keeps you fit and keeps you well.' He's right – and I would add 'keeps you warm': this is a great winter dish.

Serves 6–8

1 piece of salted silverside or brisket of beef, at least 1.8kg (4lb)
1 pig's trotter, chopped in half
2 small onions, stuck with cloves
2 small turnips, quartered
2 celery sticks, roughly chopped
1 leek, trimmed, chopped and washed
2 bay leaves
½ teaspoon black peppercorns, lightly crushed
20 baby carrots, scrubbed
225g (8oz) small new potatoes, scrubbed

For the dumplings
110g (4oz) plain flour
½ teaspoon salt
2 level teaspoons baking powder
25g (1oz) butter
1 egg
A handful of chopped parsley
Milk, to mix

Ask your butcher if you need to soak the meat overnight to draw out some of the salt. If not, start by putting it in a large pan or cast-iron casserole. Tuck the trotter, onions, turnips, celery, leek and bay leaves round it and scatter the peppercorns over the meat. Pour water over the meat until it is just covered and bring slowly to the boil. Cover the pan and simmer for about 2 hours. Remove the trotter and vegetables. Add the carrots and new potatoes and simmer for a further 20 minutes.

To make the dumplings, sift the flour, salt and baking powder together. Add the butter, chopped into small pieces, and rub it into the flour. Mix the egg with the parsley and add to the flour. Mix with a little milk into a stiff dough. Form into small balls, the size of marbles. Add to the casserole for the final 20 minutes of cooking time.

To serve, lift the meat out on to a serving dish and garnish with the carrots and new potatoes. Carve the meat, and serve with the vegetables, dumplings and broth.

AGA method

To cook the casserole, put the beef, trotter, onions, turnips, celery, leek and bay leaves into a large pan with the water and peppercorns. Bring to a rapid boil on the Boiling Plate for 5 minutes, then transfer to the Simmering Oven for 3 hours. Continue as above. Make the dumplings, then add to the casserole and move the dish to the Roasting Oven for the final 20 minutes.

Steak and Kidney Pie

Steak and Kidney Pie has a surprisingly short history for such a national institution. Beefsteak pies and puddings have been around for centuries, but Mrs Beeton gave the first recipe for a pudding with beefsteak and kidney in it in 1859. She also suggested the traditional optional extras of mushrooms or oysters. In her time, the oysters would have been cheaper than the mushrooms. Steak and Kidney Pie is a pub-menu staple and is always available from the ready-meal cabinet at the supermarket, and is even sold in tins. Make your own and it will, I promise, taste much better.

Serves 4

450g (1lb) stewing steak
175g (6oz) kidney
1½ rounded tablespoons
    seasoned flour
1 large onion, peeled and
    chopped
25–50g (1–2oz) dripping or
    3–4 tablespoons olive or
    sunflower oil
425ml (¾ pint) beef stock
1 rounded teaspoon
    mustard powder
Salt and pepper to taste
225g (8oz) shortcrust (see
    page 64) or puff pastry
A little milk

Preheat the oven to 140°C, 275°F, gas mark 1. Cut the steak and kidney into small pieces and toss in seasoned flour. Fry the sliced onion in the dripping or oil and place in a casserole. Brown the meat lightly in the fat a few pieces at a time and add to the onion. Pour over the stock, cover the casserole and stew gently in the oven for 1–1½ hours. Stir in the mustard powder and correct the seasoning to taste. You can prepare the pie ahead to this point.

Increase the oven temperature to 210°C, 425°F, gas mark 7. Turn the meat and onions into a large ovenproof pie dish. Roll out the pastry and cover the pie, using any trimmings to decorate, and make a slit in the centre. Brush the top with milk and bake for 10–15 minutes. Reduce the heat to 180°C, 350°F, gas mark 4 for a further 20 minutes until the pie is golden. Serve hot with green vegetables, jacket potatoes and mustard.

AGA method

Fry the onion and brown the meat using the AGA hotplates. Add the stock and cook in the Simmering Oven for 1½–2 hours. When you have assembled the pie, cook the dish on the fourth set of runners in the Roasting Oven for 25–30 minutes. If the pastry is browning too much, protect with the cold plain shelf.

Beef and Vegetable Pottage with Baked Norfolk Dumpling

Pottage was eaten by everyone in the Middle Ages. This is a rich man's pottage since it contains meat. Notice there are no potatoes – they hadn't yet reached Britain.

Serves 6–8

For the beef and vegetable pottage
900g (2lb) prepared
   vegetables, roughly
   chopped
700g (1½lb) shin of beef
Vegetable stock
2 tablespoons fresh mixed
   herbs or 1 tablespoon
   mixed dried herbs

For the baked Norfolk dumpling
225g (8oz) self-raising flour
Pinch of salt
175g (6oz) shredded suet
A little milk

Preheat the oven to 160°C, 325°F, gas mark 3. Prepare a mix of vegetables of some of the following: leeks, celery, onions, carrots, turnips, cabbage. Chop the meat into large chunks and pack it at the bottom of a large cast-iron casserole. Add the herbs and sufficient vegetable stock to cover the meat then bring to the boil on the top of the stove. Take the casserole off the heat and add all the chopped vegetables in a thick layer on top of the meat and stock. Cover the pan and cook slowly in the oven for at least 2 and preferably 3 hours. Simmer the pot on the top of the stove for the last 30 minutes if you are serving with Norfolk Dumpling (below), so the oven can be heated to a higher temperature. Season with salt if necessary and serve each helping topped with a wedge of dumpling.

For the dumpling, grease a 23cm (9in) flan dish. Mix together the flour, salt and shredded suet with just enough milk to make a soft dough. Knead the dough into a round, approximately 2.5cm (1in) thick, and place in the dish. Make criss-cross lines on the top and brush with milk. Turn the oven up to 190°C, 375°F, gas mark 5 and bake for 30–40 minutes. Cut into wedges to serve with the pottage.

AGA method

Prepare the casserole and bring to the boil using the AGA hotplates. Put a lid on, transfer to the Simmering Oven, and cook for 3–4 hours. Make the dumpling and bake in the Roasting Oven, on the fourth set of runners with the cold plain shelf directly above, for 30–35 minutes.

Cornish Pasties

Pasties – also known as tiddy-oggies – are made all over Cornwall. Originally they were portable meals, taken to work by the tin miners and farm labourers, and had vegetables and meat at one end and a sweet filling for pudding at the other. Forfar Bridies, Priddy Oggies, Yorkshire Mint Pasties and Bedfordshire Clangers are pasties from other parts of Britain, with many different fillings.

Makes 2 large pasties

225g (8oz) shortcrust pastry
   (see page 64)
200g (7oz) potato, peeled
   and chopped
100g (3½oz) raw turnip,
   chopped
60g (2½oz) onion, chopped
250–300g (9–10½oz) steak
   chuck or skirt, finely
   chopped (don't use
   minced beef)
Milk or egg to glaze

Preheat the oven to 200°C, 400°F, gas mark 6. Roll out the pastry to 5mm (¼in) thick and cut two dinner-plate-sized rounds. Mix the vegetables and use to cover half of each piece of pastry. Season the meat well and cover the vegetables. Wet the edges of the pastry, fold each piece in half and crimp the edges; brush with milk or beaten egg to glaze. Bake on a lightly greased tray or on baking paper, starting in a hot oven. After 15 minutes, lower the heat to 180°C, 350°F, gas mark 4 and cook for another 45 minutes.

AGA method

Make the pasties as above and bake in the Roasting Oven, on the grid shelf placed on the oven floor, for 20–25 minutes, until browned. Then slide the cold plain shelf above the pasties, on the third set of runners, and continue to bake for 30–35 minutes. For three- and four-oven models, bake in the Roasting Oven on the grid shelf placed on the oven floor for 20–25 minutes, until browned, then transfer to the centre of the Baking Oven for another 45 minutes.

Northumbrian Hodgepodge Pie

'Gees in Hoggepot' and 'Goos in hochepot' are medieval ancestors of the Hodgepodge pie. It is a close relative of the Hotpot (see page 123). Where it differs is that several different meats are included in this one dish. Where it agrees is in the slices of crisp, golden potato that top it. There are several different regional hodgepodge pies: Scottish Hodgepodge has mutton and peas in it. This Northumbrian version is thickened with pearl barley. All hodgepodges make a filling one-pot meal in a cold climate.

Serves 6

900g (2lb) stewing veal, pork
    and lamb in equal
    quantities
Dripping (if you don't have
    any dripping you can use
    untraditional olive or
    sunflower oil)
225g (8oz) onions, sliced
225g (8oz) carrots, sliced
600–850ml (1–1½ pints)
    hot water mixed with
    1 teaspoon Worcester
    sauce
2 tablespoons plain flour
2 tablespoons pearl barley
1 teaspoon mixed herbs
450g (1lb) potatoes, thinly
    sliced
50g (2oz) grated cheese
Salt and pepper to taste

Preheat the oven to 160°C, 325°F, gas mark 3. In a large frying pan brown the meat, a few pieces at a time, in the dripping or oil. Transfer the meat to a wide casserole dish. Next fry the onions and carrots for a few minutes. Stir in the flour to soak up the juices, then gradually add the hot water, stirring all the time until the liquid is smoothly blended. Pour the contents of the frying pan over the meat in the casserole – sprinkle in the pearl barley and mixed herbs and season to taste with salt and pepper. Arrange the potato slices on top in an overlapping pattern. Cover with a lid and cook in the oven for 1½ hours. Remove the lid, scatter over the grated cheese and cook for a further 50 minutes. If the top is not browning sufficiently, turn up the oven heat for the last 15 minutes or finish under the grill.

AGA method

Brown off the meat, fry the onions and carrots and make the flour base as above using the AGA hotplates. When everything is in the casserole, bring it to the boil on the Boiling Plate for 3–5 minutes. Cover with a lid then transfer to the Roasting Oven for 10 minutes. Move the casserole to the Simmering Oven and cook for 2½ hours. Sprinkle the cheese on top and continue to cook for another 50 minutes. Move to the Roasting Oven, lid off, to brown the cheese for a final 8–10 minutes.

Casserole of Pheasant with Chestnuts

Pheasants originated in the Near and Far East, but they have been part of the British diet for a long time. There is a recipe for pheasant in *The Forme of Cury*, Britain's oldest cookery book, written after the coronation celebrations for Richard II in 1390. The recipe below is inspired by *The Constance Spry Cookery Book*, which was the bible for enthusiastic cooks in the 1950s and 60s. Young pheasants are generally roasted, but if they are older you need to stew them slowly. Pheasant is in season, and readily available, in autumn and midwinter, so chestnuts, which are also harvested in the autumn, seem an appropriate addition.

Serves 4

1 tablespoon olive oil

25g (1oz) butter

2 pheasants, cut into two, lengthwise

225g (8oz) peeled and skinned chestnuts

225g (8oz) button onions

2 teaspoons plain flour

450ml (16fl oz) stock

Grated zest and juice of 1 orange

2 teaspoons redcurrant jelly

1 glass red wine

1 bouquet garni

Preheat the oven to 150°C, 300°F, gas mark 2. Heat the oil and butter in a deep casserole and brown the pheasant joints all over. Remove from the pan. Sauté the chestnuts and onions until they begin to change colour. Remove them from the pan. Mix the flour with the remaining fat and cook for a few moments until it starts to change colour. Add the stock, orange zest and juice, redcurrant jelly, red wine and bouquet garni. Bring to the boil, stirring while the liquid heats. Take off the heat, put in the pheasant pieces, chestnuts and onions and cover with a lid. Cook in the oven for about 2 hours. The meat should be very tender. Sprinkle the casserole with chopped parsley before serving.

AGA method

Brown the pheasant and sauté the chestnuts and onions using the AGA hotplates. When the dish is ready for the oven, bring to a boil on the Boiling Plate for 3 minutes, then move to the Simmering Oven for 2½–3 hours. Serve as above.

Braised Rabbit with Prunes

Tradition says William the Conqueror introduced rabbits into Britain. Certainly in the Middle Ages they were an expensive luxury and cost the equivalent of £20 in today's money. Later, once there was a wild population, rabbits became 'food for free' and farm labourers (who would justify the practice as pest control) trapped and shot them for the pot. Disease decimated the population in the late 20th century and now our rabbits are raised specifically for the pot again. This modern recipe has echoes of medieval cooking with the inclusion of prunes.

Serves 4

2 teaspoons sunflower oil
25g (1oz) butter
8 rabbit pieces (2 per
    person)
Dijon mustard
20 pickling onions, peeled
110g (4oz) smoked bacon,
    diced
1 teaspoon dried thyme
Approximately 250ml
    (9fl oz) dry white wine
2 tablespoons brandy
8 pitted prunes
Salt and freshly ground black
    pepper to taste

Preheat the oven to 180°C, 350°F, gas mark 4. Melt the oil and butter in a frying pan and brown the rabbit pieces on all sides. Remove with a slotted spoon, spread all over with Dijon mustard and put in a casserole. Brown the onions and bacon and add to the casserole with the thyme. Cover with wine, then season with salt and freshly ground pepper. Cover the casserole and cook for about an hour, then add the brandy and the prunes. Cook for a further 30 minutes. By this time the rabbit should be really tender.

AGA method

Melt the oil in a frying pan and brown the rabbit, onions and bacon as above, on the AGA hotplates. Assemble the dish for the oven as above, then bring to the boil on the Boiling Plate for 3 minutes. Cover and move to the Roasting Oven, on the fourth set of runners, for 45 minutes. Add the brandy and the prunes to the dish, cover and continue to cook for another 40–45 minutes, or until the rabbit is really tender. Alternatively, this dish can be cooked in the centre of the Baking Oven (on three- or four-oven models).

Pot-roasted Shoulder of Venison

A good dish for a chilly winter's day, this recipe is adapted from one that appears in Martha Bradley's *The British Housewife*, first published in 1756. She describes it as producing a piece of meat that 'eats moist and mellow, and excellently well flavoured'.

Serves 6–8

1 boned shoulder of venison, approximately 1kg (2¼lb)

1 thick slice of fat bacon or pancetta, approximately 110g (4oz)

6–8 black peppercorns

3 whole cloves

½ teaspoon grated nutmeg

250ml (9fl oz) dry white wine

4 bay leaves, bruised

1 bouquet garni (2 sprigs each of marjoram, thyme and rosemary, 1 slice of lemon and a few bruised juniper berries, wrapped in a piece of muslin or the green outer leaf of a leek and tied)

2 tablespoons vegetable oil or beef dripping

2 carrots, peeled and cut into chunks

¼ turnip, peeled and cut into chunks

continued

If the venison is rolled, snip the strings and open it out into a flat piece. Cut the bacon or pancetta across into thin strips or lardons. Grind the peppercorns and cloves together, using a pestle and mortar, and mix with the nutmeg. Spread this spice mixture on a plate and roll the lardons in it, until they are well coated. Then, make small incisions in the surface of the meat and push the lardons into them, so that they lie just below the surface (it is possible to manage this without a larding needle, but using one makes the job easier and neater). Roll and tie the venison into a neat shape once more.

Put the white wine and bay leaves in a large dish or casserole and add the venison and bouquet garni. Leave to marinate for about 3 hours, turning from time to time.

Preheat the oven to 140°C, 275°F, gas mark 1. Heat the oil or dripping in a large flameproof casserole. When it is hot, add the carrot, turnip and onion and fry briskly, until the vegetables begin to catch and brown in places. Then pour in the marinade from the meat and allow it to come to the boil. Turn off the heat, add the venison and the bouquet garni and cover the pot. Put in the hot oven and cook for about 3 hours, turning the meat every hour or so. At the end of this time, the venison should feel very tender when tested with a carving fork.

Lift out the venison and transfer it to a warm serving plate. Remove and discard the vegetables and bouquet

½ onion, cut into 4 chunks
15g (½oz) butter, blended
    to a paste with 15g
    (½oz) plain flour
1 tablespoon capers, rinsed
    and roughly chopped
Salt to taste

garni. Set the casserole containing the cooking juices over a high heat and bring to the boil, then continue cooking rapidly until the juices are reduced to about half their original volume. Take the casserole off the heat and drop in the butter and flour paste in small pieces, shaking the pan to mix them in. The sauce should thicken a little. Stir in the capers, check the seasoning and add salt if needed.

Slice up the venison (the meat around the lardons will appear pink or red, due to saltpetre in the bacon cure leaching into the venison) and serve with the hot sauce, accompanied by redcurrant jelly and a buttery purée of potato and celeriac.

AGA method

Prepare the venison as above. Use the AGA hotplates to fry the vegetables. Add the marinade and venison, bring to the boil on the Boiling Plate and boil for 5 minutes, then move to the Simmering Oven for 3½–4½ hours or until the venison is very tender. Continue as above, using the AGA hotplates to finish the dish.

Scotch Collops with Forcemeat Balls

A collop is a small slice of meat. Sara Paston-Williams devised this modern version from several recipes from the late 17th century, one of which begins 'Take a legg of Veale and slice it very thin…' It was served at a late-20th-century 'Georgian' dinner at Flatford in Suffolk, and was a great success.

Serves 4

For the collops
450g (1lb) veal escalope
50g (2oz) butter
25g (1oz) plain flour
300ml (½ pint) beef stock
1 glass white wine
1 teaspoon chopped fresh
    thyme
Thinly cut zest of 1 orange
Shredded zest of ½ lemon

For the forcemeat balls
200g (7oz) fresh white
    breadcrumbs
50g (2oz) shredded suet
50g (2oz) lean bacon, finely
    chopped
1 tablespoon chopped
    parsley
1 tablespoon chopped fresh
    thyme
Grated zest of ½ lemon
1 egg, beaten
Salt and pepper to taste
25g (1oz) butter for frying

Warm a large serving dish in the oven while you are preparing this dish. Cut the veal into strips 6mm (¼in) thick and approximately 13 x 5cm (5 x 2in). Melt the butter in a large frying pan and fry the veal collops for a few minutes on each side until evenly brown. Transfer to a large shallow pan or sauté pan. Stir the flour into the frying-pan juices and cook for a few seconds, then add stock together with the wine, thyme and orange zest. Bring to the boil so the sauce just thickens a little, and pour over the collops.

Now prepare the forcemeat balls. Mix together the breadcrumbs, suet, bacon, parsley and thyme, lemon zest and seasoning. Stir in the beaten egg and form into small balls about 4cm (1½in) in diameter. Melt the butter in a frying pan and fry the forcemeat balls until brown. Add to the collops and sauce. Cover and simmer gently for about 10 minutes.

Transfer to the warmed serving dish. Extract and discard the orange zest and garnish with shredded lemon zest.

AGA method

Prepare the collops and cook using the AGA hotplates. Prepare and brown the forcemeat balls and assemble the dish. Simmer gently on the Simmering Plate and continue as above.

Venison Casseroled with Apricots

The Romans first fenced game parks in Britain to raise and hunt deer and wild boar. Venison has been prized as a meat ever since.

Serves 4

50g (2oz) dried apricots

75g (3oz) butter

2 medium onions, peeled and sliced

450g (1lb) venison, cut into large cubes

2 tablespoons plain flour

2 teaspoons crushed juniper berries

300ml (½ pint) apple or apricot juice

300ml (½ pint) red wine

Salt and pepper to taste

For garnish
Chopped parsley

Greek yoghurt

Soak the apricots in cold water overnight. Preheat the oven to 160°C, 325°F, gas mark 3. In a sauté pan, melt the butter and sauté the sliced onions until soft and golden. Take out with a slotted spoon and place in a casserole. Now sauté the venison until brown and add to the onions with any cooking juices from the sauté pan. Mix the flour with the crushed juniper berries and salt and pepper to taste. Sprinkle over the meat and onions and turn them well in the flour mixture. Place the casserole in the oven for 10 minutes to cook the flour. Meanwhile heat the juice and wine gently. Remove the casserole from the oven and add the juice, wine and apricots. Stir and return to the oven. Cook gently for at least 2 hours, or until the meat is tender. This may take longer if the venison was wild rather than farmed. To serve, sprinkle with parsley and hand round a bowl of yoghurt separately for guests to add if they wish.

AGA method

Soak the apricots in cold water overnight. Melt the butter in a sauté pan and sauté the onion until soft and golden on the Roasting Oven floor. Remove them to a casserole and brown the venison in the same pan, using the AGA hotplates. Sprinkle over the seasoned flour-and-juniper mix and stir well. Place the pan in the Roasting Oven for 5 minutes to cook the flour. Heat the juice and wine on the Simmering Plate. Remove the casserole from the oven, add the liquid and apricots, cover with a lid and bring to the boil on the Boiling Plate for 5 minutes. Return to the Simmering Oven and cook for 2–2½ hours or until the meat is tender.

Game Pie

Game pie, historically, would only be made on wealthy farms or estates with large amounts of land on which the men could shoot. It can be made in the same way as Pork Pie (see page 114) with hot-water crust and jellied stock, using 450g (1lb) meat from game and the same from pork. This version is a bit of a hybrid between a raised pie and a more standard short-pastry version.

Serves 10 easily

For the filling
50g (2oz) butter
450g (1lb) venison, cubed
450g (1lb) assorted other game, cut off the bone (for example, pheasant, pigeon, partridge, rabbit, hare; cooked game can be used)
400–500g (14oz–1lb 2oz) good pork sausage meat, divided into 10–12 balls
2 level tablespoons plain flour
100ml (3½ fl oz) red wine
300ml (½ pint) stock, made from the bones and trimmings of game birds cooked with an onion and 1 bouquet garni
Salt and pepper to taste
Nutmeg
continued

Make the sauce first. Melt the butter in a large frying pan. Brown the cubed venison, the sausage meat and the other game if it is raw. Remove, leaving as much fat as possible in the pan. Stir in the flour. Add the wine, scraping the bottom of the pan to pick up all the residues from the game. Pour in the stock and simmer gently for about 20 minutes. Taste, and add salt, pepper and a scrape of nutmeg. The sauce should be well seasoned. Turn into a basin and allow to cool to tepid.

Roll three-quarters of the pastry into a large circle and place in the tin, spreading the pastry so it drapes over the sides. Ease it over the base, into the edges and up the sides, trying not to stretch it. You will have to make small pleats in places. Roll the remaining quarter ready to make the lid. Distribute the venison over the base and top with the other game. Add the sausagemeat balls. Pour in the sauce. Cover with the pastry lid, sealing with beaten egg.

Trim, crimp the edges decoratively and add decorations of pastry flowers and leaves. Game pies should be very ornamental. Glaze with beaten egg. Place on a heated baking tray in a preheated oven, 220°C, 425°F, gas mark 7, for 20–30 minutes (watch to see it doesn't brown too quickly), then turn the temperature down to 170°C, 325°F, gas mark 3 and cook for a further 1½ hours.

Remove the pie from the oven. Allow to cool in the tin overnight.

For the pastry

Shortcrust pastry made
    from 450g (1lb) plain flour
100g (3½oz) butter
110g (4oz) lard
1 teaspoon salt
100ml (3½fl oz) water

Egg, for sealing and glazing

A circular cake tin 20–22cm
    (8–9in) in diameter,
    preferably with a loose
    bottom; line the base with
    greaseproof paper.

AGA method

Make the filling on the AGA hotplates and use the
Simmering Oven to simmer the game for 20 minutes.
Assemble the pie as above, then slide the oven grid shelf
on to the Roasting Oven floor. Put the pie on to a shallow
baking tray on the grid shelf. Slide the cold plain shelf
directly above the pie and cook for 25–30 minutes. Move
to the Simmering Oven and continue to cook for another
2 hours. Remove from the oven and allow to cool in the
tin overnight.

Kidneys with a Mustard Cream Sauce

We eat less offal than our forebears did. Heads, brains, tongue and sweetbreads are seldom seen in the butchers today and virtually never in the supermarket. Liver and Bacon is still a favourite dish; it hardly needs a recipe. Neither does Grilled Kidneys, once a staple of the breakfast table of the well-to-do. In the 19th century, a version of this dish was often served at the end of the meal as a savoury on toast. I have kept the toast, but like it better as a supper dish. It needs nothing more than a green salad with a light dressing as an accompaniment.

Serves 2–3

6 lambs' kidneys
25g (1oz) butter

For the sauce
2 shallots, peeled and finely
    chopped
1 tablespoon Dijon mustard
150ml (¼ pint) vegetable
    stock
1 small glass sherry
1 tablespoon Worcester
    sauce
2 tablespoons double cream
    or crème fraîche
Salt and pepper

Slice the lambs' kidneys. Heat the butter and gently sauté the kidneys, turning them well in the butter. When they have browned, take them out with a slice or slotted spoon and keep them warm in the oven while you make the mustard cream sauce.

To make the sauce, sauté the shallots in the pan juices for a minute or two until they begin to soften. Stir in the mustard, then the vegetable stock, sherry and Worcester sauce. Adjust the seasoning; it may already be salty enough. Bring the mixture up to just below boiling point and stir in the cream or crème fraîche. Don't let it boil; it may curdle. Pour the sauce over the kidneys, give it a good stir and serve individual portions on toast.

AGA method

Make this dish as above, using the AGA hotplates.

Tripe and Onions

I have specified honeycomb tripe for this dish. This is the most tender variety of tripe, because it has already been prepared before you start cooking, with a long process of soaking and boiling before it even reaches the butcher's slab. Tripe is a very old-fashioned dish and you either like or loathe it. I once cooked a series of dishes for an elderly couple who were too frail to cook for themselves; they hated the ready meals at the supermarket so I provided ready meals for them. They were particularly ecstatic about my Tripe and Onions – partly because of the taste but mostly, I think, from nostalgia.

Serves 4

450g (1lb) honeycomb tripe
2 large onions
Approximately 600ml
   (1 pint) full-cream milk
50g (2oz) butter
25g (1oz) plain flour
Salt and pepper
2 rounded tablespoons
   chopped parsley

Cut the tripe into 2.5cm (1in) pieces and peel and slice the onions. Place the tripe and onions in a heavy-based pan, and pour over the milk. Cover the pan tightly and simmer over a gentle heat for about 2 hours or until the tripe is tender. Strain the liquid through a sieve and set aside about 600ml (1 pint) to make a sauce.

Melt the butter in a small pan, stir in the flour and cook it, stirring all the time, for about 3–4 minutes. Then gradually blend in the cooking liquid. Bring to the boil and season with salt and pepper. Scatter the parsley over the tripe and onions and then mix with the sauce. Reheat and serve immediately.

AGA method

Bring the pan of tripe and onions to a boil on the Boiling Plate, then transfer to the Simmering Oven for 2½–3 hours or until the tripe is tender. Make the sauce on the Simmering Plate and finish as above.

Liver, Bacon and Onions

Various recipes for hearty combinations of these three ingredients can be traced back to the eighteenth century. This simple version makes an excellent family supper.

Serves 4

2 tablespoons plain flour
½ teaspoon paprika
1½ teaspoons freshly
    ground black pepper
½ teaspoon salt
Approximately 300–350g
    (10½–12oz) lamb's liver,
    thinly sliced
8 rashers back bacon
    (preferably dry-cured),
    with quite a high
    proportion of fat
A little oil, dripping or lard
    (optional)
1 large onion, peeled and
    cut into rings
1 garlic clove, crushed
300ml (½ pint) beef stock

Mix the flour, paprika, pepper and salt together on a plate or in a shallow dish. Add the liver slices and turn them around in the mixture until well coated. Set on one side. Heat a large frying pan over a medium-high heat, add the bacon rashers and cook until done to your taste. Remove the bacon to a heated serving dish and keep warm. The bacon should have yielded enough fat to fry the rest of the ingredients, but if there is not very much left in the pan, add a couple of tablespoons of oil or about 25g (1oz) lard before continuing.

Put the onion rings into the pan and cook briskly, stirring all the time, until they soften. Remove to the dish with the bacon and keep warm. Now fry the floured slices of liver in the same pan. Don't overcook them – 1–2 minutes on each side should be sufficient for really thin slices; slightly longer for thicker ones. Add to the still-warm dish of bacon and onions.

Quickly prepare some gravy, using the fat and residues left in the pan. First add the garlic and cook briefly without browning. Then stir in the flour left over from dusting the liver and cook for about 1 minute. Gradually stir in the beef stock to make a rich gravy (you may not need all the stock). Serve immediately, by dividing the cooked liver, bacon and onions between four heated plates and handing round the gravy and some mashed potatoes separately.

AGA method

Use the AGA hotplates for this recipe.

Faggots

A prettier name for these meaty parcels is 'Savoury Ducks', and they are one way of dealing with some of the less glamorous bits of pig, typical of South Wales and south-west England. Caul is a thin membrane with a lacy pattern of fat, which lines the stomach cavity of the animal; it wraps the mixture neatly, adds flavour and looks pretty. Not all butchers sell caul; you may have to ask around. Laura Mason found this recipe in Glamorgan, and like many Welsh variants it uses only liver and includes apple.

Serves 4

200g (7oz) onion, peeled
    and cut in chunks
200g (7oz) cooking apple,
    peeled and cored
200g (7oz) pig's liver, cut in
    chunks
200g (7oz) breadcrumbs
50g (2oz) suet
20 sage leaves, shredded
1 teaspoon salt and some
    pepper
1 pig's caul
Stock

Mince or process the onion, apple and pig's liver. Mix with the breadcrumbs, suet, sage, salt and pepper. Soak the caul in a bowl of warm water. After a few minutes it should be soft and easy to spread out. Using scissors cut 12 neat squares from it, avoiding the fattest bits. Divide the liver mixture into 12 and wrap each in a piece of the caul. Place in a greased ovenproof dish and add a little stock. Bake at 180°C, 350°F, gas mark 4 for about an hour.

AGA method

Prepare the faggots as above and bake in the Roasting Oven, on the fourth set of runners with the cold plain shelf directly above them, for 30–35 minutes. If you have a three- or four-oven AGA, cook in the Baking Oven.

Savoury Sauces

Pork without Apple Sauce, lamb without Mint Sauce, beef without Horseradish Sauce? Unthinkable! There are twelve sauces, with variations, in this short but important section on traditional British sauces. White Sauce, a close relation to France's Bechamel, is here. Butter or Dutch Sauce and Mayonnaise are hot and cold versions of the same thing. Apple Sauce and Gooseberry Sauce are sharp, acid accompaniments, perfect with rich meat and fish, as are Horseradish Sauce and Cumberland Sauce. As for Mint Sauce, it is unknown outside this country. Onion Gravy complements the excellent meaty sausages available today. There are two new additions in this edition: Green Sauce, a sharp uncooked sauce of herbs and vinegar, versions of which date back to late medieval receipts, and Salad Cream, a distinctive British sauce for salads. Forget shop-bought versions of this and make it at home – it is delicious.

White Sauce

White Sauce is not only the basis for many other savoury sauces, but is also an accompaniment in its own right. Traditionally, it was used for coating vegetables, such as cauliflower and carrots. My preference is for half-stock, half-milk as it intensifies the flavour, but traditionally full-cream milk alone was used.

Makes 300ml (10fl oz)

300ml (½ pint) full-cream
   milk or 150ml (¼ pint)
   milk and 150ml (¼ pint)
   vegetable, fish or chicken
   stock
1 bay leaf
1 shallot, chopped
A dash of freshly grated
   nutmeg
25g (1oz) butter
25g (1oz) plain flour
Salt and pepper to taste

Put the milk (and stock, if using) with the bay leaf, shallot and a dusting of nutmeg in a pan and bring slowly to the boil. Remove from the heat, cover and leave for 15 minutes.

In a clean, heavy-based pan, melt the butter, stir in the flour and cook for 3 minutes. Strain the liquid through a sieve and gradually blend it into the flour and butter. Bring the mixture to the boil, stirring continuously. It should have thickened a little by now. Turn down the heat and cook it gently, still stirring. The harder you stir, the smoother the sauce. Adjust the seasoning and serve. You can make a white sauce ahead of time and reheat it, but you need to beat it well during reheating.

Variations

Cheese sauce: Add ½ teaspoon mustard powder and a pinch of cayenne pepper to the flour before making the sauce. Beat in 75g (3oz) finely grated mature Cheddar cheese after the sauce has thickened, until smooth.
Parsley Sauce: Add 2 level tablespoons finely chopped parsley to the sauce just before serving.
Caper Sauce: Add 1 tablespoon lemon juice to the stock before making the sauce. Add 1 tablespoon capers just before serving.

AGA method

Make the sauce using the Simmering Plate.

Mayonnaise

When making mayonnaise it is important that all the ingredients are at room temperature, to allow the eggs and oil to emulsify. Warning: recipes containing raw eggs are unsuitable for pregnant women or young children.

Makes 300ml (½ pint)

2 egg yolks
½ teaspoon Dijon mustard
300ml (½ pint) olive or
    sunflower oil
1 tablespoon lemon juice
1 tablespoon wine vinegar
Salt and pepper

Put the egg yolks and mustard into a bowl and mix thoroughly. Whisk in the oil drop by drop. This is easiest with an electric mixer or a food processor, but you can do it by hand. When you have blended in half the oil, add the lemon juice and the vinegar. Then beat in the rest of the oil. Season to taste.

Variations

Tartare Sauce: Add 1 tablespoon chopped chives, 1 tablespoon chopped parsley, 1 tablespoon chopped gherkins and 1 tablespoon chopped capers to the finished mayonnaise.
Dill Mayonnaise: Add 4 tablespoons fresh chopped dill.

Horseradish Sauce

Horseradish Sauce is addictive: addicts can't eat beef without it. Horseradish has been a staple of the British diet since the 15th century.

Makes 300ml (½ pint)

Juice of ½ lemon
2 teaspoons caster sugar
½ teaspoon mustard
  powder
4 tablespoons freshly grated
  horseradish
300ml (½ pint) double cream

Mix the lemon, sugar and mustard powder into a paste. Stir the paste into the grated horseradish. Whip the cream until thick, but not too stiff. Fold in the other ingredients, add a little salt and chill well.

Cumberland Sauce

This sauce needs to be prepared 24 hours before serving.

Serves 4–6

1 orange
1 lemon
225g (8oz) redcurrant jelly
125ml (4fl oz) ruby or tawny
  port
2 heaped teaspoons
  arrowroot
1 teaspoon mustard powder

Peel the orange and lemon and cut the peel into shreds. Bring a pan of water to the boil, add the peel and boil for 3 minutes. Drain and cover with cold water for 1 minute, drain again and set aside. Squeeze the juice from the orange and lemon, pour into a small pan, add the jelly and bring to the boil. Simmer for 5 minutes, then add the port and bring the sauce back to the boil. Remove from the heat. Mix the arrowroot and mustard powder to a paste with a little cold water and stir the paste into the mixture. Return the pan to the heat, bring the sauce back to the boil and cook for a further minute. Add the blanched peel and leave the sauce to stand for 24 hours before using.

AGA method

Make the sauce on the AGA hotplates.

Mint Sauce

**'The smell of mint does stir up the minde and the taste to a greedy desire of meat,'
wrote John Gerard in his *Herball* in 1633.**

Makes 125ml (4fl oz)

1 large pack fresh mint
   leaves (20g)
1 tablespoon sugar
2 tablespoons boiling water
White wine vinegar or cider
   vinegar, according to taste

Strip the mint leaves from their stems. Pile them on a chopping board and spoon over the sugar. Using a large, straight-bladed sharp knife, chop the mint very finely. You will find that the sugar helps to stop the leaves scattering all over the place. Every so often, scrape the mixture up into a pile again. When the mint is very finely chopped, put it into a bowl, spoon over the boiling water and stir until the sugar has dissolved. Top up the bowl with vinegar. For a less sharp and vinegary sauce, use two-thirds vinegar to one-third water. Either way, make the sauce at the last minute and the mint leaves will stay green.

Bread Sauce

**In medieval European recipes many sauces were thickened with bread. This
traditional accompaniment for roast chicken, turkey or pheasant is a direct
descendant of those sauces.**

Makes approximately 600ml (1 pint)

1 small onion, peeled and
   stuck with 6 cloves
2 bay leaves
600ml (1 pint) milk
75g (3oz) fresh white
   breadcrumbs
25g (1oz) butter
Salt and pepper to taste

Put the onion, bay leaves and milk in a pan and bring to the boil. Remove from the heat, cover with a lid and leave to infuse for 15 minutes. Add the breadcrumbs and butter, and simmer uncovered, very gently, for 10 minutes. Remove the onion and bay leaves. Season to taste with salt and pepper.

AGA method

Make the sauce using the AGA hotplates.

Onion Gravy

'We never goes home to breakfast till we've sold out; but if it's very late, then I buys a penn'orth of pudden, which is very nice with gravy.'

London Labour and the London Poor, Henry Mayhew, 1863.

For this eight-year-old selling watercress in the cold, inhospitable streets of Victorian London, gravy and pudding, bought from a street stall, was one of her few comforts. Gravy is peculiar to the British; to many of us a roast without gravy is unthinkable. This recipe for Onion Gravy, the perfect accompaniment to sausages and mash, comes from Tom Norrington-Davies' *Just Like Mother Used to Make*. He emphasises the need to fry the onions gently to extract their full sweetness – don't try to hurry this. You can make the gravy well in advance and reheat it when you want to serve it.

Serves 4

1 tablespoon olive oil
1 tablespoon butter
3 onions, sliced
4 sage leaves
300ml (100fl oz) red wine
1 teaspoon sugar
1 teaspoon Dijon mustard
Salt and pepper to taste

Heat the oil and butter in a frying pan. Add the onions and fry them gently, giving them a good stir from time to time. Shred the sage leaves and add them after 5 minutes. When the onions are soft and beginning to brown (this should be after about 15–20 minutes) add the wine and sugar and bring the mixture to the boil. Boil the onions and wine for about 5 minutes, then stir in the mustard. Taste and season with salt and pepper. If you aren't planning to serve the sauce immediately, stop cooking at this point and give it a final 5 minutes just before it is needed; otherwise continue to cook for 5 minutes and then serve.

AGA method

Heat up a frying pan on the Roasting Oven floor, add the oil and butter, and fry the onions until they are soft and golden. Remove the pan from the oven and use the AGA hotplates to finish the gravy just before serving.

Apple Sauce

It is important to use cooking apples in this traditional accompaniment for roast pork or duck. Bramleys are perfect for the zingy, sharp flavour that you need.

Makes approximately 300ml (½ pint)

450g (1lb) cooking apples
3 tablespoons water
1 tablespoon cider vinegar
1 tablespoon sugar
25g (1oz) unsalted butter

Peel and slice the apples. Put them in a pan with the water, cover and simmer until the apples are cooked and fluffy (this will take approximately 10 minutes). Take the pan off the heat and stir in the cider vinegar, sugar and butter.

AGA method

Put the apples and water into a saucepan; bring to a rapid simmer on the Simmering Plate. Cover with a lid and move to the Simmering Oven for 15–20 minutes or until they are cooked and fluffy. Finish the sauce as above.

Dutch Sauce or Butter Sauce

This sauce – similar to the French Hollandaise – has had an abundance of names over the years. This version was first published by Michael Smith in 1973.

Makes approximately 300ml (½ pint)

110g (4oz) good fresh salted butter
2 level teaspoons fine white plain flour
150ml (¼ pint) milk
1 tablespoon lemon juice or white wine vinegar

Cut the butter into small cubes, sprinkle with flour, and, either in the food processor or by hand, work into a smooth paste. Transfer into a small pan and, over the lowest heat possible, beat with a wooden spatula until it starts to melt. Gradually beat in the milk without raising the heat. Bring the sauce just to the boil and simmer for 2 minutes, beating all the time. Add the lemon juice or vinegar.

AGA method

Use the AGA Simmering Plate to make this sauce.

Gooseberry Sauce

Did you know that there have been clubs in England dedicated to growing monster gooseberries for over 200 years? The most well-known, the Egton Bridge Old Gooseberry Society in Yorkshire, still holds an annual competition for the largest berry. It is not a good contest for cooks as the way to achieve success is to strip the bush of all other fruit, leaving just one to grow and grow. The distinctive tart flavour of gooseberries provides the perfect contrast to rich meat such as goose (perhaps that is how they got their name), or oily fish, such as mackerel or salmon. The recipe below is my adaptation of Eliza Acton's recipe in *Modern Cookery for Private Families*, first published in 1845.

Serves 4

450g (1lb) gooseberries
3 tablespoons water
A pinch of ground ginger
1 tablespoon sugar
1 small cube of butter, about
    20cm (1in) square

Stew the gooseberries with the water in a small pan until very soft. There is no need to top and tail them since you are going to purée the mixture: rub it through a sieve to get rid of the skin and pips. Return the mixture to the pan, add the ginger, sugar and butter, and heat gently until the sugar is dissolved and the butter has melted. Serve the sauce hot or cold.

AGA method

Put the gooseberries and water into a saucepan, and bring to a rapid simmer on the Simmering Plate. Cover with a lid and move to the Simmering Oven for 15–20 minutes or until they are very soft. Finish the sauce as above.

Green Sauce

There are many recorded variations of this uncooked sauce, which was a late medieval favourite. What they all have in common is a flavour that is sharp and slightly peppery, but the proportions of the different herbs involved must have been varied according to taste and season. It makes an excellent accompaniment to cold fish, such as salmon or salmon trout, and is also good with cold pork, veal or chicken.

Serves 4

20g (¾oz) sorrel leaves
20g (¾oz) parsley leaves
20g (¾oz) mint leaves
2–3 sprigs thyme, leaves only
50g (2oz) good-quality
    white bread, weighed
    after crusts removed
2 tablespoons white wine
    vinegar
2 tablespoons white wine
Pinch of ground ginger
Salt and pepper to taste

Make sure all the herbs are thoroughly washed and picked over. Put all ingredients, except the salt and pepper, in a blender and process to make a vivid green sauce. It should be of a similar thickness to good homemade mayonnaise. If you feel it is a little too thick, thin by adding some extra vinegar or wine, or even a little cold stock that is appropriate to whatever you plan to serve the sauce with. Taste and season with salt and pepper as required. Other herbs, such as sage, rosemary and chives, can also be blended in if desired. Or for a hotter, more piquant result, you can add a little grated fresh horseradish.

Salad Cream

English cookery tradition includes a distinctive type of salad dressing based on cream and cooked egg yolk. Some versions also include smoothly puréed, cooked potato as well. This recipe is based on one given by Eliza Acton in *Modern Cookery for Private Families* **(1845).**

Makes approximately 200ml (7fl oz)

2 eggs
¼ teaspoon salt
A pinch of sugar
A small pinch of cayenne pepper
A small pinch of mustard powder
1 teaspoon water
150ml (¼ pint) double cream
Approximately 1 tablespoon wine vinegar
Approximately 1 tablespoon tarragon or basil vinegar, or other flavoured vinegar to taste

Put the eggs into a saucepan of cold water, bring to the boil over a medium heat, then lower the heat and leave to simmer for 10 minutes. Remove from the water and allow to cool. Shell, remove the whites and put the yolks in a bowl or mortar. Use a wooden spoon or pestle to reduce the yolks to a paste, then stir in the salt, sugar, cayenne pepper, mustard and water. Add the cream, a tablespoon at a time, stirring well to make sure that the mixture is smooth. Once all the cream is incorporated, add the vinegars, taste the mixture and add extra seasoning or vinegar if necessary.

Alternatively, you can mix all the ingredients, except the cream and vinegars, to a paste in a blender. Then, while the blender is still running, pour in the cream and continue to blend until it is all just incorporated. Don't overblend or the cream will start to thicken. Quickly blend in the vinegars, taste and, as above, add any extra vinegar plus more seasoning if needed.

AGA method

Use the AGA hotplates to boil the eggs.

Vegetables & side dishes

It is not so long ago that the British were the butt of jokes concerning the way we cooked vegetables. Watery cabbage, soggy sprouts, overcooked carrots – this was how the rest of the world saw British vegetable cooking. But there has been a sea change in the last few years, both in the home and in restaurants and cafés. Today we realise that vegetables are not only good for us, but we can appreciate their flavours and textures, when cooked appropriately.

In fact, vegetables have always played a large part in the diet of both country and town dwellers, at all levels of British society. In *Piers Plowman*, a famous narrative poem written in the 14th century, the food in the cottage of the character Hunger includes parsley, leeks and cabbage. Piers and his neighbours supplement these with peascods, beans, apples, onions and pot herbs. The market gardeners around London sold their produce on the south side of St Paul's Churchyard and, as well as the vegetables mentioned above, they sold turnips, parsnips, beet, radishes, carrots, herbs and fruit.

We know that people made pottage with these vegetables, and ate it daily. Pottage was a broth or stock in which meat and/or vegetables had been boiled, along with herbs and probably pulses and cereals. The result was something between a soup and a stew. Pease Pottage (page 178) is typical of a pottage that was thick (or 'running'), though some were even thicker (or 'stondyng'), and almost solid enough to slice. For most people, their usual pottage would have been a vegetable one, made with cabbage, lettuces, leeks, onions and garlic. 'White Porray' (leek pottage) was especially popular and, during Lent, when meat-eating was restricted, the rich ate it thickened with ground almonds. 'Green Porray' was also popular, flavoured with parsley and other herbs. There are two modern pottage recipes in this chapter: Pease Pottage, a thick, winter-warming purée from a single vegetable, and Spiced Bean Pottage (page 182), a spicy vegetable casserole that provides a main course for the hungry – continuing an old tradition. There are also some less substantial descendants of pottage in the chapter on Soups.

'Pot-herbs' had a slightly different meaning in the past. Today we take it to mean herbs – like parsley, sage, rosemary, thyme or tarragon – that can literally go in the pot. But in the Middle Ages 'pot-herbs' meant 'vegetables for the pot' and, as well as herbs, included onions, carrots, leeks and cabbage, and also salad vegetables like lettuce. Incidentally, carrots were not just orange, a colour developed by the Dutch in the Middle Ages, but also came in purple, yellow and white. Probably we have less choice of vegetables now today than people had in 1500: it has been calculated that over 100 varieties of vegetables were available to grow at that time.

Salads in medieval cookery were simple green leaves, including some – like groundsel and pimpernel – that we no longer eat today. They were decorated with edible flowers, a custom I think we should revive. Primroses, chive flowers, borage flowers, nasturtiums and violas all taste good and look even better. I haven't provided a recipe for oil and vinegar dressing, but I can't do better than quote John Evelyn in his *Acetaria*, published in 1699 and entirely devoted to salads. Evelyn defines a sallet, as he calls it, thus: 'a particular Composition of certain Crude and fresh herbs, such as usually are, or may be safely eaten with some Acetous Juice, Oyl, Salt etc. to give them a grateful Gust and Vehicle.' He calls his salad dressing an Oxoleon – although it's a strange word, the proportions work well, three centuries later: 'Take of clear, and perfectly good Oyl-Olive; three parts; of sharpest Vinegar … Limon or Juice of Orange; one Part; and therein let steep some Slices of Horse-Radish, with a little salt.' Don't worry about including the horseradish, since the dressing is perfect without it. If you like to experiment, there are two historic salads, or sallets, in this chapter. The second rejoices in the wonderful name of Salamongundy – or 'Salmagundi', or even 'Sallid Magundi'.

Naturally there is no mention of potatoes in medieval recipes. The first Europeans to come across potatoes, in 1537 in Colombia, South America, actually called them 'truffles'. And this is exactly how they were treated to begin with – as a rare, delicate luxury. They arrived in the British Isles some sixty years later, in the 1590s, probably brought back by Sir Francis Drake after one of his transatlantic voyages. Potatoes thrive in cool, damp climates, and by 1650 they were the staple diet of the Irish, so much so that the disastrous potato blight of 1845 caused widespread famine in Ireland. Irish potato recipes included here include Champ and Colcannon. Lancashire and Northumbria also grow excellent potatoes. Pan Haggerty, potatoes layered with onion and cheese and cooked in a 'pan' on the fire, is a dish from northern England, as is Leek and Potato Hotpot. Leeks are a favourite everywhere, but particularly in Northumbria, home of the largest-leek competition. Leek Pudding (a leek roly-poly), and Leek, Cheese and Bread and Butter Pudding both come from Wallington, an elegant classical house set in the beautiful Northumbrian moors. The leeks there are grown in the kitchen garden, sheltered in a fold of the rolling hills. The Potato Pudding is a modern adaptation by Sara Paston-Williams of a Georgian recipe from Somerset where the potato is flavoured with spices and sugar, and served in puff pastry.

Britain produces excellent hard cheese, which is particularly good for cooking. Macaroni Cheese and Cauliflower Cheese are both old favourites. A modern version of a very old recipe for Cheese Pudding, thickened in the old way, with breadcrumbs rather than flour, also contains beetroot and carrot. And there are some recipes for potting cheese.

In earlier centuries, fresh vegetables were in short supply by the middle of winter. During the colder months, people had to rely on root crops and what could be salted or pickled. Today we are much luckier, with vegetables available all year round, coming from all over the world. By and large the recipes in this chapter do not use exotic vegetables – they use the ones we grow best. And, by the way, the Vegetable and Nut Greate Pye, with its exotic filling of cabbage, mushrooms, dates and nuts, is a surprisingly recent invention, from Norfolk. It was made to serve 20th-century vegetarians at an 'Elizabethan banquet'.

A Salad of Herbs and Flowers

This recipe for an Elizabethan salad comes from *The Good Huswife's Jewell* by Thomas Dawson, published in 1596. At Oxburgh Hall, a fortified manor dating back to the 15th century, this salad was made as part of an Elizabethan banquet held in the spring. It consisted of Welsh onions, shallots, sage, rosemary, thyme, parsley, chives and bay garnished with cowslips, primroses and violets, all from the garden. Only the eggs were not home-produced!

'Take your herbs and pick them very fine into fine water, and pick your flowers by themselves and wash them clean, then swing them in a strainer, and when you put them into a dish, mingle them with cucumbers or lemons pared and sliced, also scrape sugar, and put in vinegar and oil, then throw the flowers on the top of the salad, and of every sort of the aforesaid things and garnish the dish about, then take eggs boiled hard, and lay about the dish and upon the salad.'

Salamongundy

More of a concept than a recipe – in 1747 Mrs Hannah Glasse wrote, 'You may always make Salamongundy of such things as you have, according to your fancy.' She added, 'If it is neatly set out it will make a pretty figure in the middle of the table, or you may lay them in heaps in a dish; if you have not all these ingredients, set out your plates, or saucers with just what you have.'

Salamongundy is basically an English composite salad, similar to the Mediterranean Salade Niçoise. Originally it consisted of cold meats combined with lettuce, grapes and anchovies, but there are many variations. Mrs Glasse refers to plates and saucers. If you want to reproduce the old effect, use a large salad plate and build up the different salads in different-sized bowls and plates. When I was a caterer, we produced a Georgian buffet for a baroque dance group and our Salamongundy consisted of bowls of different brightly coloured salads, beetroot, chopped hard-boiled egg, chopped grapes, chopped ham and chopped cucumber. We tried to keep to foods we knew were in the diet in 1700. Modern Salamongundies can range far and wide, but for authenticity keep each bowl to one colour.

In this vegetarian version the base consists of a mixture of colourful and tasty leaves such as curly endive, cos, lollo rosso, oakleaf, young dandelion leaves and spinach – whatever is available. A layer is placed on a large flat dish, then other vegetables are layered or piled on top to make a colourful display. You can use: leeks and mushrooms cooked 'à la grecque' in a little vinegar and olive oil and cooled; tiny new potatoes cooked and dressed with walnut oil and mint; raw carrot with a poppy-seed dressing; blanched green beans, etc. Hard-boiled eggs can also be added and there should always be a fruit element such as chopped red apples or grapes.

Place the dish in the centre of the table and let your guests help themselves. Served with a good selection of bread and a bottle of Gewürztraminer from Alsace, it makes a perfect summer lunch or supper.

AGA method

Make the hard-boiled eggs on the AGA hotplates, then proceed as above.

Braised Red Cabbage

Cabbage has been valued as a food since the Egyptians. The Romans considered that it was healthy and warded off drunkenness. This is the perfect vegetable to serve at Christmas, when it won't ward off drunkenness, but it can be made in advance and tastes just as good when reheated – and it is healthy.

Serves 6

900g (2lb) red cabbage
1 medium-sized onion, sliced
50g (2oz) butter
1 crisp eating apple (Cox is
   good)
1 large cooking apple
150ml (¼ pint) cheap red
   wine, or stock
1 teaspoon salt
1 tablespoon wine vinegar
6 whole cloves
½ teaspoon grated nutmeg
1 level tablespoon soft
   brown sugar
freshly ground black pepper,
   to taste

Remove the cabbage's outer leaves, white root and larger pieces of white pith, cut into quarters and shred finely. Place in a large bowl and cover with water. Drain after a minute or so.

Soften the onions in the melted butter in a large heavy pan, but do not brown. Peel, core and slice thickly the apples, and add to the pan with the wine or stock, salt, vinegar, cloves, nutmeg, plenty of black pepper and finally the cabbage. Combine and cover the pan tightly. Cook gently, stirring occasionally, for about 45 minutes; the cabbage is nicest if it still has a little bite to it. Stir in the sugar and serve.

This loses none of its flavour if reheated the following day.

AGA method

Soften the onions in an ovenproof casserole on the Simmering Plate and add the remaining ingredients. Stir well and bring up to a rapid simmer for 8–10 minutes, stirring frequently. Move to the Simmering Oven and slowly braise for 1–1½ hours.

Russian Salad

Considered part of *haute cuisine* in the late nineteenth century, this is a mixture of cooked vegetables, meat and other ingredients, bound together with a rich, creamy mayonnaise. The great chef Auguste Escoffier (1846–1935) is said to have served it garnished with caviar – a suggestion you may like to take up if your budget stretches to such luxuries.

Serves 4

50g (2oz) cooked carrot
50g (2oz) cooked new potato
50g (2oz) cooked celeriac
50g (2oz) cooked French beans
4 small gherkins
50g (2oz) unsmoked ham
50g (2oz) pressed tongue
Meat of ½ small lobster (optional)
50g (2 oz) cooked cauliflower
50g (2 oz) cooked peas
1 generous tablespoon salted capers, rinsed and dried
150ml (¼ pint) mayonnaise (see page 160)

For the garnish
1 hard-boiled egg
1 tablespoon chopped chives
4 anchovies, each halved lengthways
1 beetroot, cooked and cut into julienne strips

Cut the first seven ingredients into julienne strips and put in a large bowl. Dice the lobster meat, if using, divide the cauliflower into florets and add both to the mixture of julienned vegetables and meat in the bowl, together with the peas and capers. Gently stir in the mayonnaise. Divide the mixture between four serving plates.

To garnish, chop the white of the egg finely and scatter some over the top of each serving, followed by the yolk, that has been rubbed though a sieve. Add a sprinkling of chopped chives. Cross two anchovy halves over the top of each portion and finish by scattering beetroot strips around the edge. Serve immediately.

Pease Pottage

In the Middle Ages, 'pottage', a semi-liquid dish eaten with a spoon, was consumed by everyone. Vegetable pottages like this were for the poor; the rich enjoyed spicy meat or fish pottages. This modern recipe using frozen peas makes a good 'winter warmer'. It also makes an excellent vegetable accompaniment to poached gammon (see page 106) or Fish and Chips (see page 72), if you don't fancy mushy peas.

Serves 4

450g (1lb) frozen peas
110g (4oz) butter
1 tablespoon fresh mint
Salt, pepper and sugar to
　taste
Swirl of cream, to serve

Defrost the peas and put them in a saucepan with the butter. Put the lid on and cook very slowly until they become mushy. This will take up to 45 minutes. Season with salt, pepper and a teaspoon of sugar and stir in the fresh mint chopped very finely. Serve with an elegant swirl of cream.

AGA method

Melt the butter in a saucepan on the Simmering Plate and add the peas. Put a lid on and cook for a few minutes, then transfer to the Simmering Oven for 45–50 minutes or until mushy.

Jugged Peas

This recipe is for fresh peas – especially if you have a glut, they have all ripened at once and you aren't keeping up with eating them plain. Laura Mason suggests that they will 'go with all that lovely Devon lamb; this is good even for end-of-season, slightly-past-their-best peas'. The herbs transform the dish into something to suit 21st-century taste.

Serves 4

1kg (2¼lb) peas in the pod,
　　or 250g (9oz) shelled
　　peas
25g (1oz) butter
1 teaspoon sugar
1–2 tablespoons water
2 mint sprigs
Pinch of salt

To finish

10 green coriander sprigs
12 mint leaves
Green chilli, seeded

Put the peas, butter, sugar, salt, water and the sprigs of mint in a small casserole or a pudding basin that will hold them comfortably. Cover with a lid or some foil and place the arrangement in a saucepan of water. Bring this to a gentle boil and simmer for 30 minutes. At the end of this time, the peas should be tender and well flavoured. Chop the coriander, mint leaves and the chilli finely and stir in just before serving.

AGA method

Put all of the ingredients into an ovenproof casserole and bring to the boil on the Boiling Plate for 5 minutes. Transfer to the Simmering Oven and cook for 40–45 minutes or until the peas are tender. Finish the dish with coriander, mint and chilli as above.

Leek Pudding

Appropriately, this recipe came from Northumbria. Leeks are serious business in the North. There's a National Pot Leek Society and members compete to produce the world's largest pot leek. The World Leek Challenge offers a prize of more than £1000 for the largest pot leek in the world, assessed over four years' production. One of the leeks entered achieved 284.21 cubic inches. Don't choose these monsters for cooking; smaller and tender leeks are what you want.

Serves 4

225g (8oz) self-raising flour
½ teaspoon salt
110g (4oz) vegetarian suet
About 125ml (4fl oz) water
600g (1¼lb) leeks
2 tablespoons of one or
    more of the following:
    chopped parsley,
    marjoram and tarragon
Butter to grease the foil
Salt and pepper to taste

Preheat the oven to 350°C, 180°C, gas mark 4. Mix together the flour, salt and suet. Add enough water to produce a light, elastic dough and knead gently until smooth. Roll into a rectangle approximately 6mm (¼in) thick. Chop the leeks and sprinkle onto the pastry, leaving a margin round the edges. Sprinke the herbs over the leeks and season with salt and pepper. Roll up like a Swiss roll and seal the ends with your fingers.

Lightly butter a piece of foil or use a large piece of baking paper to wrap up the roll, not too tightly to allow for expansion. Bake in the oven for approximately 1½ hours, or until the pastry is golden and cooked through. This is delicious served with a vegetable stew.

AGA method

Prepare the leek pudding as above, slide the grid shelf on to the Roasting Oven floor, and put the pudding on to the grid shelf. Slide the cold plain shelf directly above it and bake for 30 minutes. Remove the now-hot plain shelf and bake for a further 30 minutes, or until the pudding is golden and the pastry is cooked through. Alternatively, cook in the centre of the Baking Oven (on three- or four-oven models) for about 1½ hours.

Champp

Champ is Irish. My recipe comes from Northern Ireland. There are many regional names for Champ – Bruisy, Cally, Goody and Pandy are some of them. There are also many stories surrounding the dish because it was prepared specially for Hallowe'en (31 October). It was customary to offer Champ to the fairies then. A bowl would be left out under a hawthorn bush on Hallowe'en or All Souls' Night (1 November).

Serves 4

675g (1½lb) potatoes
250ml (9fl oz) buttermilk
6 spring onions, finely
    chopped
50g (2oz) butter
Salt and pepper to taste

Peel, boil and drain the potatoes. Heat the buttermilk gently in a pan and mash the potatoes with the buttermilk until they are very smooth. Season with salt and pepper and stir in the chopped spring onions which can either be fresh or blanched for a more delicate flavour. Put a mound of champ on each plate. Make a well in the centre and fill it with a knob of butter. Serve immediately.

AGA method

Bring the peeled potatoes to a boil on the Boiling Plate and boil for 4 minutes. Drain off the water from the pan, put a lid on it and move to the Simmering Oven for 15–20 minutes, or until the potatoes are soft. Continue as above to make the champ.

Spiced Bean Pottage

This is one of the modern versions of the medieval staple, pottage, in this book. Using pulses, this is extremely nutritious. It provides quite a considerable portion of the protein required daily in our diet, so it's a good bet if you are feeding vegetarians. Originally invented by Sara Paston-Williams for a feast, it tastes every bit as good as it reads.

Serves 4

110g (4oz) chickpeas, washed and soaked overnight

175g (6oz) dried haricot beans, washed and soaked overnight

6 tablespoons sunflower or olive oil

2 red onions, diced

2 garlic cloves, peeled and finely chopped

1 teaspoon of each of the following: ground coriander, turmeric, cumin

1 fresh chilli, de-seeded and finely chopped (optional; leave it out if you prefer a less 'hot' dish)

Juice and zest of 1 lemon

2 red peppers, diced

225g (8oz) spinach, washed, stalked and shredded

50g (2oz) pine nuts

Salt and pepper to taste

Note: This recipe must be started the previous day. Soak the beans and chickpeas overnight, and drain.

Heat 5 tablespoons of the oil and sauté the onions and garlic for a couple of minutes. Then add the spices and the chilli. Cook for a further 2–3 minutes and add the lemon juice and zest and the drained haricot beans and chickpeas. Cover with water, bring to the boil, cover the pan and simmer until the beans and peas are tender. This will take about 3 hours. Heat the remaining oil and fry the peppers until tender. Add to the mixture with the spinach and pine nuts. Season with salt and pepper to taste. Serve piping hot with lots of crusty bread.

AGA method

Soak the beans and chickpeas overnight, then drain. Sauté the onions and garlic on the Simmering Plate. Add the spices and chilli. Cook for another 2–3 minutes then add the lemon juice and zest, and the drained beans and chickpeas. Cover with water and bring to the boil on the Boiling Plate for 5 minutes, then move to the Simmering Oven and cook for 4–4½ hours. Fry the peppers until tender on the Simmering Plate and continue as above with the spinach and pine nuts.

Bubble and Squeak or Colcannon

Bubble and Squeak and Colcannon are, respectively, English and Irish versions of the same dish. The Irish cooked it first and, traditionally, Colcannon is flavoured with leeks or shallots, and is served in individual bowls topped with a knob of butter. Bubble and Squeak, however, was made from leftover cooked cabbage and potatoes, fried in dripping, but it is such a good dish, it's worth making on its own account. The added twist to the recipe below is that the Bubble and Squeak is cooked in the oven in butter. I owe this idea to Tom Norrington-Davies' *Just Like Mother Used to Make* **− and I think it is inspirational.**

Serves 4

3 waxy-fleshed potatoes, cut
   into small dice
2 tablespoons butter
1 tablespoon olive oil
2 onions, chopped
Approximately half of a
   Savoy cabbage, cored and
   chopped
Salt and pepper to taste

Preheat the oven to 200°C, 400°F, Gas Mark 6 and warm a baking dish large enough to take all the ingredients. Boil the potatoes for approximately 10 minutes. Drain them well and put them in a large mixing bowl. Set to one side.

Heat half the butter with the olive oil in a large frying pan. Fry the onions for 5 minutes, stirring to stop them catching. Then add the cabbage and fry until it wilts. Take the pan off the heat and add the contents to the potatoes in the mixing bowl. Give them a good stir and season with salt and pepper. Take the baking dish out of the oven and melt the rest of the butter in it, then return it to the oven for approximately 20 minutes. The top of the Bubble and Squeak should be golden brown when cooked.

AGA method

Bring the peeled potatoes to a boil on the Boiling Plate and boil for 4 minutes. Drain off the water from the pan, put a lid on it and move to the Simmering Oven for 15 minutes, or until the potatoes are soft. Set aside. Make the bubble and squeak as above using the AGA hotplates, then bake it in the Roasting Oven, on the fourth set of runners, for 20 minutes.

Ragoo of Mushrooms

A ragoo is a stew, originally of meat and vegetables. I wanted to include this as Mushroom Stroganoff, though it is not traditional. However, picking and cooking mushrooms has been a country occupation for centuries and this is a particularly good way of cooking them. So for the purposes of this book, I've called Mushroom Stroganoff 'Ragoo of Mushrooms'. By the way, the original recipe isn't authentically Russian either, since the main ingredient should be steak.

Serves 4

50g (2oz) butter
1 tablespoon sunflower oil
1 medium onion, finely
    chopped
3 celery sticks, finely
    chopped
Pinch of thyme and a
    crumbled bay leaf
450g (1lb) button
    mushrooms
1 tablespoon wholemeal
    flour
150ml (¼ pint) vegetable
    stock
2 tablespoons medium
    sherry
2 tablespoons Greek
    yoghurt or crème fraîche
Salt and pepper to taste

For garnish
Chopped parsley
Paprika

Heat the butter and oil together and sauté the chopped onion and celery with the thyme and bay leaf until soft. Chop the mushrooms into halves or quarters and add to the pan. Add the flour and turn the vegetables so that they are well coated. Cook gently for 5 minutes, then add the stock and the sherry. Cook for another 5 minutes, taste to ensure that the flour is cooked and stir in the yoghurt or crème fraîche. Adjust the seasoning. Reheat gently, stirring all the time so that the sauce does not separate. Serve immediately on a bed of rice garnished with chopped parsley and paprika.

This is a surprisingly rich dish and only needs a green salad as an accompaniment.

AGA method

Cook the ragoo on the AGA hotplates, according to the required temperature.

Potato Pudding

Potatoes, like carrots, spinach and artichokes, were often made into sweet puddings in the 18th century. They would be served with the first course of meat and fish. The original recipe for this modern adaptation is as follows: 'Take 12oz of Potatoes, pound them very fine in a Mortar. 12 yolks of Eggs, 4 Whites, 12oz sugar, 12oz butter, some Mace and Cynnamon dry'd and powdered – a Spoonful or two of Brandy as you please. A Quarter of an Hour will bake it, put it in puff paste – round the rim.'

Serves 4

175g (6oz) shortcrust pastry
(see page 64)
1 tablespoon brandy
150ml (¼ pint) single cream
2 eggs
½ teaspoon cinnamon
450g (1lb) potatoes
(preferably Désirée)
cooked, peeled and diced
25g (1oz) butter, cut into
dice
Salt and pepper to taste

Preheat the oven to 180°C, 350°F, gas mark 4. Line a 23cm (9in) flan dish with the pastry and bake blind for approximately 15 minutes. Beat the brandy, cream, eggs and cinnamon together for a minute or two. Stir in the diced potato, mix well and fill the flan case with the mixture. Dot the top with the diced butter and put back into the oven for approximately 30 minutes, until the top is nicely brown.

AGA method

Line the flan dish with the pastry, then assemble the pudding and spoon the mix into the flan case (no blind baking required). Dot the top with the butter and bake the pudding on the Roasting Oven floor with the cold plain shelf directly above for 25–30 minutes. If it is not brown enough after 25 minutes, remove the plain shelf for the final 5 minutes of baking.

Pan Haggerty

Is Pan Haggerty a Lancashire or a Northumberland speciality? Both counties lay claim to it. Haggerty comes from the French *hacher* – to chop or slice. Traditionally, it is always served in its cooking dish, so if you want to be traditional leave the mixture in the frying pan to brown at the end. Be sure it can take the grill, though.

Serves 2

450g (1lb) potatoes
225g (8oz) onions
1 tablespoon butter
110g (4oz) Lancashire
    cheese, grated
Salt and pepper to taste

Slice the potatoes and onions very thinly. You may find this easiest in a food processor. Heat the butter in a large non-stick frying pan and put in the potatoes and onions with the grated cheese in layers, seasoning each layer lightly with salt and pepper. Fry it all gently until cooked. Place in an ovenproof casserole dish and brown under a grill. This makes a delicious supper dish served with a crisp, green salad.

AGA method

Melt the butter in the frying pan on the Simmering Plate and layer the potatoes and onions, cheese and seasonings as above. Put the frying pan on to the Roasting Oven floor and cook for 20–25 minutes.

Vegetable Cobbler

Inventive and tasty, this dish has an particular flavour due to the addition of fennel.

Serves 4

3 medium carrots, peeled
    and sliced
½ small cauliflower,
    separated into florets
75g (3oz) butter
8 small leeks, thickly sliced
2 small heads of fennel,
    sliced
25g (1oz) wholewheat flour
425ml (¾ pint) vegetable
    stock
2 tablespoons fresh parsley

FOR THE TOPPING
225g (8oz) self-raising flour
1 teaspoon mixed herbs
1 teaspoon mustard powder
2 tablespoons fresh chopped
    parsley
50g (2oz) vegetarian lard
1 egg
Milk to mix
75g (3oz) cheese, grated
Salt and pepper to taste

Preheat the oven to 180°C, 350°F, gas mark 4. Cook the carrots and cauliflower for 5 minutes in boiling, salted water and then drain. Place in a casserole. Melt half the butter and fry the leeks and fennel over a moderate heat for 3–4 minutes. Add to casserole. Melt the rest of the butter in a small pan, add the flour and cook gently for a few minutes. Gradually add the vegetable stock and season if necessary. Simmer for a minute or two, add the parsley and pour over the vegetables. Cover the casserole and bake for 30 minutes. To make the topping, sieve the flour with the mixed herbs, mustard powder and salt and pepper. Rub in the lard until the mixture resembles coarse breadcrumbs. Mix the egg with a little milk and combine to make a springy dough. Roll out to about 2cm (¾in) thick and cut into round scones with a biscuit cutter. Arrange the scones on top of the vegetables round the edge of the casserole and sprinkle with the grated cheese. Increase the oven heat to 230°C, 450°F, gas mark 8 and bake the casserole for a further 15 minutes.

AGA method

Cook the carrots and cauliflower on the Boiling Plate, then drain and put into a casserole dish. Heat a frying pan on the floor of the Roasting Oven, melt half the butter, and fry the leeks and fennel in the pan. Add them to the casserole. Make the sauce in the frying pan on the Simmering Plate. Add the parsley and pour over the vegetables. Bake for 20 minutes on the oven grid shelf on the floor of the Roasting Oven. Meanwhile, make the topping, arrange the scones as above and sprinkle with the cheese. Bake the cobbler in the Roasting Oven, on the fourth set of runners, for 15–20 minutes.

Almondines

Almondines are part of the European tradition of grand cooking. They are included here, partly because English cooking has been influenced by France, and partly because we have such a love affair with the potato and almondines are a wonderful example of the many different ways you can treat mashed potato. Snow Potatoes are boiled potatoes put through a ricer and served just as they are. Mixed with egg yolk, they become Duchesse. Formed into rolls dipped in breadcrumbs and fried, Duchesse potatoes become Croquettes. Roll Croquettes in almonds, and they become Almondines. And we love them all.

Makes about 16 Almondines

900g (2lb) potatoes
25g (1oz) butter
2 tablespoons ground almonds
1 egg, beaten
2 teaspoons chopped fresh herbs
Salt and pepper to taste
110–175g (4–6oz) flaked almonds

Preheat the oven to 190°C, 375°F, gas mark 5. Peel the potatoes and chop them roughly. Cook them in salted water until tender, drain and mash with the butter. Add the ground almonds, egg, herbs and salt and pepper to taste. Form into small balls, about the size of small plums, and roll in the flaked almonds. Chill for about 30 minutes in the fridge.

Place the almond balls on a lightly greased baking sheet and bake in the preheated oven for 15–20 minutes until they are lightly golden.

AGA method

Bring the peeled and chopped potatoes up to a boil on the Boiling Plate, and boil for 4 minutes. Drain off all the water from the pan, put a lid on it and move to the Simmering Oven for 15–20 minutes, or until the potatoes are soft. Continue as above to make the almondines. Bake in the Roasting Oven, on the fourth set of runners, for 10–15 minutes.

Cheese Pudding

This tasty dish is a Norfolk adaptation of Michael Barry's modern version of a recipe dated 1818, originally noted at Goudhurst in Kent. An example of how inspiration travels down the centuries and across counties! This is a beautiful dish, golden, light and speckled with carrot and beetroot; it makes a very good light meal for two with a salad. Serve with a spoonful of Frances's Spicy Apple and Onion Chutney (see page 388) as a relish.

Serves 2

300 ml (½ pint) milk
250g (9oz) soft white
  breadcrumbs
200g (7oz) melted butter
175g (6oz) mature Cheddar
  cheese, grated
4 eggs, separated
50g (2oz) grated beetroot
50g (2oz) grated carrot
2 tablespoons fresh parsley,
  finely chopped
Salt and pepper to taste

Preheat the oven to 190°C, 375°F, gas mark 5. Butter a 20cm (8in) china soufflé or gratin dish. Pour the milk on to the breadcrumbs in a bowl large enough to take all the ingredients. Stir in the melted butter, grated cheese and egg yolks together with the grated beetroot and carrot. Whisk the egg whites until they are nicely frothy, about 5 minutes, and fold them into the mixture together with the parsley. Season to taste. Pour into the buttered dish and bake for about 20 minutes. Serve immediately.

AGA method

Assemble the cheese pudding and bake on the oven grid shelf on the floor of the Roasting Oven for 20 minutes. If it browns too much, slide in the cold plain shelf.

Potted Stilton

This is an excellent way to extend the life of the Christmas Stilton, which may be becoming a little dry in January. It keeps well in the refrigerator for up to 2 weeks.

Fills 4 small ramekins

275g (10oz) Stilton cheese
50g (2oz) softened butter
Pinch of mace
Pinch of cayenne pepper
2 tablespoons port or milk
50g (2oz) clarified butter
  (see page 55 for
  instructions)

Blend the Stilton, softened butter, mace and cayenne together with the port or milk to make a smooth, spreadable paste. Pack into small ramekin dishes. Melt the clarified butter very gently and pour over the Stilton to seal the ramekins, taking care to leave behind the milky sediment. Chill until required.

AGA method

Melt the clarified butter at the back of the AGA or on the Warming Plate, then follow the instructions above.

Potted Cheese

Another recipe for frugal housewives. Here the potting with cream and herbs complements the texture and flavour of the cheese. These little pots should be eaten within a couple of days of mixing.

Fills 4 small ramekins

150g (5oz) Stilton cheese
150g (5oz) Cheddar cheese
2 teaspoons dried mixed
  herbs
About 150ml (¼ pint) single
  cream
Chopped parsley, for garnish

Finely grate the Stilton and Cheddar cheeses. Beat in the mixed herbs together with enough single cream to give a smoothish paste – I prefer this with a little texture to it, but a food processor can be used to make a very smooth paste. Pack into four individual pots and garnish with parsley. Serve with savoury shortbread, toast or herb scones as a snack or light lunch.

Cauliflower Cheese

The secret of this recipe for a well-loved old favourite is the amount of cheese. There is a lot of protein in this dish. Eat it as a main course, not as a vegetable accompaniment to meat. The contrast of the rich sauce with the chunks of slightly crisp cauliflower is perfect.

Serves 3–4

1 cauliflower
1 level tablespoon cornflour
300ml (½pint) milk
40g (1½oz) butter
450g (1lb) mature Cheddar
    cheese, grated
Sprinkling of cayenne pepper
Salt and pepper

Preheat the oven to 210°C, 425°F, gas mark 7. Boil or steam the cauliflower until just tender. Drain, cut into large chunks and put in an ovenproof dish. It also looks good made in individual ovenproof dishes if you have them. In a non-stick pan, cream the cornflour with a little cold milk, pour in the balance of the milk and add the butter. Bring to the boil, stirring continuously until the sauce has thickened. Add two-thirds of the cheese, season to taste with salt and pepper and simmer gently for 5 minutes, or until the cheese has melted. Pour over the cauliflower, sprinkle the top with the remainder of the cheese and dust with cayenne pepper. Cook in the oven, uncovered, until the top is golden brown – approximately 15 minutes.

AGA method

Cut the cauliflower into chunks and boil using the Boiling Plate, until just tender. Make the sauce in a pan on the Simmering Plate. Pour the sauce over the cauliflower and sprinkle with cheese and cayenne pepper. Cook in the Roasting Oven, on the fourth runners down, for about 15 minutes, until golden.

Cheese Soufflé

At least three quite different methods for making cheese soufflés are recorded in nineteenth-century cookery books. This version gives a result similar to choux pastry – slightly less spongy than the more familiar béchamel sauce-based soufflés, with a lovely crisp outer crust.

Serves 4

75g (3oz) butter, plus a little extra for greasing
125ml (4fl oz) water
½ teaspoon salt
¼ teaspoon black pepper
75g (3oz) flour, sifted
4 eggs, separated
75g (3oz) strong cheddar cheese, finely grated

Preheat the oven to 200°C, 400°F, gas mark 6. Lightly butter the inside of a 1.2 litre (2 pint) soufflé dish. Put half of the butter, all the water and the salt and pepper in a pan and bring slowly to the boil, stirring to make sure the butter melts completely and is evenly distributed throughout the mixture. Remove from the heat and quickly stir in the flour to make a stiff paste.

Allow the paste to cool until tepid, then mix in 1 egg yolk, followed by some of the remaining butter and some of the cheese. Repeat this process until the other 3 yolks and all the butter and cheese have been thoroughly incorporated into the mixture. Whisk the egg whites until they form soft peaks and stir approximately a quarter of them into the paste to slacken it off a little. Gently but thoroughly fold in the remaining egg whites. Tip the mixture, which should still be quite stiff, into the prepared soufflé dish and bake in the hot oven for 35–40 minutes. About halfway through the cooking time, check if the soufflé is browning evenly and turn it round, if necessary. Towards the end of the cooking time, it should rise spectacularly. Serve immediately, before it falls.

AGA method

Prepare the soufflé as above. Bake in the Roasting Oven, on the fourth set of runners, for 25–35 minutes. If it browns too much, slide the cold plain shelf on to the first set of runners.

Cheese and Onion Pasties

An old saying states that a Cornishwoman will put anything in a pasty. This recipe is for a vegetarian version. Try to use good Cornish potatoes and clotted cream in the filling.

Makes 2 large pasties

Plain flour, for dusting
250g (9oz) shortcrust pastry
    (see page 64)
200g (7oz) potatoes, peeled
    and thinly sliced
100g (3½oz) mature
    Cheddar cheese, thinly
    sliced
1 small onion, peeled and
    thinly sliced
2 generous tablespoons
    clotted cream
1 scant tablespoon finely
    chopped parsley or
    parsley plus a little
    tarragon
1 egg, beaten
Salt and pepper

Preheat the oven to 220°C, 425°F, gas mark 7. Dust a work surface with flour. Divide the pastry into two and roll out each piece very thin, about 5mm (¼in), and as near a circle as you can get it. Arrange half of the potato slices in a layer over one half of one of the pastry circles and arrange the remaining potato slices in a similar way over one half of the other pastry circle. Season each potato layer with a little salt and quite a lot of pepper, then top each with half of the Cheddar, then half of the onions. Heap a tablespoon of the clotted cream on top of each pile of vegetables and cheese and sprinkle over the chopped herbs. Brush around the edges of the pastry circles with some of the beaten egg. Fold the uncovered halves of pastry over to enclose the filling and crimp the edges of the pastry together firmly to form two pasties. Brush more beaten egg over the top of the pasties, then carefully transfer them to a lightly greased baking tray. Cook in the hot oven for 15–20 minutes (the pastry should crisp and brown but not scorch, so keep an eye on it). Then turn the heat down to 160°C, 325°F, gas mark 3 and cook for another 20–25 minutes. The pasties are best eaten hot or while still warm, with a salad.

AGA method

Prepare the pasties ready to go into the oven. Slide the oven grid shelf on to the floor of the Roasting Oven and place the baking tray on top. Cook for about 20 minutes, until browned, then slide the cold plain shelf directly above the tray and bake for 30–40 minutes.

Mock Crab

The idea of calling this pleasant light lunch or supper dish 'mock crab' may have evolved during the Second World War, when the real thing was difficult to find away from the coast. It can be put together very quickly from ingredients that most people have readily to hand. For a vegetarian version, omit the anchovies and add a little chopped fresh basil.

Serves 2

2–3 large, well-flavoured tomatoes, about 200g (7oz) in total

50g (2 oz) butter

1 small onion, very finely chopped

40g (1½oz) strong Cheddar cheese, finely grated

2 eggs

2 tablespoons fresh white breadcrumbs

4–6 anchovy fillets, chopped into small pieces (optional)

Salt and pepper to taste

Crusty bread or toast, to serve

Put the tomatoes in a bowl, cover with boiling water and leave to stand for 1–2 minutes. Drain and peel off the skins. Cut in half and remove and discard the pips. Cut the flesh into slivers or cubes. Melt the butter in a saucepan. Add the onion with the tomatoes and stew gently over a low heat for about 5 minutes, until the onion is soft and transparent. Stir in the cheese.

Beat the eggs together in a small bowl, then mix in the breadcrumbs. Stir this into the tomato mixture, together with the anchovies, if using, and continue to cook very gently, stirring all the time, until the eggs thicken. Remove from the heat, taste and season. Serve immediately with toast or some good crusty bread, or allow to cool and use as a sandwich filling.

AGA method

Use the AGA hotplates for this recipe, moving from the Boiling Plate to the Simmering Plate as necessary.

Glamorgan Sausages

Traditional to South Wales, these are a mixture of cheese and breadcrumbs, seasoned with chopped leeks (or sometimes onions or chives). They make a good vegetarian alternative (cooked with vegetable oil, of course) to conventional sausages. The proportions, especially of cheese to breadcrumbs, vary from recipe to recipe – increase or decrease them according to taste.

Serves 4–6

250g (9oz) fresh white
  breadcrumbs
125g (4½oz) Caerphilly or
  Lancashire cheese,
  coarsely grated
50g (2oz) very finely
  chopped leek
1 generous tablespoon
  chopped parsley
6 sprigs fresh thyme (leaves
  only) or ½ teaspoon
  dried thyme
1 scant teaspoon salt
¼ teaspoon freshly ground
  black pepper
1 teaspoon mustard powder
2 eggs, separated
Milk or water, to mix
Plain flour, for coating
Bacon fat or vegetable oil,
  for frying

Set aside 75g (3oz) breadcrumbs on a plate or in a shallow bowl. Mix the remainder with the cheese, leek, herbs, salt, pepper, mustard, both egg yolks and one of the whites. Stir well, and if the mixture seems dry, add a little milk or water – it should hold together but not be sloppy.

Flour a work surface generously, turn the mixture on to it and divide into 12 equal pieces. Roll each piece gently in the flour to make a sausage shape. Put the remaining egg white in a shallow bowl and whisk to break it up a little, but not until frothy. Put the plate or bowl of reserved breadcrumbs next to it. Pass each sausage through the bowl of egg white, then roll in the breadcrumbs until well coated.

Heat a couple of tablespoons of bacon fat or oil in a large frying pan. Add half the sausages and cook gently, turning so that they brown and crisp all over. When they are golden, remove from the pan and drain on kitchen paper. Keep warm while frying the remaining sausages. These were traditionally eaten with potatoes, but a crisp green salad would make a good lighter alternative.

AGA method

Use the AGA hotplates to fry the sausages. Alternatively, heat the oil in the frying pan on the floor of the Roasting Oven, add the sausages and fry, turning occasionally, until golden brown.

Leek and Cheese Bread and Butter Pudding

Bread puddings, savoury and sweet, are part of our heritage. This recipe from Northumberland uses the superlative local ingredients to good effect.

Serves 6

Butter for greasing

2 tablespoons vegetable oil

4 medium leeks, trimmed, washed and finely sliced

8 slices herb-flavoured bread, sliced and buttered (if unavailable, use plain bread and add 1 teaspoon dried mixed herbs to the leeks when sautéing)

6 eggs, well beaten

600ml (1 pint) milk

300ml (½ pint) double cream

1 tablespoon finely chopped fresh chives (use chive flowers when in season)

225g (8oz) Northumberland cheese, grated

Salt and pepper to taste

Preheat the oven to 180°C, 350°F, gas mark 4. Butter a large ovenproof dish. Heat the oil and gently sauté the leeks until soft. Lay the bread in the dish interspersed with the softened leeks. Whisk together the eggs, milk and cream, stir the chives and grated cheese into the mixture and season to taste. Bake for approximately 50 minutes until golden and set but still wobbly in the middle. Serve at once with a green salad.

AGA method

Heat the oil in a frying pan on the floor of the Roasting Oven and fry the leeks in the pan until they are soft. Assemble the rest of the dish and bake in the Roasting Oven, on the fourth set of runners with the cold plain shelf directly above, for 30 minutes. Remove the plain shelf and continue to bake for another 15–20 minutes, or until golden. Alternatively, cook in the centre of the Baking Oven (on three- and four-oven models) for about 40–50 minutes.

Welsh Rarebit

There are at least three basic versions of this toasted cheese dish. This is one of the more elaborate ones. I like the use of beer in it: ale and cheese complement each other beautifully.

Serves 4

200g (7oz) strong cheese:
    Cheddar or a good
    Cheshire, grated
25g (1oz) butter
1 level teaspoon mustard
    powder
2 teaspoons plain flour
4 tablespoons beer
Pepper to taste
4 slices of bread, toasted on
    one side only

Put everything except the bread in a saucepan. Stir well and heat gently until all is melted and well amalgamated. Spread over the untoasted side of the bread and brown under the grill.

AGA method

Use the Simmering Plate to make the cheese topping. Spread over the untoasted side of the bread, put on to a shallow baking tray, and slide onto the top set of runners in the Roasting Oven.

Vegetable and Nut Greate Pye

Alison Sloane invents delicious modern versions of historic recipes. This is a small version of the truly 'great pyes' that were so popular in the Middle Ages and later. They were large enough for practical jokes: when a pie was cut into, birds or frogs might jump out, the origin of the nursery rhyme 'Sing a Song of Sixpence/ A pocketful of rye/Four-and-twenty blackbirds baked in a pie.'

Serves 4

225g (8oz) Shortcrust
  Pastry (see page 64)
¾ white cabbage, shredded,
  cooked and well drained
225g (8oz) sliced raw
  mushrooms
50g (2oz) vegetarian suet
75g (3oz) pine nuts or
  walnut pieces
50g (2oz) ground almonds
75g (3oz) chopped dates
½ teaspoon cinnamon
½ teaspoon nutmeg
75g (3oz) Parmesan cheese,
  grated
Milk or beaten egg, to glaze

Preheat the oven to 180°C, 350°F, gas mark 4. Line a 23cm (9in) flan tin with two-thirds of the pastry. Prick the base and chill while you mix all the other ingredients together for the filling. Roll out the remainder of the pastry. Pile the filling into the tin – it should be fairly full – and cover with the pastry lid. Brush with milk or beaten egg to glaze. Bake for approximately 35–40 minutes or until the pastry is golden. The juices from the raw mushrooms flavour the pie as they cook during baking.

AGA method

Make the pie as above and cook on the Roasting Oven floor with the cold plain shelf directly above it for 30–40 minutes or until the pastry is golden.

Homity Pies

Homity Pies originated in the West Country during World War II, when meat was rationed. They were made popular later by Cranks, one of the first successful all-vegetarian restaurants.

Serves 6

For the pastry
175g (6oz) plain wholemeal flour
50g (2oz) plain white flour
Pinch of salt
50g (2oz) butter
50g (2oz) vegetarian lard
2 tablespoons cold water

For the filling
350g (12oz) potatoes
450g (1lb) onions
3 tablespoons vegetable oil
25g (1oz) butter
1 tablespoon parsley, chopped
110g (4oz) Cheddar cheese, grated
2 garlic cloves, crushed
1 tablespoon milk
Salt and pepper to taste

Preheat the oven to 220°C, 425°F, gas mark 7. First make the pastry. In a large bowl, mix together the flours and salt. Cut the fats into pieces and then, using your fingers, rub the fats until the mixture resembles breadcrumbs. Add the water and gently gather the pastry together into a ball. Knead lightly, then wrap the pastry ball in clingfilm and chill in the fridge for 30 minutes. Roll out the pastry and line six 10cm (4in) individual tins – Yorkshire pudding tins are ideal. Boil or steam the potatoes for the filling until tender. Chop the onions, sauté in the oil until soft but not coloured. Then combine the potatoes and onions, add butter, parsley, half the cheese, garlic, milk and salt and pepper to taste. Cool, then use to fill the cases. Sprinkle with the remaining cheese and bake in the oven for 20 minutes, until golden.

AGA method

Make the pastry as above and leave it to rest. Bring the peeled potatoes up to a boil on the Boiling Plate, then boil for 4 minutes. Drain off all the water from the pan, put a lid on, and move to the Simmering Oven for 15–20 minutes or until the potatoes are soft.

Line the tins ready for filling. Use the AGA hotplates to fry the onion and combine the potatoes, onions, butter, parsley, half the cheese, garlic, milk, salt and pepper. Cool, then fill the pastry cases. Sprinkle with the remaining cheese and bake on the Roasting Oven floor for 15–20 minutes, until golden. If the pies brown too much, slide in the cold plain shelf.

Leek and Potato Hotpot

This Leek and Potato Hotpot comes from Lancashire. It's a Fatherless Pie. Vegetarian hotpots were made when the earner of the family was out of work and money was short. The Lancashire plain was full of market gardens and potato fields, so the leeks and potatoes were plentiful and good value. A pity this excellent dish was viewed as second best. Now we can appreciate it in its own right.

Serves 4

450g (1lb) leeks
1 tablespoon sunflower oil
50g (2oz) butter
25g (1oz) plain flour
150ml (¼ pint) milk
1 teaspoon mustard powder
175g (6oz) Cheddar cheese, grated
450g (1lb) new potatoes, cooked
Finely chopped parsley, to serve

Preheat the oven to 160°C, 325°F, gas mark 3. Trim, slice and wash the leeks in a colander. Sauté gently in the sunflower oil until soft but not mushy. Make a cheese sauce: melt the butter, and stir in and cook the flour for a couple of minutes. Gradually add the milk, stirring all the time, until the mixture comes to the boil and a thick sauce is made. Add the mustard and cheese and heat gently until melted into the sauce. Arrange half the potatoes in the bottom of each dish, then the leeks, then cover with the cheese sauce. Arrange the balance of the potatoes on top, brush with a little extra oil and bake uncovered in the oven for 20 minutes. Serve with a scattering of chopped parsley.

AGA method

Use the hotplates to sauté the leeks and make the cheese sauce. Assemble the dish and bake in the Roasting Oven, on the third set of runners, for 25–30 minutes.

Macaroni Cheese and Tomato Bake

Britain has always had an affection for *maccheroni*, pasta tubes. We even anglicized its name to *macaroni*. At the beginning of the 19th century, our dandies were called 'macaronis' because they wore wigs with white curls that were supposed to resemble macaroni. Macaroni Cheese has long been a supper standby. Combining cheese sauce with basil and tomatoes makes this dish especially appetising.

Serves 4

225g (8oz) dried macaroni
1 medium onion, chopped
1 tablespoon oil
400g (14oz) tinned
    tomatoes, drained
4 teaspoons tomato purée
Fresh basil
75g (3oz) butter
50g (2oz) plain flour
1 teaspoon mustard powder
425ml (¾ pint) milk
225g (8oz) cheese, grated
Salt and pepper to taste

Preheat the oven to 200°C, 400°F, gas mark 6. Boil the macaroni in the usual way according to the instructions on the packet and drain well.

Fry the chopped onion gently in the oil and add the drained tomatoes, tomato purée and plenty of basil. Cook together for a few minutes, breaking the tomatoes with a wooden spoon and adding salt and pepper to taste. Make a cheese sauce: melt the butter in a saucepan, stir in the flour with the mustard and cook for a minute before pouring in the milk. Stirring all the time, bring to the boil and add 175g (6oz) of the grated cheese.

Stir the tomatoes into the cooked macaroni and spoon either into individual baking dishes or one large dish. Cover each dish or the large dish with the cheese sauce and sprinkle the remaining grated cheese on top. Bake in the oven for 20 minutes or until golden brown.

AGA method

Boil the pasta and make the tomato sauce and cheese sauce using the AGA hotplates. When the dish is assembled, bake in the Roasting Oven, on the third set of runners, for 20–25 minutes or until golden brown.

Parsley and Lemon Stuffing

This recipe is my own favourite basic stuffing. I like a light stuffing and I prefer to cook it separately from the meat or poultry, either rolled into balls or pressed into a well-buttered china dish or tin and cut into squares or slices to serve. I nearly always add extra ingredients such as herbs, nuts or fruits to this stuffing and I have listed some variations to the basic method. This recipe is also the basis for the Sage and Onion Stuffing recipe on page 87.

Serves 4

50g (2oz) butter
1 small onion, peeled and
   finely chopped
2 celery sticks, chopped
Zest and juice of 1 unwaxed
   lemon
150g (6oz) fresh white
   breadcrumbs
Large handful of fresh
   parsley, chopped
1 large egg, well beaten

Preheat the oven to 180°C, 350°F, gas mark 5. Melt the butter in a medium-sized pan. Fry the chopped onion and celery for about 5 minutes or until slightly softened but not coloured. Take the pan off the heat and stir in the lemon zest and juice, breadcrumbs and parsley. Mix well, season with salt and pepper to taste and bind together with the beaten egg. Either press the mixture into a buttered ovenproof dish or make it into patties the size of a golf ball. Put these on a baking tray lined with baking parchment.

Bake for 30 minutes. The top of the mixture or the patties should be golden brown.

AGA method

Use the Simmering Plate to soften the onion and bake the stuffing balls in the Roasting Oven, on the third set of runners, for 20–25 minutes. If they brown too much, cover with foil.

Variations

Tarragon and Apple Stuffing: Add a large handful of chopped French tarragon and a finely chopped crisp apple to the mixture at the same time as the breadcrumbs.

Almond and Oregano Stuffing for Turkey: When making stock from turkey giblets, keep back the liver and use it for this stuffing. Chop the liver and fry it with 25g (1oz) of flaked almonds and the chopped onion and celery. Add 1 tablespoon of chopped fresh oregano or marjoram at the same time as the breadcrumbs. You can also add a handful of fresh cranberries at this point.

Yorkshire Pudding

In Yorkshire, pudding was always served at the beginning of the meal – with gravy – to take the edge off the appetite and enable the cook to serve smaller helpings of expensive meat. It may be called Yorkshire, but batter puddings were eaten everywhere. Nor is gravy the only accompaniment. Sugar, vinegar, jam, golden syrup and mustard were all eaten with pudding. Northerners often accuse Southerners of not being able to make a good Yorkshire pudding. This may simply be a difference in taste. Northerners like their puddings very crisp, while Southerners prefer a slightly softer pudding. Two essentials: you must let the batter stand before using and the fat in the pan must be smoking hot.

Serves 4–6

2 eggs, well beaten
175g (6oz) plain flour
Water to mix
300ml (½ pint) milk
Salt and pepper to taste
Approximately 25g (1oz)
    hard vegetable fat such
    as Trex

In a mixing bowl, stir the eggs into the flour and add sufficient water to make a smooth paste. Beat in the milk until the consistency of the mix is similar to unwhipped double cream; season. Leave to stand for 30 minutes.

Preheat the oven to 220°C, 450°F, gas mark 7. You can use either a 20 x 16cm (8 x 6in) oblong tin, or individual pudding tins. Put a knob of fat in the tin or tins and heat in the oven until the fat smokes. Divide the mixture among the tins and bake for 15 minutes, until risen and golden brown. If cooking one large pudding this will probably require an extra 5 minutes.

Essentials for a good Yorkshire Pudding are very hot fat, not too much of it and a good hot oven.

AGA method

Make the batter as above. Put a knob of fat in the tin or tins and heat in the Roasting Oven until the fat smokes. Remove the tin from the oven and rest on the Boiling Plate while you pour in the batter. Put the tin onto the fourth set of runners in the Roasting Oven, and bake for 15 minutes or until risen and golden.

Savoury Pudding

Puddings of this type, based on highly seasoned bread or oatmeal mixtures, are found in various parts of the British Isles. This is one that is traditional to Yorkshire, where it was served (like the better-known Yorkshire pudding) with the gravy from a roast, before the meat itself. It is especially good as an accompaniment to roast pork.

Serves 4

Butter for greasing
1 large onion, finely chopped
125g (4½oz) fine white
   breadcrumbs
1 heaped tablespoon coarse
   oatmeal
60g (2¼oz) suet
1 heaped tablespoon
   chopped fresh herbs,
   including some sage (the
   traditional combination of
   parsley, sage, rosemary
   and thyme is delicious)
   or 1 teaspoon dried sage
2 eggs, beaten
½ teaspoon salt
Pinch of pepper
A little milk or water (about
   100ml/3½fl oz), to mix

Preheat the oven to 190°C, 375°F, gas mark 5. Grease a shallow ovenproof dish, about 20 x 20cm (8 x 8in) with butter. Mix all the ingredients together until well combined, adding a little milk or water at the end if the mixture seems on the dry side. Spread the mixture in an even layer in the greased dish and cover with greaseproof paper or a piece of foil. Cook in the hot oven for 20 minutes, then remove the paper and cook for another 5–10 minutes to allow the top to crisp and brown. Serve immediately.

AGA method

Prepare the pudding as above. Slide the oven grid shelf on to the floor of the Roasting Oven and place the dish on top. Slide the cold plain shelf directly above the tray and bake for 20–30 minutes. Remove the plain shelf and paper from the top of the pudding and cook for another 5–10 minutes to crisp and brown. Alternatively, cook in the Baking Oven (on three- and four-oven models), on the second set of runners, for 20 minutes, then remove the paper and cook for a further 5–10 minutes until crisp and brown.

Hot Puddings

Queen of Puddings, Sussex Pond Pudding, Chocolate Fudge Pudding, College Pudding, Christmas Pudding, Custard Tart – even the names conjure up pictures of sweet indulgence. With your hunger already assuaged by the previous courses, the only real justification for eating pudding is pleasure. And a memorable pleasure too: the chances are that any childhood memory of a delicious meal is going to feature pudding. Steamed puddings, both savoury and sweet, are a British speciality – one that amazed sophisticated 17th-century European visitors. Monsieur Misson de Valberg's ecstatic comments on puddings, in 1690, must be the most-quoted culinary comment on this particularly British food: 'Blessed be he that invented pudding! For it is manna that hits the palates of all sortes of people, better even than that of the wilderness. Ah! What an excellent thing is an English Pudding! To come in pudding-time is as much as to say to come in the most lucky moment in the world.'

The Oxford Companion to Food agrees that 'Pudding may be claimed as a British invention', but how did it all start? Certainly the British were already enjoying milk puddings such as syllabubs, possets, flummeries and fools by the reign of Elizabeth I. And they were already baking tarts, pies and puddings – both sweet and savoury – in bread ovens, in large houses and cookshops. But that British speciality, the steamed pudding (actually a descendant of savoury faggots, haggis and sausages) came into its own at the beginning of the 17th century, with the invention of the pudding cloth. A 1617 recipe for sweet Suet Pudding, also called College Pudding, proclaims: 'Let your liquor boil and throw your pudding in, being tied in a fair cloth; when it is boiled enough, cut it in the midst, and so serve it.'

There are seven steamed puddings in this chapter, including a modern version of College Pudding, and a recipe for Christmas Pudding that I have been making for Christmas since I was given it eleven years ago. Cooks have been known to compete to make the best version of a particular recipe. Sussex Pond

Pudding is a steamed suet crust enclosing butter, sugar and a whole lemon. Cut into it and it releases a delicious rich lemon syrup. But add currants and it becomes Kentish Well Pudding, a slightly different variation.

I did not ask my donors where their recipes came from, but I am willing to bet that more than a few had the same sort of history as Gerty's Treacle Pudding. When I was compiling this book, my eldest daughter said 'you must put in the treacle pudding that Granny used to cook'. My mother had cooked it for me as a child, too, and I had often watched her make it – a suet roly-poly pudding, spread with golden syrup and then baked in milk in the oven. We ate it with clotted cream on Sundays, as a final treat at the end of roast lunch, and it remains a culinary high spot in my memory. My mother told me that she was given the recipe by Gerty, her parents' cook, back in the 1920s in Norfolk. To my knowledge, the recipe had never been written down, but I found the almost identical Hollygog Pudding in *Traditional Puddings*, a collection of British recipes by Sara Paston-Williams, later reissued as *Good Old-Fashioned Puddings*. Many of the recipes in this and the next chapter come from this invaluable book. The author has not only researched the recipes, she has gone further and tracked down the village or county where these puddings were first tasted. Hollygog Pudding was written down in Oxfordshire, so I wonder how it managed to reach Norfolk? As far as I know, Gerty had never travelled out of the county.

Fritters, or Fritours, are some of the earliest puddings, pre-dating the invention of the pudding cloth, and fried directly over an open fire. They have been found in menus from medieval banquets. The recipe here is for Apple Fritters, but parsnip and carrot fritters were also popular. Pancakes date from the same time. Today we prefer them wafer-thin, but they were originally a thick round of fried batter flavoured with herbs and spices. Since they were made with eggs and milk, and fried in butter, they could not be eaten during Lent, the forty-day fast before Easter when meat and dairy products were forbidden. Today, some people still make pancakes on Shrove Tuesday, the day before Lent, but they do so because they are delicious, and fun to make, rather than to use up the 'illegal' ingredients. Some recipes seem very old, but are actually quite recent: I wonder who, accidentally or on purpose, first tipped sweet pastry ingredients – mixed but not yet kneaded – on top of fruit, then baked the result and found it good? It seems extraordinary that Fruit Crumble may only have been around for sixty years or so.

Sugar, milk or cream and eggs are the ingredients necessary for a true custard. Forget using ready-made custard powder – it doesn't take long to make the real thing, and is well worthwhile, and the recipe is at the end of this chapter. The filling for Sweet Egg Pie, popular since Elizabethan times, is a version of custard. Add breadcrumbs and you have the base for the wonderful Queen of Puddings, an 18th-century English recipe that was hijacked by Charles Francatelli, 'maître d'hôtel and chief cook in ordinary' to Queen Victoria, and renamed in her honour. To the French, custard is known as Crème Anglaise, and you can indeed serve it, hot or cold, as an alternative to cream. There are also recipes for Fruit Sauce, and for Brandy Butter (a hard sauce made from spirits, sugar and butter), that essential accompaniment to Christmas Pudding or Mince Pies.

Nobody could dispute the fact that the British make a great variety of very good puddings. Indeed there are so many puddings that there are two separate chapters in this book, for hot and cold versions.

Abbot's Fruit Pudding

Abbot's Fruit Pudding is named after the Abbot of the Cistercian monastery at Buckland Abbey in the far west of Devon. It was given to Sally Whitfield, the Head Gardener there, by an old lady who was already 90, and it had been handed down to her. Sally gave it to me. So many pudding recipes are handed down by word of mouth.

Serves 4–6

25g (1oz) sago
Butter for greasing
150ml (¼ pint) milk
225g (8oz) breadcrumbs
225g (8oz) mixed fruit
175g (6oz) dark brown
  sugar
1 teaspoon bicarbonate of
  soda
1 teaspoon mixed spice

Soak the sago overnight in the milk. Butter a 1.25 litre (2 pint) pudding basin. In a bowl large enough to take all the ingredients, dissolve the bicarbonate of soda in a little extra milk, add all the rest of the ingredients, mix well and put in the pudding basin. Cover with a layer of greaseproof paper and foil and steam for 2 hours. Serve with an Egg Custard Sauce (see page 257).

AGA method

You will need a saucepan with a trivet large enough to hold the pudding basin – an AGA Cake Baker is ideal.

Assemble the pudding and cover with the greaseproof paper and foil. Put the pudding basin on to a trivet and lower into the saucepan. Pour boiling water around the basin so that it comes halfway up the sides, then bring back to the boil on the Boiling Plate. Boil for 5–8 minutes and cover with a lid. Transfer to the Simmering Oven for 3–3½ hours.

Baked Jam Roll

This pudding is also known as Jam Roly Poly. It used to be boiled, in a cloth or even the sleeve of a shirt, but nowadays it is generally baked. Baking gives the pudding a crisp, golden-brown crust – a good contrast to the hot, sweet, jammy interior.

Serves 4

225g (8oz) self-raising flour
Pinch of salt
110g (4oz) shredded suet
About 7 tablespoons cold
    water
450g (1lb) pot of jam
    (strawberry, apricot,
    blackcurrant, etc)

Preheat the oven to 190°C, 375°F, gas mark 5. Grease a 450g (1lb) loaf tin or line it with baking paper. Sift the flour and salt in a bowl, then sprinkle in the suet and mix lightly with your hands to distribute evenly. Add enough cold water to give a light, elastic dough and knead gently until smooth and the mixture leaves the sides of the bowl clean. Roll out into an oblong about 12mm (½in) thick. Spread evenly with jam and roll up. Trim the edges, use any pastry trimmings to decorate the top, and place in the greased loaf tin. Brush the top with beaten egg and milk and bake for approximately 30 minutes until a pale golden brown. Serve hot with Egg Custard Sauce (see page 257).

AGA method

Assemble the jam roll as above and bake in the Roasting Oven, on the fourth set of runners with the cold plain shelf directly above, for 20 minutes. Remove the plain shelf and continue to cook for another 10 minutes, or until golden brown.

Fruit Crumble

Whenever I cook this recipe for guests from abroad, they are very enthusiastic and very surprised when told how simple the recipe is. Fruit Crumble is an essentially British dish. Its history probably does not go back further than sixty years, according to *The Oxford Companion to Food*, but it is well established now in the British canon of puddings.

Serves 6

700g (1½lb) of fruit –
  apples, plums and rhubarb
  are all good choices. You
  can also use a mixture of
  fruit; blackberries and
  apples is a particular
  favourite.
Sugar to taste

For the crumble topping
110g (4oz) plain flour
1 teaspoon mixed spice
110g (4oz) butter
110g (4oz) brown sugar
50g (2oz) chopped walnuts
  or almonds

Preheat the oven to 200°C, 400°F, gas mark 6. Layer the fruit in an ovenproof dish with sugar (the amount depending on the sharpness of the fruit).

Sieve the flour with the spice. Rub the butter into the flour with your fingers until the mixture is the texture of fine breadcrumbs (you can also do this in a food processor). Mix in the sugar and the nuts and sprinkle in a thick, even layer over the fruit. Bake in the oven for 30–40 minutes. Serve hot with pouring cream or yoghurt.

AGA method

Make the crumble as above and bake in the Roasting Oven, on the lowest set of runners, for 25–30 minutes. If it browns too much, put a piece of foil over the top, or transfer to the Simmering Oven to finish cooking the fruit. Alternatively, cook in the centre of the Baking Oven (on three- or four-oven models) for about 30 minutes.

Steamed Ginger Sponge Pudding with Ginger Sauce

This delicious, warming recipe is from Cornwall.

Serves 4

For the pudding
110g (4oz) butter
110g (4oz) caster sugar
2 eggs
175g (6oz) self-raising flour
50g (2oz) stem ginger, finely
    chopped
3 tablespoons golden syrup

For the ginger sauce
300ml (½ pint) full cream
    milk
1 tablespoon fresh ginger,
    grated
25g (1oz) butter
25g (1oz) plain flour
50g (2oz) caster sugar

Butter an 850ml (1½ pint) pudding basin. Cream together the butter and sugar until pale and fluffy. Beat in the eggs, adding one spoonful of flour with each egg. Fold in the remaining flour and the chopped ginger. Spoon the syrup into the bottom of the pudding basin, then the pudding mixture on top. Smooth the top. Cover with a layer of greaseproof paper and foil and steam for 1–1½ hours.

While the pudding is steaming, make the sauce. Bring the milk to the boil with the ginger. Let the mixture stand for at least 30 minutes to infuse, then strain off the milk. Melt the butter slowly and stir in the flour; cook gently for 2–3 minutes then add the milk gradually, stirring all the time. Bring the sauce to the boil and simmer for at least 5 minutes, stirring constantly. Add the sugar and stir until dissolved.

Turn the pudding out and serve the sauce separately. Serve both warm – there is no need to burn tongues – the gentle spiciness will add its own heat.

AGA method

You will need a saucepan with a trivet large enough to hold the pudding basin – an AGA Cake Baker is ideal. Assemble the pudding and cover with the greaseproof paper and foil. Put the basin on to a trivet and lower into the saucepan. Pour boiling water around the basin so that it comes halfway up the sides, then bring it back to the boil on the Boiling Plate. Boil for 5–8 minutes and cover with a lid. Transfer to the Simmering Oven for 2–2½ hours. Make the ginger sauce on the Simmering Plate.

Custard Tart or Sweet Egg Pie

This pie has been popular since Elizabethan days when the filling was made with vegetables or fruit, eggs, thick cream and lots of spices. Originally the pastry case was literally to provide a 'coffyn', or container, in which to cook the custard.

Serves 4–6

For the pastry
175g (6oz) plain flour
75g (3oz) unsalted butter
50g (2oz) caster sugar
1 egg yolk
1–2 tablespoons ice-cold
    water

For the filling
3 eggs
1 level teaspoon cornflour
425ml (¾ pint) single cream
    or milk
1 vanilla pod, pierced
Grated nutmeg or ground
    cinnamon for sprinkling

Preheat the oven to 190°C, 375°F, gas mark 5. Sieve the flour into a mixing bowl. Rub the butter into the flour using fingertips. Stir in 10g (½oz) of the sugar. Beat the egg yolk with cold water and add to the flour and butter mixture. Collect into a dough, knead very lightly and set aside in a cool place to chill for 30 minutes. Then roll out on a lightly floured board and line a 20cm (8in) flan tin. Chill again. Bake blind for 15–20 minutes until the pastry is almost cooked. Remove from the oven, and leave to cool while you make the filling. Lower the oven to 150°C, 300°F, gas mark 2.

Beat the eggs and mix in the cornflour and remaining sugar. Beat until the sugar granules have dissolved. Heat the cream or milk with the pierced vanilla pod until it reaches boiling point. Pour on to the egg mixture, whisking continuously. Remove the vanilla pod. Strain through a sieve into the flan case and sprinkle with grated nutmeg or ground cinnamon. Bake in the centre of the oven for about 45 minutes or until the custard is set (test with a fine skewer, which should come out clean). Remove from the oven when set and leave to cool a little before removing from the flan tin. Serve warm or cold, decorated with a few fresh flowers.

AGA method

Make the tart as above, using the AGA hotplates to make the filling. Bake the tart on the Roasting Oven floor with the cold plain shelf directly above it for 20 minutes, then transfer to the Simmering Oven for a further 30 minutes or until the custard has set.

Exmoor In and Out

This Devon recipe is essentially a spiced apple pudding with a flavourful almond sponge topping.

Serves 6

900g (2lb) cooking apples
   (preferably Bramleys)
50g (2oz) demerara sugar
   mixed with 1 teaspoon
   cinnamon
4 tablespoons apple juice
   mixed with a few drops
   of almond essence

For the topping
110g (4oz) butter
110g (4oz) demerara sugar
2 eggs
110g (4oz) self-raising flour
50g (2oz) ground almonds
A handful of flaked almonds

Preheat the oven to 180°C, 350°F, gas mark 4. Peel and slice the apples into an ovenproof dish and drizzle the sugar, cinnamon and apple juice over the apples. Cover with a damp cloth while mixing the topping. Beat the butter and demerara sugar together until light and beat in the eggs gradually (this can be done in a food processor). Then fold in the flour and ground almonds. Spread on the apples and scatter over the handful of flaked almonds. Bake until golden brown – about 40 minutes.

AGA method

Assemble the pudding as above. Put the grid shelf on the floor of the Roasting Oven. Slide the pudding dish on to the grid shelf. Slide the cold plain shelf directly above and bake for 30–40 minutes, or until golden brown. You may need to take the plain shelf out after 25 minutes for it to brown. Alternatively, cook in the centre of the Baking Oven (on three- and four-oven models) for about 40 minutes.

Gingerbread Pudding

Gingerbreads, popular over many centuries, always spiced with ginger and sometimes containing chunks of preserved ginger, vary enormously throughout Britain. Many towns had their own specialities. Ashbourne in Derbyshire has a 'white' gingerbread, Ormskirk in Lancashire a 'dark' one. Grasmere gingerbread is like a shortbread. This gingerbread recipe comes from Warwickshire, so presumably it is local to that county.

Serves 6

110g (4oz) butter
75g (3oz) sugar
225g (8oz) golden syrup
1 tablespoon orange
    marmalade
1 large egg
150ml (¼ pint) milk
225g (8oz) self-raising flour
1 teaspoon ground ginger
1 teaspoon ground
    cinnamon
1 teaspoon bicarbonate of
    soda

Preheat the oven to 160°C, 325°F, gas mark 3. Grease a 20cm (8in) square tin. Put the butter, sugar, golden syrup and marmalade into a saucepan and heat until the sugar has dissolved. Leave to cool. Beat the egg with the milk and add to the syrup mixture. Sift the flour with the ginger, cinnamon and bicarbonate of soda, pour into the mixture and beat until smooth. Turn into the prepared tin and bake for 45 minutes, or until firm. Serve hot with cream.

AGA method

Prepare the pudding as above. Bake in the Roasting Oven, on the fourth set of runners, for 20 minutes, then move to the Simmering Oven for another 30–35 minutes or until firm. Alternatively, cook on the oven grid shelf set on the floor of the Baking Oven (on three- or four-oven models) for about 40 minutes, until firm.

Apple Pie

Everyone has their favourite apple pie. I like the sharpness of the filling here, the use of the citrus fruits and the spice. It tastes delicious.

Serves 4–6

350g (12oz) shortcrust
   pastry (see page 64)
700g (1½lb) Bramley apples,
   peeled and thinly sliced
25g (1oz) soft brown sugar
   (use more if you like a
   sweeter filling)
Grated zest and juice of half
   an orange and half a
   lemon
¼ teaspoon ground cloves
½ teaspoon ground
   cinnamon
Milk to glaze
Caster sugar for decoration

Preheat the oven to 200°C, 400°F, gas mark 6. Roll out a little more than half the pastry and line a 23cm (9in) enamel pie plate, pressing it gently and firmly all round. Cover the pastry shell with the sliced apples, sprinkling in the brown sugar, zests, ground cloves and cinnamon between the layers. Pour over the juices when finished. Roll out the other half of the pastry to form a lid. Dampen the bottom layer of pastry round the edge with milk, then fix the lid in position, pressing it very firmly all round. Cut slits in the top crust to release steam. Brush with milk and sprinkle with a little sugar before baking for 40 minutes. Serve warm with cream or yoghurt.

AGA method

Make the pie as above and cook on the Roasting Oven floor, with the cold plain shelf directly above it, for 30–40 minutes or until golden.

Dolbury Pudding

This steamed pudding recipe comes from the restaurant at Killerton, a delightful 18th-century house set in the rich green countryside of East Devon. The person who named it thought the pudding's shape reminded them of Dolbury Hill, which rises behind the house.

Serves 4–6

110g (4oz) butter
25g (1oz) lard
150g (5oz) soft brown sugar
3 eggs, beaten
200g (7oz) chopped apples
200g (7oz) mincemeat
225g (8oz) self-raising flour
A little milk, if necessary

Grease a 1.2–1.5 litre (2–2½ pint) pudding basin well and put a round of greased greaseproof paper in the base. Cream together the fats and sugar until pale and fluffy. Add the beaten eggs, a little at a time, and beat well after each addition. Stir in the apples and mincemeat and gently fold in the flour. If necessary, pour in a little milk to give a dropping consistency – the mixture should be moist. Cover the basin loosely with a double layer of greaseproof paper or a piece of foil and secure with string. Place in a pan of boiling water (which should come halfway up the pudding basin) and steam for 2 hours. Serve with any sort of fruit sauce, custard or cream.

AGA method

You will need a saucepan with a trivet large enough to hold the pudding basin for this recipe – an AGA Cake Baker is ideal. Assemble the pudding and cover with the greaseproof paper and foil. Put the pudding basin on to a trivet and lower into the saucepan. Pour boiling water around the basin so that it comes halfway up the sides. Bring it back to the boil on the Boiling Plate, then boil for 5–8 minutes and cover with a lid. Transfer to the Simmering Oven for 3–3½ hours.

Christmas Pudding

The making and the eating of Christmas Pudding has become thick with tradition. It should be made on Stir-Up Sunday, the Sunday before Advent, and all the family should give it a stir and make a wish. Silver coins and charms are cooked with it.

Makes 2 puddings serving 6, or 1 large pudding serving 12

225g (8oz) raisins
175g (6oz) sultanas
175g (6oz) currants
50g (2oz) candied peel
25g (1oz) flaked almonds
25g (1oz) flour
1 teaspoon mixed spice
1 teaspoon cinnamon
½ teaspoon nutmeg
110g (4oz) caster sugar
110g (4oz) fresh white
    breadcrumbs
Grated zest and juice of
    1 lemon
25g (1oz) butter, diced
2 eggs
150ml (¼ pint) orange juice

In a large bowl mix together the raisins, sultanas, currants, candied peel and almonds. Sieve the flour with the mixed spice, cinnamon and nutmeg. Add to the fruit, together with the sugar and breadcrumbs, grated zest and juice of the lemon, and the diced butter. Mix thoroughly. Beat the eggs well with the orange juice and stir into the mixture. Leave to stand overnight. The next day, pack the mixture into pudding basins. There is probably enough mixture for one large or two medium-sized basins. Leave at least 2.5cm (1in) at the top for expansion. Cover with greaseproof paper and foil and tuck it down round the rim. Stand the basins on top of upturned saucers in a pan. Fill the pan with water to halfway up the basins and simmer for at least 3 hours.

The puddings will then keep for as many months as you want. On Christmas Day, re-cover with fresh paper and foil and steam for an hour before serving.

AGA method

You will need a saucepan with a trivet large enough to hold the pudding basin – an AGA Cake Baker is ideal. Assemble the pudding and cover with the greaseproof paper and foil. Put the pudding basin on to a trivet and lower into the saucepan. Pour boiling water around the basin so that it comes halfway up the sides. Bring it back to the boil on the Boiling Plate for 5–8 minutes and cover with a lid. Transfer to the Simmering Oven for 4–5 hours. On Christmas Day, wrap the pudding in foil and put it into the Simmering Oven about 4–5 hours before you want to eat it.

Apple Cake

Apple cakes are a speciality of the West Country, where orchards cover the rolling hills. Some cakes also contain cider. I chose this example because I like the idea of eating it warm first as a pudding.

Serves 6

175g (6oz) self-raising flour
1 teaspoon mixed spice
225g (8oz) sugar
225g (8oz) butter
700g (1½lb) cooking apples
2 eggs, beaten
A little milk

Preheat the oven to 190°C, 375°F, gas mark 5. Grease a 23 x 23cm (9 x 9in) tin. Sift the flour and mixed spice together and put into a bowl with the sugar. Roughly chop in the butter but do not rub in or cream. Peel the apples and slice into the mixture. Add the beaten eggs and enough milk to make a fairly stiff batter. Bake in the tin for about 1½ hours – until golden brown. This can also be made with pears or plums. It is delicious served hot with thin cream; any left over can be eaten as cake.

AGA method

Bake in the Roasting Oven, on the fourth set of runners with the cold plain shelf directly above, for 40–50 minutes until firm. If it is browning too much, slide a sheet of foil between the cake and the plain shelf. If the cake is not cooked all the way through after 50 minutes, move it to the Simmering Oven for another 25–30 minutes. Alternatively, cook in the centre of the Baking Oven (on three- and four-oven models), for about 1½ hours.

Apple Hat

Sara Paston-Williams wrote this recipe, a sweet version of Steak and Kidney Pudding. She lives in Cornwall, where clotted cream is good and available. This also tastes very good without it though.

Serves 6

225g (8oz) self-raising flour
Pinch of salt
110g (4oz) shredded suet
6–8 tablespoons cold water
700g (1½lb) cooking apples,
    peeled, cored and sliced
50g (2oz) raisins or sultanas
75g (3oz) brown or white
    sugar
3 cloves
Pinch of ground cinnamon
Pinch of ground ginger
Grated zest and juice of ½
    lemon or 1 orange
50g (2oz) unsalted butter,
    plus extra for greasing

Butter well a 1.2 litre (2 pint) pudding basin. Sieve the flour with salt into a mixing bowl. Stir in the suet and mix with sufficient cold water to make a soft, light dough. Knead lightly and roll out on a floured board about 6mm (¼in) thick. Use two-thirds of the pastry to line the prepared basin. Fill the lined basin with layers of apples, raisins or sultanas, sugar and spices. Add lemon or orange zest and juice and the butter, cut into small pieces. Cover the basin with the reserved piece of pastry, dampening the edges and pressing together firmly. Cover with a piece of pleated, well-buttered greaseproof paper followed by a piece of buttered foil with a pleat in the centre, at right angles to the greaseproof paper to allow room for the pudding to rise. Tie down securely with string. Steam for 2–2½ hours, topping up with boiling water as necessary. Turn out on to a warmed serving plate.

AGA method

You will need a saucepan with a trivet large enough to hold the pudding basin for this recipe – an AGA Cake Baker is ideal. Assemble the pudding as above. Put the pudding basin on to a trivet and lower into the saucepan. Pour boiling water around the basin so that it comes halfway up the sides. Bring it back to the boil on the Boiling Plate for 5–8 minutes and cover with a lid. Transfer to the Simmering Oven for 2½–3 hours. Make sure there is sufficient room in your covered saucepan so that it does not obstruct the pudding from rising.

Apple Fritters in Ale Batter

'Frutours' or 'fritours' were a great favourite on medieval menus. They usually appeared as part of the last course and were dusted with sugar. Sweet root vegetables such as parsnips, as well as almonds and edible flowers, were also battered and fried. This recipe was researched by Sara Paston-Williams for *A Book of Historical Recipes* (National Trust).

Serves 4

4 medium cooking or crisp, tart eating apples
1 tablespoon lemon juice
caster sugar

For the batter

110g (4oz) plain flour
½ teaspoon ground cinnamon
2 tablespoons sunflower oil
150ml (¼ pint) pale ale, or still, dry cider
2 egg whites
oil for deep-frying
caster sugar and ground cinnamon for sprinkling

Make the fritter batter first so that it has time to rest for at least 30 minutes before using. Sieve the flour and cinnamon together into a bowl. Make a well in the centre and pour the oil into this, followed by the pale ale or cider. Gradually beat the liquids into the dry ingredients, to make a smooth, creamy batter. Set aside for 30 minutes.

When ready to cook, heat the oil for deep-frying to 190°C (375°F). Peel, core and slice the apples into 5mm (¼in) thick rings and sprinkle with lemon juice and caster sugar. Whisk the egg whites until stiff and fold them into the batter to make it extra light. Make the fritters in small batches, three or four at a time. Pat the apple slices with kitchen paper to mop up any excess lemon juice, dip them into the batter using a skewer or kitchen tongs, then shake off any excess batter. Lower carefully into the hot fat and fry for about 4 minutes or until golden brown and crisp. Drain well on kitchen paper and keep hot in a single, uncovered layer in a cool oven until all are cooked. Serve piping hot, sprinkled with caster sugar and cinnamon.

AGA method

Heat the oil and fry the fritters on the AGA hotplates.

Baked Almond Pudding

Sweet almonds arrived here with the Romans. The nuts have been great favourites in British cooking every since. Marchpane, which was used in medieval banquets to sculpt wonderful table decorations known as 'subtleties', is made from ground almonds and sugar. Macaroons, large almond biscuits that are crispy and sticky at the same time, are also traditional (see page 354).

Serves 6

Butter for greasing
300ml (½ pint) single cream
300ml (½ pint) milk
Grated zest of 1 lemon
1 piece of cinnamon stick
1 blade mace or 1 pinch of
    powdered mace
75g (3oz) caster sugar
175g (6oz) fresh white
    breadcrumbs
110g (4oz) ground almonds
110g (4oz) almond biscuits,
    broken into small pieces
    (use Amaretti or
    something similar with a
    good flavour)
4 eggs
½ teaspoon grated nutmeg
Pinch of salt

Preheat the oven to 190°C, 375°, gas mark 5. Butter a 23cm (9in) gratin dish. Bring the cream and milk to the boil, reduce the heat and add the lemon zest, cinnamon stick, mace and sugar. Stir well and simmer for 10 minutes. Mix the breadcrumbs, ground almonds and almond biscuits in a large bowl and pour in the milk and cream mixture through a sieve. Mix thoroughly and allow to cool to lukewarm. Beat the eggs until foamy, add nutmeg and salt and stir into the almond mixture. Pour into the gratin dish and bake for approximately 45 minutes until firm. Serve warm from the oven.

AGA method

Make the pudding as above using the AGA hotplates. Bake in the Roasting Oven, on the fourth set of runners, for 30–40 minutes until firm. If it is browning too much, slide in the cold plain shelf. Alternatively, cook in the centre of the Baking Oven (on three- or four-oven models) for 45 minutes, until firm.

Almond, Orange and Lemon Tart

This has a subtle, unusual flavour. It is an adaptation of an old recipe from the *Common Place Book* kept by Mrs Margaretta Ackworth, who lived with her husband Abraham in London during the 18th century. Her book records all kinds of 'receipts', not only for eating, but also for cleaning and simple household remedies. This tart is an unusual mixture for today's cooking, but do try it – it looks beautiful and tastes delicious.

Serves 6

175g (6oz) shortcrust pastry (see page 64)
450ml (¾ pint) whipping cream
75g (3oz) caster or granulated sugar
75g (3oz) ground almonds
¼ teaspoon almond essence
¼ teaspoon orange-flower water
1 tablespoon candied peel
3 large egg whites
2 small unwaxed lemons
2 small unwaxed oranges

Preheat the oven to 160°C, 325°F, gas mark 3. Roll out and line a 25cm (10in) deep flan dish with the shortcrust pastry. Bring the cream up to the boil with a slice of lemon zest. Take off the heat and allow to cool. In a bowl large enough to hold all the ingredients, mix the sugar, ground almonds, flavourings and candied peel. Whisk the egg whites until stiff and gently fold into the cooled cream, then fold the egg whites and cream into the rest of the ingredients. Pour into the pastry case. Slice the oranges and lemons thinly and cover the whole of the top of the flan with the slices. Scatter the top with a little extra sugar and bake for 1–1¼ hours or until just set. Serve warm or cold.

AGA method

Make the tart as above, using the AGA hotplates to make the filling. Bake the tart on the Roasting Oven floor, with the cold plain shelf directly above it, for 40–50 minutes or until just set. You may need to move the tart up on to a grid shelf, as it has such a long cooking time. Take care that the pastry does not burn on the bottom. Alternatively, cook the tart for 20–25 minutes on the floor of the Roasting Oven, then transfer to the Simmering Oven for a further 30 minutes.

Bread and Butter Pudding

This is an everyday version of this old favourite – served hot or warm from the dish. A good sauce to go with it is the Fruit Sauce on page 258.

Serves 6

4–5 slices of white bread,
    buttered
2 tablespoons demerara
    sugar
110g (4oz) sultanas
4 eggs
700ml (1¼ pints) milk
Freshly grated nutmeg

Preheat the oven to 180°C, 350°F, gas mark 4. Grease a 1.2–1.5 litre (2–2½ pint) ovenproof dish. Cut the buttered bread slices in half and arrange, buttered side up, in layers in the ovenproof dish, sprinkling the layers with the sugar and sultanas. Finish with a layer of bread and sugar. Whisk the eggs lightly and add to the milk. Pour the whole lot over the bread, sprinkle some freshly grated nutmeg on top and bake for 30–40 minutes until set and lightly brown. Serve warm.

AGA method

Bake in the Roasting Oven, on the grid shelf on the floor of the oven, with the cold plain shelf on the second set of runners, for 25–30 minutes, or until firm. Alternatively, cook in the centre of the Baking Oven (on three- and four-oven models) for 25–30 minutes, or until firm.

Apricot Bread and Butter Pudding

This is a grander, richer affair. The apricots add a welcome tang.

Serves 6

175g (6oz) dried apricots
75g (3oz) sultanas
450g (1lb) medium-sliced
    white bread, lightly
    buttered
Grated nutmeg or
    powdered cinnamon
225ml (8fl oz) milk
225ml (8fl oz) single cream
175g (6oz) caster sugar
Vanilla essence
3 eggs, lightly beaten
1–2 teaspoons lemon juice

Preheat the oven to 180°C, 350°F, gas mark 4. Soak the apricots in 600ml (1 pint) water overnight. Butter a 1.5 litre (2½ pint) soufflé dish. Soak the sultanas in hot water for 10 minutes, drain and mix with 50g (2oz) apricots (retain the rest of the apricots and liquid for the sauce). Remove the crusts from the bread and cut into triangles. With the buttered side up, line the sides of the soufflé dish and place the rest in the dish, layered with the sultanas and apricots and a sprinkling of nutmeg or cinnamon. In a saucepan heat together the milk, cream and 110g (4oz) of the caster sugar to boiling point. Take off the heat, add a few drops of vanilla essence and stir in the beaten eggs. Pour over the bread mixture and wait a few minutes for it to be absorbed. Cover the dish with foil and place in a large, deep roasting tin. Pour boiling water around the dish so that it comes halfway up the sides. Bake for 50 minutes or until set and firm. Remove from the oven and allow to cool a little before turning out on to a serving dish.

To make the sauce, put the remaining apricots and their liquid into a saucepan and simmer for around 15 minutes. Add the rest of the sugar and lemon juice and stir until dissolved. Blend in a liquidiser and serve separately.

AGA method

Prepare using the AGA hotplates. To bake the pudding, place the dish into a large, deep roasting tin. Pour boiling water around the basin so that it comes halfway up the sides. Put the grid shelf on to the Roasting Oven floor. Slide the roasting tin on to the grid shelf and bake for 30–40 minutes, or until the pudding is set and firm. Make the sauce on the AGA hotplates.

Bread Pudding

Bread Pudding was – and still is – made in bakeries to use up yesterday's bread. The difference with a bread pudding made at home is that you can make up your own mix of dried fruit. I think it should always contain some candied peel, but how about crystallised ginger, chopped prunes and dates? Or halved crystallised cherries and dried apricots? Try it and see.

Serves 6

425ml (¾ pint) milk

150ml (¼ pint) cold strong
  tea

110g (4oz) butter, melted

1 tablespoon mixed spice

3 eggs, well beaten

350g (12oz) mixed dried
  fruit

450g (1lb) fresh
  breadcrumbs

Preheat the oven to 180°C, 350°F, gas mark 4. Either grease a tin 5cm (2in) deep and 20 x 28cm (8 x 11in) wide or line it with baking paper. Combine the milk, tea, melted butter, mixed spice, beaten eggs and dried fruit and mix well. Mix in the breadcrumbs and leave to soak for at least an hour or overnight if you wish. Spread the mixture into the prepared tin and bake for 1¼ hours. Cool and serve cut into squares.

AGA method

Prepare the pudding as above, then put the grid shelf on to the Roasting Oven floor. Put the bread pudding on to the grid shelf and slide in the cold plain shelf directly above. Bake for 40–45 minutes. If it needs more baking time, transfer it to the Simmering Oven and bake for another 40 minutes. Alternatively, cook in the centre of the Baking Oven (on three- and four-oven models) for about 1 hour.

Chocolate Fudge Pudding

The first chocolate in the form of a drink reached Britain soon after the restoration of Charles II to the throne in the 1660s. However, there are few recipes using chocolate until the 20th century. Even Mrs Beeton has just one steamed pudding and a soufflé. We have made up for it since then. This is a magical recipe where the sauce is poured over the sponge mixture, the pudding is baked and – to my endless astonishment – the sauce is underneath and the sponge is on top.

Serves 4

For the pudding
110g (4oz) butter
110g (4oz) caster sugar
2 eggs
175g (6oz) self-raising flour
2 level tablespoons cocoa
A little milk, if necessary

For the chocolate base
300ml (½ pint) water
75g (3oz) brown sugar
3 level tablespoons cocoa

Preheat the oven to 180°C, 350°F, gas mark 4. Butter an ovenproof dish, approximately 10cm (4in) deep and 20 x 23cm (8 x 9in) wide. Cream the butter and sugar until pale and fluffy. Beat in the eggs, adding one spoon of the flour with each egg. Fold in the remaining flour and cocoa, sifted together. If the mixture seems too stiff, fold in a little milk until it is a suitable mixture to spread in the bottom of the dish.

Gently heat the water, brown sugar and cocoa in a saucepan until the sugar is dissolved and the mixture resembles a thinnish sauce. Pour the sauce over the pudding mixture and bake for 45–60 minutes, until the top is crisp and brown.

Serve warm. The pudding will have risen through the sauce, combining a rich, dark, moist base with a crisp top. For total indulgence serve with extra pouring cream.

AGA method

Assemble the dish using the AGA hotplates. Bake in the Roasting Oven, on the fourth set of runners with the cold plain shelf directly above, for 30–40 minutes, until the top is crisp and brown. Alternatively, cook on the oven grid shelf, set on the fourth set of runners in the Baking Oven (on three- and four-oven models) for about 45–55 minutes.

Pears in Red Wine Syrup

Pears were very popular in the Middle Ages. The pear most available then was called a Warden. Wardens were large, hard and responded well to poaching. I prefer to use small pears, which are easier to poach, and allow two per serving. Sara Paston-Williams developed this from a recipe dated around 1430.

Serves 6

About 500ml (18fl oz) dry
   red wine
110g (4oz) caster sugar
½ teaspoon ground
   cinnamon
Pinch of ground ginger
12 small pears, ripe or
   unripe
Red food colouring
   (optional)
Small bay leaves to decorate

Put the wine, sugar and spices in an enamel-lined or stainless-steel saucepan just large enough to hold pears standing upright. Heat gently until the sugar has dissolved, then bring to the boil and simmer for 5 minutes.

Meanwhile, peel the pears as thinly as possible, leaving the stalks on. Put the pears into the hot syrup, cover and simmer very gently for 20–30 minutes, or until just tender, basting them occasionally with the syrup. Transfer the pears to a serving dish with a slotted spoon. Taste the syrup and stir in a little more sugar to taste, then boil rapidly without covering until reduced by half and of a coating consistency. Cool a little, then spoon over the pears to give them an attractive reddish gleam. If the colour of the syrup does not seem bright enough, intensify it with 2 or 3 drops of red food colouring. Continue to baste the pears with the syrup until cold, then chill until ready to serve. Decorate with bay leaves stuck into the stalk ends of the pears.

AGA method

Make the syrup on the AGA hotplates. Put the pears into the syrup and bring to the boil on the Boiling Plate, then transfer to the Simmering Oven for 35–40 minutes or until tender. To reduce the syrup, use the Boiling Plate.

Rice Pudding

This unusual rice pudding is made on top of the stove and takes far less time than a baked rice pudding. It is also made with long-grain rice, as used in savoury dishes. Try making it with the best basmati – it will have a delicious flavour.

Serves 6

350g (12oz) long-grain rice
1–1.5 litres (1¾–2½ pints)
    milk
Knob of butter
110g (4oz) sugar
Pinch of salt
½ teaspoon ground nutmeg
125ml (4fl oz) single or
    double cream

For garnish
Jam
Freshly grated nutmeg

Put the rice in a heavy-bottomed pan. Add the milk, butter, sugar, salt and nutmeg, bring to the boil and simmer very gently, stirring frequently, for 30–40 minutes or until the rice is soft. If your stove is rather fierce the rice may tend to stick. Should this happen, change the pan halfway through to a clean one. Just before serving, stir in the cream and pour into individual bowls. Add a swirl of jam and a dusting of nutmeg. A very unusual method, but it works beautifully.

AGA method

Bring the rice pudding to the boil on the Boiling Plate, then move to the Simmering Plate and cook for 8 minutes. Put a lid on the saucepan and move to the Simmering Oven for 1–2 hours, stirring about halfway through the cooking time.

Old English Baked Rice Pudding

For me, the best part of a rice pudding is the golden skin that forms on the top as it cooks slowly, so slowly in the oven. You can't hurry a baked rice pudding; best make the other pudding here if time is short. This recipe is based on one from 1685.

Serves 6

50g (2oz) raisins
2 tablespoons brandy (optional)
50g (2oz) butter
50g (2oz) caster sugar
110g (4oz) pudding or short-grain rice
700ml (1¼ pints) full-cream milk
300ml (½ pint) single cream
1 vanilla pod
Zest of 1 lemon
Freshly grated nutmeg

Preheat the oven to 160°C, 325°F, gas mark 3. Soak the raisins in the brandy while you are preparing the pudding. This part of the recipe is optional; you can stir in the raisins straight from the packet if you prefer.

Melt the butter in a pan and dissolve the sugar in it. Add the rice and boil up until the mixture is golden and bubbly. Pour on the milk and cream and heat gently. Split the vanilla pod. Add to the mixture with the lemon zest and stir well until just boiling. Remove from the heat, stir in the raisins (and the brandy, if using) and pour into a shallow earthenware dish. Grate some fresh nutmeg over the top. Bake for 2 hours. By this time, the mixture should be almost set and there will be a golden skin on the top. Serve warm or at room temperature.

AGA method

Bring the rice pudding mixture to the boil on the Boiling Plate, then move to the Simmering Plate and cook for 4–5 minutes. Pour into a shallow dish and move to the Simmering Oven for 2–3 hours, or until it is almost set and the skin is golden.

Spicy Ground Rice Pudding

This recipe, from *Good Old-Fashioned Puddings* by Sarah Paston-Williams, is based on one by Eliza Acton, one of the best known of the 19th-century cookery writers. Pies and puddings were often 'iced' or topped with egg whites as in this recipe.

Serves 4–6

40g (1½oz) ground rice or semolina

600ml (1 pint) full-cream milk

Strip of lemon zest

1 vanilla pod

1 bay leaf

Pinch of ground nutmeg

25g (1oz) caster sugar or ½ tablespoon honey

2 eggs, separated

25g (1oz) butter, plus extra for greasing

Grated nutmeg or ground cinnamon for sprinkling

110g (4oz) caster sugar

Preheat the oven to 180°C, 350°F, gas mark 4. Butter well a 1.2 litre (2 pint) ovenproof dish. Mix ground rice or semolina to a smooth paste with a little of the milk in a basin. Boil the rest of the milk with the lemon zest, vanilla pod, bay leaf and pinch of nutmeg. Pour on to the ground rice or semolina, stirring continuously. Rinse the pan in which the milk was boiled and leave a film of cold water on the bottom. Return the rice and milk and bring slowly to the boil again, stirring all the time, so that it does not burn on the bottom of the pan. Cook gently for 10 minutes. Add the sugar or honey. Beat the egg yolks and beat into the rice. Remove the vanilla pod, bay leaf and lemon zest. Pour into the prepared pie dish. Dot with the butter and sprinkle with nutmeg or cinnamon. Bake in the centre of the oven for about 25 minutes. Whisk the egg whites until stiff and whisk in 50g (2oz) of the caster sugar. Fold in the remaining caster sugar. Pile the sweetened egg whites on top of the pudding and bake for a further 20 minutes until the meringue is crisp and lightly browned.

AGA method

Make the dish using the AGA hotplates then put the grid shelf on to the Roasting Oven floor. Slide the pudding dish on to the grid shelf and bake for 20–25 minutes, then top with the egg whites. Slide the cold plain shelf above the pudding and continue to bake for another 20–25 minutes, or until the meringue is crisp and lightly browned. Alternatively, cook in the centre of the Baking Oven (on three- and four-oven models), then pile on the meringue and bake for a further 20 minutes.

Queen of Puddings

Queen of Puddings, or Queen's Pudding, is an 18th-century milk, breadcrumb and egg pudding. It was given this particular name during the reign of Queen Victoria.

Serves 6

75g (3oz) fresh white
   breadcrumbs
600ml (1 pint) full cream
   milk
25g (1oz) butter, plus extra
   for greasing
175g (6oz) caster sugar
Zest of 1 lemon, grated
3 eggs, separated
3 tablespoons raspberry jam

Preheat the oven to 180°C, 350°F, gas mark 4. Butter generously either a 1.2 litre (2 pint) shallow ovenproof dish or 6 ramekins. Sprinkle the breadcrumbs in the bottom of the dish or dishes. Put the milk, butter and lemon zest in a pan and bring slowly to the boil. While it is heating, whisk the egg yolks and 50g (2oz) of the sugar in a bowl until they are pale and thick. Take the milk off the heat, let it cool a little, then whisk in the egg yolks. Strain the custard over the breadcrumbs and leave to soak for 15 minutes. Stand the dish or dishes in a roasting tin and fill with water halfway up the dish or dishes. Bake in the oven until set. This will take about 25 minutes. Allow to cool slightly.

Turn the oven temperature down to 150°C, 300°F, gas mark 2. Warm the jam and spread over the top of the pudding(s). Whisk the egg whites until very stiff, then whisk in the remaining sugar, a little at a time. Pile the meringue mixture on top of the jam. Sprinkle with a little extra caster sugar and bake for a further 15 minutes until the meringue topping is crisp and lightly browned.

AGA method

Prepare using the AGA hotplates. To bake, place the dish into a large, deep roasting tin. Pour boiling water around the basin so that it comes halfway up the sides. Put the grid shelf on to the Roasting Oven floor. Slide the roasting tin carefully on to the grid shelf and bake for 25 minutes. Allow to cool slightly. Continue to make the dish as above, then transfer to the Simmering Oven and bake for another 20–30 minutes. Lastly, put into the Roasting Oven for a few minutes to crisp up and lightly brown the top.

Baked Apples

Baked apples, often cooked in cider or wine, have been a country favourite for centuries. They can be filled with any dried fruit and topped with sugar, honey, jam or marmalade. The secret of a good baked apple is to use a good-quality cooking apple, preferably a Bramley. These apples were first grown in Nottinghamshire by Matthew Bramley, an innkeeper and butcher from Southwell. The Bramley is a late cropper and is large with a shiny green skin. This recipe comes from Sara Paston-Williams's *Good Old-Fashioned Puddings*.

Serves 6

6 Bramley cooking apples
50g (2oz) chopped dates
50g (2oz) sultanas
50g (2oz) raisins
25g (1oz) chopped almonds
    or hazelnuts
Grated zest and juice of
    1 orange
75g (3oz) soft brown sugar
1 level teaspoon ground
    mace or mixed spice
40g (1½oz) butter
150ml (¼ pint) sweet sherry
    or Madeira

Preheat the oven to 180°C, 350°F, gas mark 4. Wash and core the apples. Score the skin around the middle of each apple to prevent it bursting during baking and stand close together in a well-buttered ovenproof dish. Mix the chopped dates, sultanas, raisins and nuts with the sugar, orange rind, juice and spices. Pack the centres of the apples with this mixture. Top with a knob of butter. Pour the sherry or Madeira around the apples and bake in the centre of the oven for 45 minutes, basting occasionally. Serve hot or warm with pouring cream.

AGA method

Prepare the apples as above, then put the oven grid shelf on to the Roasting Oven floor. Slide the apples on to the grid shelf and bake for 30–40 minutes, basting occasionally. Alternatively, cook in the centre of the Baking Oven (on three- and four-oven models) for about 45 minutes.

Pancakes

Pancakes have been part of our diet since the Middle Ages. Cooked in a pan, no oven required, they could be made in even the simplest household. Pancakes are always eaten on Shrove Tuesday, the day before Lent begins.

Serves 4

300ml (½ pint) milk
2 eggs
20g (¾oz) caster sugar
Pinch of salt
Grated zest of ½ lemon
110g (4oz) plain flour
20g (¾oz) melted butter
oil for frying
caster sugar for dusting

Place the milk, egg, sugar, salt and grated lemon zest in a liquidiser and switch on to maximum for 10–20 seconds. Sieve the flour and add to the liquidiser. Continue liquidising for a further 15 seconds. Switch off. If any flour remains sticking to the sides of the liquidiser, scrape it into the batter with a plastic spatula. Liquidise for a further 10 seconds, then pour the batter into a bowl. Let it rest for at least 30 minutes – the starch cells will swell and the batter will thicken.

Just before the batter is required, stir the melted butter into it (butter adds a richness to the pancake batter). Pancakes need a fierce heat, so heat an omelette (or crêpe) pan with a little oil until the oil smokes. Do not use butter as the frying agent – it will burn at too low a temperature. Pour off the oil into a dish and keep it for the next pancake. Hold the pan at 45° and add 1 full tablespoon of batter. The batter will quickly run over the bottom of the pan. Swirl the pan around so that the pancake is paper thin. The pancake should be golden brown on the bottom within 30 seconds. Quickly turn the pancake over with a spatula and cook on the other side. Turn out on to a plate and dust with caster sugar. Eat with a squeeze of lemon juice and sugar, syrup or jam.

AGA method

Make the batter as above, then either use a frying pan on the AGA hotplates, or place a piece of Bake-O-Glide silicone liner directly on to the Simmering Plate and cook the pancakes directly on it.

Sussex Pond Pudding

This pudding consists of a suet crust enclosing butter, brown sugar and a whole lemon. When the pudding is cut open, a rich, sweet syrup – the pond – oozes out. The recipe appears in *Good Old-Fashioned Puddings* by Sara Paston-Williams.

Serves 6

225g (8oz) self-raising flour
Pinch of salt
25g (1oz) caster sugar
110g (4oz) shredded suet, grated
1 large thin-skinned lemon, plus the zest of another
6–8 tablespoons cold water
2–3 cloves
110g (4oz) unsalted softened butter
110g (4oz) soft dark brown sugar

Sieve the flour and salt into a mixing bowl. Stir in the sugar. Add the suet and 1 teaspoon grated lemon zest. Add just enough water to mix to a soft, but not sticky, dough using a palette knife. Roll out on a lightly floured board. Butter a 1.2 litre (2 pint) pudding basin and line with the suet crust, reserving about one-third for the lid. Sprinkle the remaining lemon zest into the bottom of the basin. Press the cloves into the lemon and prick it all over with a darning needle. Pat the softened butter around the lemon and roll in the sugar. Place the coated lemon in the lined basin and pack any remaining butter and sugar around it. The basin should be full (if the lemon is large you may have to cut the end off). Dampen the pastry edges and fit the lid. Seal by pressing the edges together. Cover with buttered kitchen foil, making a pleat across the centre to allow the pudding to rise. Tie down securely with string. Steam for 3–3½ hours or until the suet is cooked and well risen. Allow to rest for a few minutes before turning out on to a warmed serving plate.

AGA method

You will need a saucepan with a trivet large enough to hold the pudding basin and with enough room at the top for the pudding to rise – an AGA Cake Baker is ideal. Assemble the pudding as above. Put the pudding basin on to a trivet and lower into the saucepan. Pour boiling water around the basin so that it comes halfway up the sides. Bring it back to the boil on the Boiling Plate for 5–8 minutes and cover with a lid. Transfer to the Simmering Oven for 3½–4 hours or until the suet is cooked and well risen.

Gerty's Treacle Pudding

This recipe was passed down to me by my mother. She was given it by her mother's cook, Gerty, who was born, brought up and lived in Fakenham, Norfolk. Until today, no one, as far as I know, has written it down. It was passed on by word of mouth. Sara Paston-Williams, in *Good Old-Fashioned Puddings*, says Hollygog Pudding, which is very similar, was first made in Kiddington in Oxfordshire. I would love to know how many times the recipe was passed on before it arrived in Norfolk.

Serves 4–6

225g (8oz) self-raising flour
A pinch of salt
2 tablespoons caster sugar, plus a little extra for dusting
150g (6oz) butter, cut into small pieces
Golden syrup
Milk, for baking and glazing

Preheat the oven to 200°C, 400°F, Gas Mark 6. Sift the flour, salt and sugar together and rub the butter into the flour. Mix with a little water to make a stiff dough. Roll out the dough to make a rectangle, roughly 30 x 20cm (12 x 8in). Spread the dough thickly with golden syrup to within 2.5cm/1in of the edge. Brush the edges with milk and roll up to form a sausage. Butter a deep pie or gratin dish and lay the sausage in it, with the join underneath. Brush the top with milk and scatter a little sugar over it. Pour in sufficient milk to come approximately halfway up the pudding. Bake uncovered for 30–45 minutes, until the pudding is golden brown. Serve hot with cream.

AGA method

Prepare the treacle pudding as above. Put the oven grid shelf on to the Roasting Oven floor. Put the pudding on to the grid shelf and bake for 30–40 minutes. If it browns too much, slide in the cold plain shelf.

College Pudding

Also called Cambridge Pudding, this is reputed to have been the first pudding boiled in a cloth rather than in animal guts or a vegetable container. It was served to students at Cambridge University in 1617. Nowadays, it is easier to cook this pudding in a basin. It should be dark and spicy. This recipe is also from *Good Old-Fashioned Puddings*.

Serves 6

75g (3oz) self-raising flour
75g (3oz) fresh white or brown breadcrumbs
1 teaspoon mixed spice
75g (3oz) shredded suet
Pinch of salt
75g (3oz) raisins
50g (2oz) currants
25g (1oz) chopped candied peel
50g (2oz) brown sugar
1 egg
6 tablespoons milk

Generously butter a 1.25 litre (2 pint) pudding basin. Mix together all the dry ingredients in a bowl. Beat the egg and add to the dry ingredients with enough milk to produce a soft dropping consistency. Spoon into the prepared basin and cover with buttered kitchen foil, making a pleat across the centre to allow the pudding to rise. Tie the foil firmly in place with string, making a handle across the top so that you can lift the pudding easily. Steam for 2–2½ hours, topping up with boiling water when necessary. Remove from the heat and allow to shrink slightly before turning out on to a warmed serving plate. Serve very hot with Egg Custard Sauce (see page 257).

AGA method

You will need a saucepan with a trivet large enough to hold the pudding basin and with enough room at the top for the pudding to rise – an AGA Cake Baker is ideal. Assemble the pudding as above. Put the pudding basin on to a trivet and lower into the saucepan. Pour boiling water around the basin so that it comes halfway up the sides. Bring it back to the boil on the Boiling Plate for 5–8 minutes and cover with a lid. Transfer to the Simmering Oven for 2½–3 hours.

Sweet Sauces

Egg Custard Sauce

Our own sweet sauce, which is known in France as *Crème Anglaise*. An essential ingredient of the Trifles on pages 276 and 282, it is also a wonderful accompaniment to a variety of tarts, puddings and pies.

Serves 6–8

600ml (1 pint) full cream
   milk
2 large eggs
1 level tablespoon
   caster sugar
1 level tablespoon cornflour
Drops of vanilla essence

Heat the milk in a pan to almost boiling. Whisk the eggs, sugar and cornflour together while the milk is heating. Add a couple of drops of vanilla essence to the mixture. Then whisk in the hot milk. When it is blended, wash out the pan and return the mixture to the pan. Heat very gently (stirring hard all the time) until the sauce has thickened. Serve hot with puddings or cool for a trifle. The custard will develop a skin as it cools, but this can be whisked smooth when the sauce is needed.

AGA method

Make the egg custard sauce on the AGA hotplates.

Fruit Sauce

I make this fruit sauce to serve instead of cream with chocolate puddings or cakes, or sliced ripe fruit, such as mangoes or peaches. It is also delicious with ice cream. It is an essential ingredient in Peach Melba (see page 274), the grand and delicious pudding invented by Georges Auguste Escoffier, the great chef at the Savoy Hotel, as a tribute to Dame Nellie Melba, the Australian opera diva.

Makes 300ml (½ pint)

225g (8oz) raspberries
    (fresh or frozen)
100g (4oz) fresh
    strawberries
75g (3oz) caster sugar
Juice of 1 lemon

Heat the fruit, sugar and lemon juice gently, stirring continuously until they come to the boil. Remove from the heat, press through a sieve and leave to cool. Refrigerate until you need it.

AGA method

Make the sauce on the AGA hotplates.

Brandy Butter

As a small girl I didn't really like Christmas Pudding, but I ate it because I adored Brandy Butter and was allowed to have a teaspoonful with the pudding (but not without), and because I might be lucky enough to find a silver charm or threepenny piece in my portion.

Brandy Butter can be made a week ahead of use and will keep for a couple of weeks in the fridge. It must be well sealed as it easily picks up other flavours, which will spoil its delicate taste. It is an essential accompaniment for Christmas Pudding (see page 231). Try a small teaspoon on the top of warm mince pies – absolutely delicious! There's a recipe for Mince Pies on page 373.

Provides a spoonful for six with the Christmas pudding, plus leftovers for mince pies

75g (3oz) unsalted butter, softened
75g (3oz) icing sugar
Grated zest of ½ orange
2–3 tablespoons brandy

Either put the butter, about half of the sugar and the orange zest in a food processor and process until the mixture is smooth and creamy, or beat half of the sugar and the orange zest into the butter by hand, with a wooden spoon. Stir in the brandy, then beat in the rest of the sugar. The mixture should be soft enough to spoon, but stiff enough to stand up in peaks when you fork it into a bowl for serving.

Cold Puddings

Perfect for warm summer days, the names of these puddings slip off the tongue almost as easily as the puddings themselves go down. Syllabub and Snow, Flummery and Fool, Tart and Trifle, Posset and Blancmange. Many of these delights are direct descendants of the sweets served as the dessert, or 'banqueting course', at great Tudor feasts. As the last part of a feast, the puddings were special, and only the host or hostess's closest, most important guests were invited to eat this course, which used the richest, most expensive ingredients.

Syllabubs would have been one of the delicacies offered on such occasions. Traditionally, a country syllabub was made by milking the cow directly into a punchbowl containing ale or cider that was already sweetened and spiced. The warm milk and alcohol formed honeycomb curds and alcoholic whey, and the syllabub was served in a special 'syllabub pot', that allowed you to drink the whey from the spout, and eat the curds with a spoon. I have included one Syllabub recipe that uses red wine and ale, a very old combination. My other recipe is a complete contrast, made with white wine and flavoured by bruising and steeping lemon-geranium leaves in lemon juice.

Fine Almond Blancmange is a very old recipe – versions of it probably even pre-date the Tudor banqueting course – while, over the centuries, the recipes for the traditional fools, flummeries, creams, snows and possets have all merged a little. Those I have been given are all light concoctions, made from different fruit purées combined with eggs, sugar and varying amounts of cream.

Tarts have definitely been on the menu quite as long as syllabubs. Tafferty Tart is an apple lattice tart – sadly, I don't know the origin for the delightful name. The original recipe for Maids of Honour Tarts may have originated in the kitchens of Hampton Court, where these little cakes are said to have been a favourite of King Henry VIII. The 'official' recipe is a closely guarded secret, but here is one of the many unofficial recipes, a Victorian version collected by Laura Mason.

On the colder side, there are three recipes for Ice Cream. We British have always preferred ice cream to water ices, or sorbets, unlike our neighbours the French. A few ice-cream recipes appear as far back as the 18th century, such as Damson Ice Cream. The first recipe for Brown Bread Ice appeared in 1772, while Vanilla Ice Cream (see page 294) is essential for making Peach Melba – so I really couldn't leave it out.

The pudding course has always provided an opportunity for chefs to show off their talents, and then name their creation in honour of a place or famous person. Eton School and Clare College, Cambridge are probably still arguing over who first mixed strawberries, cream and crushed meringues together, and then flavoured them with orange liqueur. Is it Eton Mess or Clare College Mush? Either way, it is scrumptious. Boodles Orange Fool was first eaten by the members of Boodles gentlemen's club, and Peach Melba was the invention of the great French chef, Escoffier, who created it at the Savoy Hotel, in honour of Dame Nellie Melba, the famous Australian opera singer.

Finally, with some trepidation, I have included two trifle recipes. I could not leave it out – after all, in his book on trifles, Alan Davidson calls it 'Britain's supreme contribution to the dessert tables of the world'. But everyone has a favourite recipe that they believe is the 'right' trifle, and they are all different! The contributions here are an 18th-Century Trifle – Sara Paston-Williams has researched and rewritten a trifle recipe from its golden age – and Sherry Trifle, my own recipe. For many years I cooked for parties, and this particular trifle was our recipe of choice: I happen to think it is the best in the world.

Baked Quinces in Honey

The quince is a relative of the apple and pear. It is usually large, yellow and knobbly. It is also very hard and is nearly always cooked. It has an extraordinary subtle and special flavour, for which it is highly prized. If you are offered quinces, which are seldom in the shops, take them. Not only will they taste delicious, but they also turn a delicate pink when you cook them.

Serves 6

275g (10oz) honey
300ml (½ pint) orange or
    grapefruit juice
6 quinces, peeled, cored and
    quartered

Preheat the oven to 160°C, 325°F, gas mark 3. Mix the honey into the fruit juice. Lay the quince quarters in a casserole or gratin dish and pour over the liquid. It should well cover them. Put in the oven and bake until the quinces are tender, which will take about 2 hours. Check the dish after an hour or so and if they are getting too dry, add a little water and cover the dish with a lid or foil for the rest of the cooking time. Allow to cool and serve cold. The grainy texture of the quinces provides a good contrast to the sweet syrup.

AGA method

Assemble the dish as above, then cover with a lid or a piece of foil and bake in the Roasting Oven, on the fourth set of runners, for 10 minutes. Move to the Simmering Oven and continue to bake for 2½–3 hours. Check after 2 hours.

Apricot, Honey and Rosemary Mousse

This is a modern recipe using ingredients that were popular in the Middle Ages, even before Henry VIII's gardener brought the first apricot tree to Britain in 1542. Dried 'apricocks' feature in much earlier recipes. Honey was the universal sweetener before sugar, while rosemary, a Mediterranean herb, was brought here by the Romans.

Serves 6

50g (2oz) butter
450g (1lb) semi-dried
    apricots
Water
75g (3oz) honey
2 fresh rosemary sprigs
1 tablespoon gelatine
300ml (½ pint)
    double cream

For decoration
Rosemary sprigs
Chopped apricot

Melt the butter in a pan, add the apricots and turn in the butter. Add water just to cover the fruit, bring to the boil, reduce the heat, simmer until tender, then purée. Heat the honey so it can be measured in a measuring jug, and add to the purée. Add the rosemary and leave in the fruit mixture to infuse while it cools.

When the purée is completely cold, remove the rosemary. Melt the gelatine in a little hot water and stir into the purée. Whip the cream and fold into the purée. Pile into glasses and garnish with a tiny sprig of rosemary and a little chopped apricot.

AGA method

Use the AGA hotplates when making this mousse.

Eton Mess or Clare College Mush

The original recipe for this pudding is said to have come from Clare College, Cambridge. It is a combination of raspberries, cream and crushed meringues and can be flavoured with an orange liqueur, Kirsch, Framboise, brandy or vanilla.

Serves 6

2 large egg whites
110g (4oz) caster sugar
900g (2lb) fresh raspberries
25g (1oz) icing sugar
3 tablespoons Kirsch, orange
  liqueur or raspberry
  liqueur
425ml (¾ pint) double or
  whipping cream

To make the meringues, whisk the egg whites in a clean bowl, with a balloon, rotary or electric whisk. Be careful not to overbeat. Whisk until the whites are stiff enough not to fall out of the bowl when it is turned over. Add the caster sugar, spoonful by spoonful, whisking in between each addition. With a tablespoon, drop even amounts of meringue mixture on to a lightly greased baking tray. Bake in a very cool oven (130°C, 250°F; gas mark ½) for about 1½ hours, or until the meringues are cream-coloured with a slightly soft, chewy centre. Remove from the oven and leave to cool. Chop up the raspberries roughly or leave whole if small. Save a few perfect berries for decorating. Sift the icing sugar over the strawberries and sprinkle with the liqueur. Chill for at least 1 hour. Just before serving, whip the cream until it holds its shape. Gently fold in the raspberries and their juices. Crush the meringues into pieces and fold into the cream and raspberry mixture. Taste, and add more sugar if desired. Pile into a glass bowl or individual glasses and decorate with raspberries.

AGA method

To bake the meringues, slide the baking tray into the Simmering Oven for 1½–2 hours. If you like your meringues very dry, turn each meringue on its side when you remove them from the oven and place the baking tray on to the Simmering Plate lid, protecting it with a tea towel or AGA Chef's Pad. Leave to dry out for another 45 minutes to an hour. Alternatively, dry out the meringues in the Warming Oven (on the four-oven AGA) for 2½ hours.

Lemon Geranium Syllabub

Syllabubs are in cookery books from the 16th century onwards. They are always confections of cream, lemon and alcohol – wine, ale or cider. What makes this syllabub special is the lemon-geranium leaves, which impart a very unusual flavour. Note: some people can be slightly allergic to geraniums.

Serves 6

8 lemon-geranium leaves
Juice of 1 lemon
6 tablespoons white wine
3 tablespoons caster sugar
300ml (½ pint) thick double
   cream

For decoration
Zest of lemon
Fresh lemon-geranium
   leaves

Bruise the lemon-geranium leaves and infuse them in the lemon juice, white wine and sugar. Chill for at least 30 minutes in the fridge (if the infusion is very cold it will whisk more easily with the cream). Discard the leaves and stir the cream into the infusion. Whisk until thick. This can take some time; it depends on the weather! If it is hot and thundery, whisk gently and gradually to prevent the mixture curdling. When thick, pile into glasses and decorate with lemon zest and lemon-geranium leaves. This is the most delectable flowery syllabub.

Summer Fruit Moulds

These are essentially individual summer puddings. Mixing the bread and fruit together makes them firmer and easier to turn out.

Makes 6 ramekins

900g (2lb) prepared fresh
   soft fruit (eg blackcurrants
   and redcurrants, stripped
   from their stems;
   strawberries; blackberries;
   raspberries; gooseberries,
   topped and tailed)
12 thick slices of milk loaf
600ml (1 pint) water
Sugar
4 tablespoons cassis or
   elderflower cordial

To decorate
Extra fruit
Fresh mint or lemon-balm
   sprigs

First put a piece of baking paper, cut to size, in the base of each ramekin. This will make them easier to turn out.

Try to use at least two varieties of soft fruit. Cut the crusts off the bread and cut the slices into large dice. Put the fruit in a pan, cover with the water and simmer until the fruit is tender. Gooseberries and blackcurrants need 5 minutes or so; strawberries, blackberries and raspberries just need to be brought up to the boil and then removed from the heat immediately. Remove the fruit from the juice with a slotted spoon and add sufficient sugar to the juice to make a syrup. This will vary according to the fruits and taste. Bring the syrup to the boil and simmer for 5 minutes. Allow to cool and add the cassis or elderflower cordial. Mix the fruit and bread together. Put a little syrup in the bottom of each ramekin, then pack in the fruit and bread, pressing the mixture down well. Spoon a little syrup over the top of each ramekin. Chill until required.

To serve, run a knife round the inside of each ramekin and unmould on to a dessert plate. Take off the paper and pour over the rest of the juice and then decorate with more fresh fruit and fresh mint or lemon-balm sprigs.

AGA method

Use the AGA hotplates to cook the fruit and to reduce the syrup.

Blackcurrant Flummery

The name Flummery originally came from the Welsh *llymru*, a dish of oats cooked until they were almost solid, eaten with honey or a sweet sauce. Later it became a jelly or blancmange, sometimes made in elaborate moulds for table centres, such as a Flummery in the shape of fish in a pond of jelly. I think this modern recipe is borrowed from its American cousins, where the name means a thickened berry dessert. Warning: recipes containing raw eggs are unsuitable for pregnant women or young children.

Serves 6

450g (1lb) blackcurrants
300ml (½ pint) double
  cream
225g (8oz) caster sugar
1 egg white
Whipped cream for
  decoration

Make a thick sieved purée of the blackcurrants, stewed with a little water. Allow to cool. Whip the cream with the caster sugar. Whisk the egg white separately and fold into the cream. Gently stir the cream mixture into the purée so as to give a marbled effect and serve in individual glasses garnished with a rosette of whipped cream. Chill before serving. This is also excellent made with gooseberries.

Elderflower and Gooseberry Fool

The earliest record of a cultivated gooseberry is said to be a fruiterer's bill from the court of King Edward dated 1276. Elderflowers have been used in our cookery since medieval times. The two have a perfect affinity, the one enhancing the taste of the other. The name Fool comes from the French *fouler*, to crush. Fools have been made for many centuries, always from stewed fruit because people feared that only cooked fruit was 'safe'. Early recipes were much more elaborate and involve eggs, cream, spices and wine. The simple fruit purée and cream fool that we enjoy today has been a favourite since the 19th century.

Serves 6–8

700g (1½lb) fresh
   gooseberries
175g (6oz) sugar
2 tablespoons elderflower
   wine or cordial
300ml (½ pint) double or
   whipping cream
Fresh mint leaves, egg white
   and caster sugar for
   decoration (optional)

Wash the gooseberries and put them into a pan without any extra water (the juice running out of the gooseberries will provide all the liquid you need). Simmer for approximately 15 minutes, or until cooked and squashy. Add the sugar. Pour into a blender or food processor and purée. Then sieve the purée to remove the pips etc. Allow to cool, then stir in the elderflower wine or cordial. Whip the cream until it is thick but not stiff and fold gently into half the gooseberry purée. Spoon the two mixtures in layers into individual glasses, starting with a layer of the gooseberry and cream mixture, then the rest of the gooseberry purée in another layer and then the remainder of the gooseberry and cream mixture. Chill before serving.

For a special occasion you could decorate the glasses with frosted leaves. Beat a little egg white, paint it on each of the mint leaves and coat with caster sugar. Leave to dry on a paper towel until crisp before decorating.

AGA method

Use the AGA hotplates to heat the gooseberries for 3–4 minutes, then transfer to the Simmering Oven for 20 minutes to cook through.

Peach Melba

Peach Melba was invented in London in the late 19th century at the newly opened Savoy Hotel. It was named after Dame Nellie Melba, the Australian opera star.

1 ripe peach per person

For the raspberry sauce
225g (8oz) raspberries
75g (3oz) caster sugar
Juice of 1 lemon

For the vanilla ice cream
450ml (16fl oz) single cream
1 vanilla pod or a few drops
 of vanilla extract
3 egg yolks
110g (4oz) caster sugar
150ml (¼ pint) double
 cream

Heat the single cream with the vanilla pod very gently until it just reaches boiling point. Take off the heat. Beat the egg yolks and sugar together until thick, pale and creamy, then whisk in the hot cream. Return the mixture to the pan and heat very gently until it thickens. It should just coat the back of a wooden spoon. Do not let it boil. Take off the heat, remove the vanilla pod if you are using one or flavour the custard with the vanilla extract, pour the mixture into a bowl and let it cool completely. When it is cold, whip the double cream until it stands in peaks and fold it into the cold mixture. Put the bowl in the freezer. After about an hour take the bowl out and whisk, preferably with an electric whisk, to break up the ice crystals. Return the bowl to the freezer until it is firm.

To make the raspberry sauce, heat the raspberries, sugar and lemon juice gently, stirring continuously, until they come to the boil. Remove from the heat, press through a sieve and leave to cool. Refrigerate until required.

To assemble, first cut a ring round each peach with a knife. Then put them in a deep bowl and cover with boiling water. Leave for 1 minute, then remove from the water and allow to cool. Peel away the skin, slice in half and remove the stone. Put two balls of ice cream in each bowl. Top each ball with half a peach and pour the raspberry sauce on top. Serve immediately.

AGA method

Use the AGA hotplates to make the egg base for the ice cream and the raspberry sauce.

An 18th-century Trifle

Sara Paston-Williams devised this trifle using a recipe from an ancient cookbook. Pre-18th-century trifles were more like a cooked cream or a fool, but this recipe has biscuits, wine, custard and whipped cream.

Serves 6–8

For the base
18 boudoir biscuits or
    sponge fingers
3–4 tablespoons medium-
    dry sherry or white wine

For the custard
300ml (½ pint) double
    cream
3 large egg yolks
1 level teaspoon cornflour
25g (1oz) caster sugar

For the topping
Finely grated zest and juice
    of 1 lemon
4 tablespoons medium-dry
    sherry or white wine
1 teaspoon orange-flower or
    rose-water
50g (2oz) caster sugar
300ml (½ pint) double
    cream
Redcurrant or blackcurrant
    jelly, to decorate
Finely shredded orange,
    lemon or citron zest, to
    decorate

Prepare the topping several hours in advance. Put the lemon zest and juice, sherry or wine, orange-flower or rose-water and caster sugar into a bowl. Cover with clingfilm and leave for a few hours to let the oils from the zest impregnate the liquor. Meanwhile make the custard. Heat the cream in a small non-stick pan. Beat the egg yolks with the cornflour and sugar in a small basin until smooth, then pour on the hot cream, stirring all the time. Return the custard to the pan and stir it with a wooden spoon over a low heat until thick. Place the pan on a cold surface or in a bowl of cold water to remove any heat that might curdle the custard. Leave to cool while you prepare the base. Break the biscuits in half and place in the bottom of a shallow glass or china dish. Sprinkle over the sherry or wine, then pour over the custard. Cool completely. To make the topping, strain the prepared liquor into a clean bowl and stir in the cream, gradually beating it with a whisk until it stands in soft peaks (be careful not to overbeat or the syllabub will separate). Decorate with small blobs of jelly and zest.

AGA method

Make the custard using the Simmering Plate.

Old English Syllabub

This recipe harks back to Elizabethan times, when ale was used far more in cooking than it is now. It is a very good idea to chill all the ingredients for at least an hour before making the syllabub.

Serves 6

300ml (½ pint) double
    cream
100ml (3fl oz) red wine
100ml (3fl oz) light ale
50g (2oz) caster sugar
Tot of whisky (optional)
Grated nutmeg
Boudoir biscuits or small
    shortcake biscuits, to
    serve

Whip the cream, wine, ale and sugar until thick. Do not worry if the cream separates – it will taste just as good. Fold in the whisky if used. Pour into serving glasses and put into the fridge to chill for approximately 1 hour. Sprinkle with grated nutmeg and serve with boudoir biscuits or small shortcake biscuits.

Fine Almond Blancmange

I can't do better than quote Sara Paston-Williams's short history and recipe from her book *Good Old-Fashioned Puddings*. She writes: 'Although its actual name is undoubtedly of French origin, blancmange has been known in Britain for many centuries. It is mentioned in some of the oldest cookery books as "Blewe Manger" or "Blank Mange" or "white food". Chaucer, in *The Canterbury Tales*, describes it as a mixture of "minced capon with flour, cream and sugar". In fact, it was made with any white meat stewed with rice, dried fruits, almonds and spices. Exactly when the meat was omitted is not known, but by Elizabethan times the dish had become a mixture of cream, sugar and rose-water, thickened with egg yolks. The English blancmange of the 18th century was a kind of jelly, stiffened with isinglass or hartshorn and flavoured with almonds and rose-water. By the early 1820s, arrowroot was being exported to Britain from the West Indies and became the thickening agent. Boiling milk, sweetened and seasoned with cinnamon, mace and lemon peel, was poured on to a solution of arrowroot. It was set in elaborate moulds – and here was the true forerunner of our modern cornflour blancmange. Try experimenting with different flavourings like chocolate, coffee, lemon, orange, brandy or other liqueurs, and vanilla.'

Serves 4–6

40g (1½oz) cornflour
300ml (½ pint) milk
300ml (½ pint) single cream
1 bay leaf
Strip of lemon zest
2 tablespoons caster sugar
4–5 drops almond essence
25g (1oz) toasted flaked
    almonds

Mix the cornflour to a smooth paste with a little of the milk. Heat the rest of the milk and cream in a pan with the bay leaf and lemon zest and gradually blend in the cornflour mixture. Bring to simmering point and cook for about 3 minutes, stirring continuously until thickened. Remove from the heat and sweeten to taste. Stir in the almond essence. Pour into a fancy 600ml (1 pint) mould, rinsed out with cold water. Put in the fridge to set. Unmould on to a plate, decorate with toasted almonds and serve with Fruit Sauce (see page 258).

AGA method

Use the AGA hotplates to heat the milk and cream as described above.

Blackcurrant and Rum Posset

The earliest form of posset was milk, lightly curdled by adding wine, ale or lemon or orange juice. Later, possets became more solid. By the 19th century, the posset had become closely related to the fool or syllabub. Rum and blackcurrant work well together – today you can order a rum and blackcurrant cordial at a bar. Warning: recipes containing raw eggs are unsuitable for pregnant women or young children.

Serves 6–8

225g (8oz) blackcurrants
50g (2oz) caster sugar
2 tablespoons water
2 tablespoons rum
600ml (1 pint) whipping or
   double cream
3–4 egg whites

Place the blackcurrants and sugar in a pan and stew lightly with the water. Sieve the cooked fruit, saving a few whole blackcurrants, and add the rum. Whip the cream and fold into the blackcurrant purée. Whisk the egg whites until stiff and gently fold into the cream and fruit mixture. Spoon into individual glasses and decorate with a few whole blackcurrants. Serve well chilled.

AGA method

Use the AGA hotplates to soften the blackcurrants, as required.

Sherry Trifle

Trifle is one of those dishes for which no one can agree on the correct recipe. Grown men remember with affection the trifle made by their mothers and grandmothers and come to blows over whether or not jelly and/or jam should be ingredients. Alan Davidson and Helen Saberi's book, *Trifle*, traces the recipe back to 1596, and includes versions from as far afield as Laos and India. The recipe below is for a modern trifle that features neither jelly nor jam, includes fruit (non-traditional) and has given pleasure to many over the years.

Serves 8

Crème pâtissière or Egg
    Custard Sauce (see
    page 257)
6 trifle sponge cakes
4 tablespoons whisky or
    sherry
1 small ripe pineapple
1 small punnet of
    strawberries
1 small punnet of
    raspberries
8 ratafia biscuits or small
    macaroons
300ml (10fl oz) double
    cream
25g (1oz) flaked almonds

Make up the crème pâtissière or custard. Leave it to cool while you continue making the trifle. Break up the sponge cakes and use them to fill the bottom of a large glass fruit bowl. Spoon the whisky or sherry over the sponge base. Peel the pineapple, then core and dice the fruit; hull and quarter the strawberries. Scatter the pineapple dice, the strawberries and the raspberries over the sponge base, interspersed with the ratafia biscuits or crumbled macaroons.

When the custard is cool, spoon it over the trifle and smooth the top. Whip the cream and spread it over the custard. Toast the almonds until golden, cool and scatter on the top of the trifle. Chill until required.

AGA method

Use the AGA hotplates to make the crème patissière or custard.

Summer Pudding

Quintessentially English, this pudding was known as Hydropathic Pudding in the 19th century, when it was served at health resorts where pastry was forbidden. This recipe is for a large pudding. A tip: don't make the pudding in the basin too liquid; it might collapse when you unmould it. You can always add liquid once it is safely on its dish.

Serves 6

7–8 medium slices of white bread, with the crusts cut off

700g (1½lb) prepared mixed soft fruit (i.e. blackcurrants and redcurrants, stripped from their stems; strawberries; blackberries; raspberries; gooseberries, topped and tailed)

300ml (½ pint) water

About 150g (5oz) caster sugar

Thick double cream to serve

Lightly butter a 900ml (1½ pint) pudding basin. Line the base and sides of the pudding basin with the bread, making sure that there are no gaps between the slices. Reserve two slices for the top. Put the fruit in a pan, cover with water and simmer until the fruit is tender. Gooseberries and blackcurrants need 5 minutes or so; strawberries, blackberries and raspberries just need to be brought up to the boil and then removed from the heat immediately. Lift the fruit into the bowl with a slotted spoon. Add the sugar to the juice and reheat it to make a syrup. The amount of sugar may vary according to the mixture of fruits and your taste. Then pour over the syrup so that it comes just below the top of the bowl. This should leave you with a small amount of extra juice. Cover the top with the reserved bread slices. Put a small plate or saucer over the pudding (one that fits inside the rim of the bowl), place a weight on top and chill overnight.

Unmould by holding a serving dish with a rim (a china quiche dish works well) over the top and turning the pudding over. Use the reserved juice to spoon over and soak any bits of bread that still look white. Serve cut into slices with some thick cream. Best made in season, but try it with frozen fruit for a taste of summer in the winter.

AGA method

Use the AGA hotplates to cook the fruit.

Marbled Rose Cream

This delicate raspberry cream is flavoured with rose-water, which you can buy at grocers and chemists. It was a favourite flavouring in Tudor and Stuart cookery. Rose bushes, specifically for making rose-water, were grown in the kitchen garden alongside fruit bushes. Any soft fruits can be used in this recipe. It can be frozen and served as an ice cream.

Serves 8–10

900g (2lb) fresh or frozen
    raspberries
250g (9oz) caster sugar
2 tablespoons cold water
600ml (1 pint) double cream
2 tablespoons rose-water or
    Kirsch
Frosted mint leaves (see
    page 273)

Put 450g (1lb) raspberries into a saucepan with 175g (6oz) caster sugar and the water. Bring gently to the boil and simmer for a few minutes, or until the raspberries start to yield their juice. Push through a sieve and leave to cool. Whip the cream until thick and add the remaining caster sugar gradually. Mash the remaining raspberries, reserving a few of the best berries for decoration. Mix very thoroughly into the whipped cream and stir in the rose-water or Kirsch. Now add the cooked raspberry pulp, stirring just enough to give a marbled effect. Pour into a glass bowl and put into the fridge for at least 3 hours before serving. Decorate with reserved berries and frosted mint leaves.

AGA method

Use the AGA hotplates to heat up the raspberries.

Boodles Orange Fool

A speciality at Boodles, a London club in St James's Street, which was founded in 1762. The idea of combining sponge with fruit fool dates back to the 18th-century version with ratafias. In this pudding, the lemon and orange fool, the cream and juice separate so that the sweet, sharp juice soaks the sponge at the bottom.

Serves 4–6

4 trifle sponge cakes
Grated zest and juice of
   1 lemon
Grated zest and juice of
   2 oranges
50–75g (2–3oz) caster sugar
600ml (1 pint) double cream

For decoration
Crystallised orange slices
Crystallised angelica

Cut the sponge cakes into 1cm (½in) strips and line the base of a glass serving dish, or individual glass dishes. Mix the zest and juice of the fruit with the sugar and stir until dissolved. Whip half the cream until thick, but not stiff, and beat the juice into the cream slowly. Taste for sweetness. Spoon over the sponge cakes and chill thoroughly for 2–3 hours, until the juice has soaked into the sponge and the cream has set. Whip the remaining cream until stiff, and pipe or spoon on top of the pudding to decorate. Garnish with crystallised orange slices and angelica.

Burnt Cream or Trinity Pudding

This pudding, also known as Cambridge Cream, was traditionally served at dinner during May week at Trinity College, Cambridge. It was brought in on a large silver dish and the caramelised top was cracked with great ceremony.

Serves 6–8

850ml (1½ pints) double
  cream
1 vanilla pod
6 egg yolks
75g (3oz) caster sugar
Caster sugar for caramelising
Fresh flowers to decorate

Preheat the oven to 150°C, 300°F, gas mark 2. Put the cream and vanilla pod into a pan and bring very gently to the boil. Leave to cool a little. Remove the vanilla pod, wash and reserve for future use. Cream the egg yolks and sugar together in a basin until almost white. Pour the hot cream on to the yolks in a steady stream, whisking all the time. Strain into a shallow ovenproof dish, or individual dishes, and place in a roasting tin half-filled with hot water. Bake for 1–1¼ hours or until just set. Remove the dish and leave until cold. Chill in the fridge overnight.

Just before serving, coat the top of the pudding with an even layer – about 6mm (¼in) thick – of caster sugar, using a sugar dredger. Heat the grill until really hot. Put the pudding in a roasting tin or large dish of ice cubes (this will make sure that your custard does not spoil when you are caramelising the top). Slip under the hot grill and watch carefully, turning if the sugar is browning unevenly. When the sugar has completely melted and is an even caramel colour, remove the tin and leave to cool. Serve chilled.

AGA method

Use the AGA hotplates to make the custard. Assemble the pudding as above. Put the dish into a deep roasting tin and pour boiling water around the dish so that it comes halfway up the sides. Transfer to the Simmering Oven for 2–2½ hours or until just set. You will need a blowtorch or grill to make the 'burnt' part of the cream, or cook the caramel separately, allow to cool slightly, and then pour on to the cooked custard.

Claret Jelly

Cooks have been setting liquids with gelatine, isinglass and hartshorn since the Middle Ages. These early jellies sometimes contained meat and they were often highly spiced, and also sometimes sweetened and flavoured with rose-water. They are the ancestors not only of sweet jellies but also of the vegetable, fish and meat terrines and mousses still made today.

Dessert jellies often contain fruit but this is very different. Jellies made with wine or port were very popular with the Victorians. I often make wine jellies in individual glasses, so you can pour a little thin cream on top and eat the jelly through the cream. Delicious.

Serves 6

600ml (1 pint) claret
Zest and juice of 1 lemon
15–30g (½–1oz)
    powdered gelatine
75–110g (3–4oz) sugar

For decoration
Black grapes
Egg white
Caster sugar

Place 4 tablespoons of the claret and the lemon juice in a small basin and stir in the gelatine. If you wish to serve your wine jelly in glasses, 15g (½oz) gelatine will be sufficient, but if you wish to turn it out of a fancy mould, add an extra 15g (½oz) to make certain, but do check quantities on the packet, because different brands can vary in strength. Leave for 5 minutes until swollen and soft, then stir this into half the remaining claret in a pan. Add the sugar and lemon zest, then bring slowly almost, but not quite, to the boil, stirring all the time. Strain into a bowl and gently stir in the remaining claret. Pour into glasses, a wetted mould or a pretty bowl and leave to set in a cool place. Serve slightly chilled. Decorate with small bunches of black grapes which have been frosted with egg white and caster sugar (see page 273). A little thin cream poured on top of the jelly is a perfect accompaniment.

AGA method

Use the AGA hotplates to heat up the claret.

Damson Ice Cream

Ice creams have been part of our diet (at least in rich households) since long before refrigeration. The ice-cream syrup in this recipe can be used for most fruit purées. Damsons are tart and their deep red flesh produces a sharp-tasting, beautifully coloured ice cream.

Serves 6–8

For the ice-cream syrup
700ml (1¼ pints) water
425g (15oz) sugar
Juice and thinly pared zest of
    1 lemon
2 drops vanilla essence

For the ice cream
600g (1¼ pints) damsons
150ml (¼ pint) whipping or
    double cream

Make the ice-cream syrup as follows. Bring the water and sugar to the boil in a heavy-bottomed pan. While the mixture is heating up, add the lemon zest. When at boiling point, leave the syrup to bubble for exactly 1 minute. Remove from the heat, add the lemon juice and vanilla essence, then pour into a cold container and leave to cool. When cold, strain. Cover and store in the fridge, where it will keep for up to 2 weeks.

Poach the damsons in 1 litre (1¾ pints) syrup for about 10 minutes until the fruit is soft. Leave to cool overnight. When cold, strain, remove the stones and liquidise the pulp with the reserved syrup to a fine purée. Set to freeze. After 1 hour, remove, whip the cream until stiff and add to the mixture. Beat thoroughly and replace in the freezer. Repeat until the mixture hardens into ice cream. The process will take about 4–5 hours.

AGA method

Use the AGA hotplates to make the ice-cream syrup and poach the damsons.

Damson Snow

Damsons are small, sharp-tasting plums. They are not an eating variety; they must be cooked but they have an intense, rich flavour unique in the plum family. If you are offered damsons, or see them in the greengrocer, seize them, because they make wonderful jams and jellies, they pickle beautifully, and make delicious puddings like this one.

Serves 6–8

900g (2lb) damsons
175g (6oz) caster sugar
150ml (¼ pint) cold water
425ml (¾ pint) double
   cream
2 tablespoons brandy or
   Marsala
3 egg whites

Put the washed and de-stalked damsons into a pan with the sugar and water. Bring slowly to the boil and cook gently for 10–15 minutes or until the fruit is tender. Rub through a sieve and leave the damson pulp to get cold. Lightly whip the cream with the brandy or Marsala until thick. Whisk the egg whites until stiff and fold into the cream mixture. Stir in the damson pulp, reserving 1 tablespoon for decoration. Pour into individual glasses and chill well. Just before serving, stir in the reserved damson pulp to give a marbled effect, or just top with damson pulp. Serve with any homemade biscuits.

AGA method

Heat the damsons on the Simmering Plate for 5 minutes, then transfer to the Simmering Oven for 30 minutes. Continue as above.

Variation

Edinburgh Fog: Omit the damson pulp and replace the brandy with sweet sherry. Sweeten with 50g (2oz) caster sugar and stir in 50g (2oz) ratafias. Chill well, and serve with a bowl of fresh raspberries or strawberries and sprinkled with toasted flaked almonds.

Brown Bread Ice Cream

Ice creams became popular in the 18th century. Country houses of this period were designed with ice houses, insulated brick vaults where ice was stored. The ice was used not only to prolong the life of fish and meat but also to make iced desserts. The first recipe for Brown Bread Ice was given by Mary Smith in 1772. It became very popular in late Victorian and Edwardian days, when it was served as a country weekend treat. Warning: recipes containing raw eggs are not suitable for pregnant women or young children.

Serves 6–8

75g (3oz) wholemeal
    breadcrumbs
50g (2oz) unsalted butter
75g (3oz) caster or soft
    brown sugar

For the ice cream

4 eggs, separated
115g (4oz) caster sugar
2 tablespoons rum, brandy
    or Madeira
425ml (¾ pint) double or
    whipping cream

Preheat the oven to 180°C, 350°F, gas mark 4. Spread the breadcrumbs on a baking tray lined with baking paper. Add the melted butter and sprinkle with the sugar. Bake for about 30 minutes or until crisp. Cool and then crush.

To prepare basic Ice Cream, beat the egg yolks with the sugar and the brandy, rum or Madeira. Whip the cream until it holds its shape and add to the egg mixture. Whisk the egg whites until stiff and fold into the cream and egg mixture. Freeze in a lidded container for about 1 hour.

Stir in the prepared breadcrumbs and freeze again. Remove from the freezer and place in the fridge at least 30 minutes before serving. Scoop into glasses.

AGA method

Bake the breadcrumbs on the Roasting Oven floor for 5–8 minutes, watching them like a hawk so that they do not burn. Continue as above.

Killerton Chocolate Pot

Recipes using chocolate usually date from no earlier than the 20th century. However, chocolate puddings are now part of our tradition. I like the concentration of flavour that these little pots provide. You could also make the cocoa-and-sugar paste with strong instant coffee for a change, and stir in a tablespoon of rum or Tia Maria.

Serves 4

4 tablespoons cocoa, the
    best quality you can find
225g (8oz) soft brown sugar
Boiling water to mix
1 tablespoon Grand Marnier
    or Cointreau
600ml (1 pint) double cream
Grated orange zest, to
    garnish
Thin cream, to serve

Mix the cocoa and sugar into a thick paste with boiling water. Leave to cool, then chill in the fridge until really cold. Put the liqueur and cocoa mixture into a mixing bowl. Using an electric rotary whisk, beat in the cream slowly, being careful not to overbeat the mixture. When all is combined, fill small ramekins with the chocolate mixture and garnish with grated orange zest. This is very rich and creamy and keeps excellently for a day or two in the fridge. Serve with a jug of thin cream to pour on top of the pots.

Treacle Tart

Treacle Tart is not now made with black treacle (otherwise known as molasses) but with golden syrup. I found different recipes using oats and no breadcrumbs and recipes involving nuts. I have chosen a recipe given to me by the chef in the Regatta Café at the National Maritime Museum in Greenwich. I particularly liked the inclusion of grated apple or pear. Not because it makes the tart any healthier – one of the guilty treasures of Treacle Tart is its sweetness – but because I think it introduces just a hint of a different taste and texture.

Serves 6–8

350g (12oz) shortcrust
    pastry
450g (16oz) golden syrup
Zest and juice of 1 lemon
225g (8oz) fresh white
    breadcrumbs
1 crisp apple or pear, peeled
    and grated
1 teaspoon mixed spice
1 egg yolk beaten with a
    little water
Pouring cream, crème
    fraîche or yoghurt,
    to serve

Preheat the oven to 180°C, 350°F, gas mark 4. Roll out the pastry. Grease a 25cm (10in) flan dish and line with the shortcrust pastry, reserving a quarter for the top. Warm the syrup and lemon in a pan. Stir in the breadcrumbs, the grated fruit and the mixed spice, then pour into the uncooked pastry case. Use the last quarter of the pastry to cut into strips to make a lattice on top. Crimp the edge of the tart with a fork, pressing the lattice strips on firmly. Brush the lattice on top with beaten egg yolk and water. Bake for approximately 35 minutes or until set. Serve with pouring cream, crème fraîche or yoghurt.

AGA method

Make and assemble the tart as above, using the AGA hotplates to make the filling. Bake the tart on the Roasting Oven floor for about 25 minutes, or until the pastry is golden and the filling is just set.

Toffee and Apple Crumble Tart

A tart with an apple crumble and toffee sauce filling. Total self-indulgence.

Serves 4

For the pastry
225g (8oz) plain flour
4 tablespoons caster sugar
110g (4oz) butter
4 egg yolks

For the filling
900g (2lb) cooking apples
50g (2oz) butter
50g (2oz) sugar
75g (3oz) soft brown sugar
150ml (¼ pint) golden syrup
150ml (¼ pint) double
   cream
2 drops vanilla essence

For the crumble
75g (3oz) butter
110g (4oz) flour
110g (4oz) porridge oats
75g (3oz) soft brown sugar

Preheat the oven to 180°C, 350°F, gas mark 4. First make the pastry as follows. Sift the flour with the sugar, rub in the butter and stir in the egg yolks to bind the dough. Roll out, line a greased 25cm (10in) flan tin and prick the bottom. Chill while you prepare the filling and the crumble. Peel and slice the apples thinly. Arrange on the bottom of the pastry case. Melt the butter and dissolve the sugars and the syrup over a very low heat in a saucepan. Cook very gently, stirring well, for 5 minutes. Remove the pan from the heat and stir in the cream and the vanilla. Beat well until the sauce is smooth. Let it cool to lukewarm, then pour it over the apples. To make the crumble, rub the butter into the flour and oats until the mixture is crumbly, stir in the sugar and spread the mixture evenly over the filling. Bake for approximately 30–40 minutes. The top should be golden and crunchy. This is also delicious made with pears.

AGA method

Make and assemble the crumble as above, using the AGA hotplates to make the filling. Bake on the floor of the Roasting Oven, with the cold plain shelf on the second set of runners, for about 25–30 minutes, or until golden and crunchy. If it is not browning enough, remove the plain shelf for the last 5–10 minutes.

Maids of Honour

Tradition says these little sweet cheese tarts are named after the ladies-in-waiting to Queen Caroline, wife of George II, who reigned from 1727 to 1760. She lived in a palace in Richmond, Surrey, where, on Richmond Green, a terrace of lovely houses still stands called Maids of Honour Row. Not far down the road, Newens, the last of the famous Kew tea rooms, sells Maids of Honour, made to a secret recipe. This not-so-secret 19th-century recipe comes from Laura Mason's *National Trust Farmhouse Cookbook*.

Makes about 24

500ml (18fl oz) whole milk
Pinch of salt
Rennet
100g (3½oz) butter at room
    temperature
2 egg yolks
2 teaspoons brandy
12 almonds, blanched and
    chopped
25g (1oz) sugar
1 teaspoon ground
    cinnamon
Juice and zest of ½ lemon
4 tablespoons currants
250g (9oz) puff pastry

The day before you want to bake the Maids of Honour, heat the milk to blood temperature, stir in a pinch of salt and add rennet as directed on the bottle. When the curd has set and cooled, transfer it to a clean square of muslin or a jelly bag and allow the whey to drip out overnight. Next day, rub the curd through a sieve with the butter. Beat in the egg yolks and brandy, then stir in the almonds, sugar, cinnamon and the lemon juice and zest.

Next day, preheat the oven to 220°C, 425°F, gas mark 7. Roll the pastry out very thinly and cut into rounds with a plain cutter. Using a fork, prick the centres of the rounds lightly a few times, otherwise your maids may go head-over-heels in the oven. Line the patty tins with the rounds and put a generous teaspoon of mixture in each. Scatter a few currants on top of each one. Bake for 7 minutes, until the pastry is risen and nicely browned.

AGA method

Start this pudding the day before serving, heating the milk using the AGA hotplates. Bake the Maids of Honour in the Roasting Oven, on the third set of runners, for about 7 minutes.

Tafferty Tart

This is a modern version of a 16th-century recipe. Sadly, the origins of its charming name have been obscured.

Serves 6

350g (12oz) shortcrust
   pastry

For the filling
Approximately 6 large
   cooking apples, thinly
   sliced
150g (5oz) sugar blended
   with the grated zest of
   1 lemon and the lemon
   pulp, finely chopped
25g (1oz) butter

For the topping
110–175g (4–6oz) icing
   sugar
1 tablespoon milk
1 tablespoon lemon juice

Preheat the oven to 200°C, 400°F, gas mark 6. Butter a 25cm (10in) pie plate. Roll out two-thirds of the pastry and line the plate, pressing it gently and firmly into place. Arrange the thinly sliced apples in layers, sprinkling each layer with the lemon and sugar mixture. Dot with butter and cover with the remainder of the pastry arranged in lattice strips. Place in the oven on a baking sheet and bake for 45–50 minutes until lightly brown.

While still warm, drizzle with the topping made by mixing the icing sugar, milk and lemon juice together to produce a pouring consistency.

AGA method

Put the tart on to a shallow baking tin and cook on the Roasting Oven floor, with the cold plain shelf directly above, for 20–30 minutes.

Breads, Teabreads and Scones

Bread – the staple of life. The finer the flour, the whiter the bread – and the farther up the social scale you were, if you could afford it. For hundreds of years that was the way things were, until the gourmets and the doctors agreed, for once, that bread with the bran left in not only tasted better, but was better for you, too.

The finest bread in the Middle Ages was *paindemaigne* or *manchet*, a pale cream in colour. Middling bread of varying quality was *trete*, *cocket*, or *wastel*, while the brownest bread, made from unbolted flour, was *panisenter* or *tourte*. An English law, known as the Assize of Bread, attempted to standardise loaf prices, fixing a common weight of bread known as a penny loaf, but in general you got more bread for your penny if you bought the lower-quality bread, and prices were by no means fixed. And not all bakers were honest – through the centuries there were prosecutions for adulteration: alum, root vegetables, sand, gravel and dried beans are just some of the substances bakers put in to eke out their flour.

So it was generally much better to bake bread at home, and know exactly what was in it. While only the well-off had hearths that were big enough to house a bread oven, a griddle was within most people's reach. In Scotland, and northern England, a homestead or croft might be far from a baker's shop and, as also in Wales, there is still a tradition of griddle cooking in these areas today. No griddle? Then you would probably have eaten your grain as porridge, frumenty or gruel.

There are four recipes for bread in this chapter. One of them comes from Northern Ireland, where bread is taken very seriously. Indeed, throughout Ireland, an ability to bake a good loaf is considered almost as important as a good character (well, perhaps I'm exaggerating a little!). A fresh loaf of Wheaten Bread, buttered with sweet Irish butter, is so good that it is tempting to make a meal of it. And, of course, that's what many people did. Wheaten

Bread is raised with baking powder, while Oatmeal Soda Bread is raised with bicarbonate of soda and cream of tartar. These loaves don't keep as well as yeast-based bread, but since they usually disappear so quickly, this doesn't really matter. The Soda Bread recipe comes from Buckland Abbey, in the far west of Devon – again an isolated part of the world where village bakers were few and far between, and a household had to bake for itself if possible. The two yeast-based recipes here are for Granary Bread or Rolls (page 307) and Wholemeal Bread (page 310). Granary flour is a modern British flour mix, and the resulting bread – a slightly crumbling, soft brown loaf, speckled with crisp malted grains – is surely one of our better inventions.

How can you tell the difference between a cake and a teabread? Maybe the dictionary definition of a teabread is a little narrow: 'Yeast-leavened baked goods considered suitable for either afternoon tea or high tea in Britain, including many spiced, fruited and enriched breads and buns.' Being yeast-based, Chelsea Buns (see page 323) fit this definition perfectly, but so many of the recipes I've been given were raised in other ways. Besides, I think the home cook often finds yeast complicated and long-winded to use, and the time required for the mix to rest is, so often, unavailable in today's busy world. So my preferred definition for a teabread is 'food for teatime that tastes best buttered', and I think that covers all the teabreads, scones and griddle cakes here. Bara Brith, or 'Speckled Bread', is probably the most famous teabread of all, and my recipe came from its home, North Wales. Soak the fruit in the best Earl Grey Tea and the resulting loaf will taste subtle and delicious.

Griddle cooking, a method that evolved from the age-old idea of cooking on a flat, hot stone in the fire, is still popular today. By the Middle Ages, large round metal griddles were hung above the fire, and various breads were cooked on them. Welsh Cakes, Pikelets, Staffordshire Oatcakes, Scotch Pancakes and the delightfully named Singin' Hinnies are all griddle-cooked.

Scone recipes are very special, and cooks guard them closely. Perhaps this is because the basic ingredients are so simple – just flour, liquid, fat and a raising agent – so any variations generally come from minute adjustments of quantities. There are recipes here for both savoury and sweet scones. Savoury scones are a speciality in Northumberland, where many people prefer to eat a scone with soup rather than bread. Some scones include local specialities: Old Hannah's Cheshire Potato Cakes, Erddig Apple Scones and Leek and Onion Scones from Souter Lighthouse are three of these.

And I can't write about scones without admitting that my whole writing career started with a scone recipe! Years ago, I was asked to cook a lunch for 125 people, to celebrate the opening of a lovely maritime museum at Cotehele, on the Cornish side of the River Tamar. I was given use of the tea room's kitchen for my preparation. Glancing around this busy kitchen, knowing I was being sized up by the band of local cooks and helpers, I realised that I must get the cook in charge, Mrs Laver, on my side if lunch was going to happen. I'd been given a cup of coffee and a buttered scone, more to keep me out of the way than anything else. The scone was delicious, so I complimented Mrs. Laver and asked for her recipe – the rest was plain sailing. That experience led me to thinking that there must be other good traditional food being cooked in tea rooms right across Britain. Ten years later, my first collection of recipes from National Trust cooks was published.

Unless otherwise stipulated, all breads, teabreads and scones should be cooled on a wire rack.

Wheaten Bread

In Ireland, breadmaking and scone-making is highly esteemed. Characters are assessed through the quality of their bread. Families even fall out over their bread recipes. This wheaten bread sliced warm from the oven and spread with Ulster butter is irresistible.

Makes 2 small or one large loaf

225g (8oz) wholemeal flour
225g (8oz) strong white
    flour
1 teaspoon baking powder
110g (4oz) butter
110g (4oz) sugar
350ml (12fl oz) buttermilk
1 egg, beaten
Milk, for brushing

Preheat the oven to 200°C, 400°F, gas mark 6. Grease either 2 x 450g (1lb) loaf tins or 1 x 900g (2lb) loaf tin. Sift together all the dry ingredients except the sugar. Rub in the butter until the mixture resembles coarse breadcrumbs. Add the sugar and stir well. Make a well in the centre and gradually work in the buttermilk and egg until you have a soft dough. Knead lightly. Form into one large loaf or two smaller ones. Place in the tins, brush with milk and bake until well risen and golden brown. The bread should sound hollow when knocked and a skewer should come out of the loaf clean. For a 900g (2lb) loaf this may take 1¼ hours, but the smaller loaves need a little less time; have a look at them after 45 minutes.

AGA method

Prepare the bread as above. Place the bread tins on the oven grid shelf on the Roasting Oven floor and bake for approximately 30–45 minutes. Check them after 20 minutes – if they are browning too much, slide the cold plain shelf in, on the second set of runners.

Granary Bread and Rolls

Granary bread is named after the flour used, a British flour composed of mixed brown wheat and rye flour with malted cracked-wheat grains. This recipe comes from Killerton, a National Trust property in East Devon. Originally the home of the Acland family, it is a thriving agricultural estate. The bread in the restaurant is famously good and people come some distance to eat it in the elegant tea room in the 18th-century house.

Makes two 450g (1lb) loaves or approximately 16 rolls

800g (1¾lb) granary
   bread flour
2 teaspoons salt
25g (1oz) fresh yeast or
   1 teaspoon dried yeast
2 teaspoons molasses
   dissolved in 75ml (3fl oz)
   of hand-hot water
600ml (1 pint) warm water

Put the granary flour and salt in a large bowl and warm together in the oven at its lowest temperature for a few minutes. Cream the fresh yeast with molasses and hand-hot water or sprinkle the dried yeast in and mix well. Add the yeast mixture to the warmed flour with 600ml (1 pint) of warm water; combine thoroughly but do not knead. The mixture should be very wet. Spoon into well-greased 450g (1lb) loaf tins or, for rolls, into well-greased patty tins. Prove in the oven for 15 minutes, still at the lowest temperature possible. Raise the oven to 180°C, 350°F, gas mark 4 and bake for 20–30 minutes for the rolls and 50 minutes for the loaves. To test if a loaf is done, turn the tin on its side, slide out the loaf and tap it on the bottom. If it sounds hollow, it is cooked; if not, leave it out of the tin and bake for another 10 minutes or so. Leave to cool on a wire rack.

AGA method

Prepare the dough and put into the tins. The first proving should be done near the AGA or on the Simmering Plate lid, protected with a tea towel or AGA Chef's Pad. Place the bread tins directly on the Roasting Oven floor and bake for approximately 35–45 minutes. Check them after 20 minutes; if they are browning too much, slide the cold plain shelf directly above. Cook rolls on the cold plain shelf, slid on to the third set of runners, for 15–20 minutes.

Oatmeal Soda Bread

Oats grow best in cool climates; they were the principal cereal crop in Wales and Scotland. The Romans were rude about oats, thinking them only suitable for barbarians. Dr Johnson, in his famous dictionary, was even ruder, defining oats as 'a grain which in England is given to horses, but in Scotland supports the people'. However, it has the most protein (16%) of any grain and the undoubted success of Scots men and women throughout history is sometimes put down to the consumption of oats in the form of porridge. This oatmeal soda bread is easy to make and is delicious to eat straight from the oven or cold with a salad, pasta or nut roast. Soda bread does not keep well and should be eaten in one or two days.

Makes I large soda bread

450g (1lb) wholemeal flour
110g (4oz) fine oatmeal
1½ teaspoons cream of
    tartar
1 teaspoon bicarbonate of
    soda
25g (1oz) butter
425ml (¾ pint) milk and
    water mix (half and half)
1 teaspoon salt

Preheat the oven to 350°F, 180°C, gas mark 4. Mix together the flour, salt, oatmeal, cream of tartar and bicarbonate of soda. Using your fingers or a food processor, rub in the butter to resemble fine breadcrumbs. Add the milk and water and mix to a soft dough. Turn out the mixture on to a lightly floured surface and knead slightly into a loaf shape or slightly flattened round ball. If you wish, the surface can be deeply scored with a knife in portions. Place on a greased baking sheet and bake in the oven for 30–35 minutes.

AGA method

Prepare the dough and put on to a greased baking tray. Place the tray directly on to the Roasting Oven floor and bake for approximately 25–30 minutes. If it is browning too much, slide the cold plain shelf directly above.

Wholemeal Bread

This is a standard handmade wholemeal bread recipe.

Makes 1 loaf

250ml (9fl oz) tepid water
1 teaspoon sugar
2 teaspoons dried yeast or
   10g (½oz) fresh yeast
450g (1lb) 100% wholemeal
   flour
or 350g (12oz) wholemeal
   flour and 110g (4oz)
   strong plain flour
1½ teaspoons salt
15g (½oz) vegetarian lard

Preheat the oven to 200°C, 400°F, gas mark 6. If using the dried yeast, place half the tepid water in a measuring jug and dissolve the sugar. Sprinkle the yeast over the top and leave in a warm place for 5–10 minutes until frothy (fresh yeast can be mixed in the water and used straight away). Put the flour(s) and salt into a mixing bowl and rub in the lard. Add the frothed-up yeast and the balance of the water and mix with a wooden spoon to give a fairly soft dough (add more water, if necessary). Turn out on to a clean work surface and knead for 10 minutes until the dough is smooth and supple. Place in a well-greased 450g (1lb) loaf tin, pushing the dough well down into the corners and sides of the tin to encourage it to form a dome-shaped loaf. Put the tin in a warm place covered with a damp tea towel or placed in a lightly greased polythene bag, tied loosely, and leave to rise for 30–40 minutes or until the loaf has doubled in size and is within 6mm (¼in) of the top of the bread tin.

Bake for about 40 minutes. Turn out the bread and, if cooked, the loaf will sound hollow when tapped underneath. Put it back for 10 minutes if it is not ready. Leave to cool on a wire tray.

AGA method

Prepare the dough and put into the tin. The first proving, until the loaf has doubled in size, should be done near the AGA. Place the bread tin directly on the Roasting Oven floor and bake for approximately 35–45 minutes. Check after 20 minutes; if it is browning too much, slide the cold plain shelf directly above. Turn the loaf out and, if cooked, the loaf will sound hollow when tapped underneath.

Pikelets

The current Welsh name for Pikelets is *Pice'r Pregethwr*, but they used to be known as *Bara Pyglyd*, which means 'pitchy bread'. Like Welsh Cakes (see page 322), these were cooked on a griddle, but you can use a heavy-based frying pan very successfully. Pikelets are made with a batter similar to the one used for crumpets and look, when cooked, like a cross between a pancake and a crumpet. Originally, the batter was yeast-based, but now many recipes, like this one, are soda-based.

Makes approximately 12 pikelets

225g (8oz) self-raising flour
110g (4oz) caster sugar
1 egg, well beaten
Approximately 300ml
    (½ pint) full-cream milk
50g (2oz) butter
½ teaspoon bicarbonate of
    soda
1 teaspoon vinegar

Sieve the flour and sugar together. Add the beaten egg and milk and mix to form a thick batter. Melt the butter, add the bicarbonate of soda and vinegar and then mix into the batter.

Drop a tablespoon on to a hot, greased griddle or heavy-based frying pan. Cook until bubbles appear and the bottom is brown. Then turn the pikelet over and cook the other side. Serve warm and well buttered.

AGA method

Prepare the pikelets as above. Place a piece of Bake-O-Glide silicone liner directly on to the Simmering Plate. Grease sparingly, then drop tablespoonfuls of the pikelet mixture on top and cook until bubbles appear and the bottom is brown. Turn the pikelet over and cook for another minute or so.

Ulster Cheese Cakes

These buttery little tarts aren't cakes and contain no cheese. Perhaps they did long ago. They now seem most closely related to the Bakewell Tart (see page 348). I was given this recipe at Mount Stewart, a wonderful house on Strangford Lough, south of Belfast.

Makes approximately 16

225g (8oz) shortcrust pastry
(see page 64)
Sunflower oil
175g (6oz) butter
175g (6oz) caster sugar
3 eggs, well beaten
175g (6oz) plain flour
Strawberry or raspberry jam
Caster sugar, for dusting

Preheat the oven to 160°C, 325°F, gas mark 3. Roll out the pastry and use to line small tartlet tins brushed with sunflower oil. Prick the bottoms and leave to rest while making the filling. Cream the butter and sugar together until light and fluffy. Beat in the eggs gradually, adding a little flour if the mixture should start to curdle. Then fold in the remaining flour.

Place a small teaspoonful of jam on each pastry base and fill with the sponge mix. Bake for approximately 20 minutes, until golden brown. Allow to cool and dust with caster sugar before serving.

AGA method

Prepare the cakes as above. Slide the oven grid shelf on to the floor of the Roasting Oven and bake there, with the cold plain shelf directly above, for 15–20 minutes or until golden brown.

Staffordshire Oatcakes

Biddulph Grange is a spectacular garden, with a tearoom where I had an oatcake for lunch. I asked for the recipe and found out that at Biddulph the oatcakes were made by a local baker, whose recipe is a secret. I have adapted this recipe from Elizabeth David's _English Bread and Yeast Cookery_. She describes the oatcakes as 'an intensely local delicacy unheard of north of Leek, unimagined south of Banbury'. The tearoom at Biddulph, seven miles west of Leek, serves them for lunch with vegetables. They can also be eaten with butter and honey or with bacon and eggs for breakfast.

Makes 16–18 16–18cm (6–7in) oatcakes

225g (8oz) bread flour
225g (8oz) fine oatmeal
2 teaspoons salt
10g (½oz) bakers' yeast
425ml (¾ pint) warm milk
425ml (¾ pint) warm water
Butter for greasing frying
    pan or griddle

Put the flour and oatmeal in a bowl with the salt. Cream the yeast with a little of the warm milk. Stir into the flour, add the rest of the liquid and beat well with a wooden spoon. If it seems too thick add a little more warm water. Cover the bowl and leave to rise for an hour or so.

Heat a griddle or heavy-based frying pan until very hot. Grease sparingly and make the oatcakes as you would pancakes. Put a ladle of mixture into the pan, cook for a minute or two until bubbles appear in the mixture, then flip over and cook for another minute or two. The oatcakes can be kept warm in a folded damp cloth.

AGA method

Prepare the oatcakes as in the recipe above. Place a piece of Bake-O-Glide silicone liner directly on to the Simmering Plate. Grease sparingly, then drop spoonfuls of the oatcake mixture onto the Simmering Plate and cook for about 1½–2 minutes per side. Alternatively, use a frying pan or grease the Simmering Plate with a little oil on a piece of kitchen paper, then cook direct on the plate (the nearest you can get to the authentic 'bakestone').

Cheese and Herb Scones

Like the scones opposite, this is a Northumbrian recipe for scones to be served with soup. This recipe comes from Wallington, a classical mansion set deep in the bleak, beautiful Northumbrian moors north of Newcastle.

Makes approximately 20 scones

450g (1lb) self-raising flour, sifted
10g (½oz) baking powder
1 teaspoon salt
110g (4oz) mature Cheddar cheese, grated
10g (½oz) mixed dried herbs
50g (2oz) butter
225ml (8fl oz) milk and water mix (half and half)

Preheat the oven to 230°C, 450°F, gas mark 8. Either grease and flour a metal baking sheet or line it with baking parchment. Put the flour, baking powder, salt, half the grated cheese and the dried herbs in a large bowl. Rub the butter into the dried ingredients until the mixture resembles breadcrumbs. Make a well in the centre, add the milk and water slowly, and knead until you have a soft dough. Roll out the dough and cut into 12 x 7.5cm (3in) rounds. Knead together lightly the leftover dough and cut into rounds. This should give you, approximately, 8 more scones. Sprinkle the rest of the cheese on the top of each scone. Bake for approximately 17 minutes. Keep an eye on them: oven temperatures vary and this is very hot.

AGA method

Arrange the scones on to the prepared baking tray and brush with milk. Bake in the Roasting Oven, on the second set of runners, for 10–15 minutes or until golden. Remove from the oven and cool on a wire rack.

Leek and Onion Scones

This recipe comes from the Souter Lighthouse on the rugged Northumbrian coast, where a leek scone is served with a steaming bowl of Vegetable Barley Broth (see page 16) to keep out the cold. Northumbrians also eat leek scones, rather than bread or biscuits, with their good local cheese.

Makes approximately 24 scones

1 tablespoon olive oil
1 large leek, cleaned and
   chopped fine (you can
   use the whole leek)
1 small onion, finely chopped
Pinch of sugar
450g (1lb) self-raising flour
Salt to taste
110g (4oz) butter
250ml (9fl oz) milk

Preheat the oven to 230°C, 450°F, gas mark 8. Either grease a baking sheet or line it with baking paper. Heat the oil and sauté the chopped leek and onion with the pinch of sugar until soft. Sift the flour with salt and rub in the butter until the mixture resembles fine breadcrumbs. Stir in the leek and onion and sufficient milk to form a soft dough. Turn out on to a floured surface and knead lightly. Roll out to approximately 2.5cm (1in) thick. Use a round cutter to stamp out 14 x 5cm (2in) rounds. Knead together lightly the leftover dough and cut into rounds. This should give you, approximately, 10 more scones. Place on the baking sheet and brush the tops with milk. Bake for approximately 12 minutes, or until golden brown.

AGA method

Arrange the scones on to the prepared baking tray and brush with milk. Bake on the second set of runners in the Roasting Oven for 10–15 minutes, or until they are golden. Remove from the oven and cool on a wire rack.

Ulster Scones

Baking is a huge tradition in Ulster and still very important. Bakers' shops are full of different shapes and sizes of scones, teabreads, tray cakes and soda-bread varieties not seen in the rest of the UK. Ulster bakers swear by buttermilk, and I am glad to say that you can now buy it in most supermarkets. In Ulster you can also buy soda-bread flour, a combination of brown and white. I asked my daughter, who is married to an Irishman, for the proportion she uses, which I have given here, but really it is a matter of taste and what works for you. It is a hotbed of controversy in Ireland, where cooks are assessed on their breads and everyone has a different key to success.

Makes about 24 scones

250g (9oz) wholemeal flour
250g (9oz) strong white
    flour
½ teaspoon bicarbonate of
    soda
75g (3oz) sugar
50g (2oz) chopped glacé
    cherries or 50g (2oz)
    sultanas (optional)
75g (3oz) butter
350ml (12fl oz) buttermilk
1 egg, beaten
Milk, to brush

Preheat the oven to 220°C, 425°F, gas mark 7. Grease or line a baking sheet with baking paper. Sift the two flours together with the bicarbonate of soda and sugar (if you are making fruit scones, add the cherries or sultanas at this point and mix them in well). Rub in the butter. Stir in the buttermilk and egg and knead the mixture until it forms a soft dough. Do not overwork the dough. Roll the dough out to about 2.5cm (1in) thick and cut the scones into rounds or triangles. This should make about 24. Brush the tops with milk and bake for 10–15 minutes, until golden brown and risen.

AGA method

Arrange the scones on to the prepared baking tray and brush with milk. Bake on the second set of runners in the Roasting Oven for 10–15 minutes, or until golden. Remove from the oven and cool on a wire rack.

Wholemeal Sultana Scones

This is a slightly sweet scone to eat buttered, with or without jam. It can also be a part of that great British tradition, the cream tea, which consists of scones, clotted cream and jam, a cake of some kind and a large pot of good tea. Eaten at around 4 to 5 o'clock, it takes care of hunger for several hours.

Makes approximately 12 scones

225g (8oz) wholemeal flour
13g (½oz) baking powder
50g (2oz) lard, diced
25g (1oz) soft brown sugar
38g (1½oz) sultanas
1 egg
50ml (2fl oz) milk
Flour or milk to brush
(optional)

Preheat the oven to 220°C, 450°F, gas mark 8. In a large mixing bowl sift the flour and the baking powder – add any bran left in the sieve. Rub in the diced fat with your fingertips until the mixture resembles coarse breadcrumbs. Add the sugar and sultanas and combine evenly. Make a well in the centre and slowly add the egg and milk, beaten together. Stir the mixture with a fork to make a smooth dough. Knead slightly to make a ball and place on a floured board. Roll out to a thickness of not less than 2.5cm (1in) and cut out the scones using a 5cm (2in) cutter. Place on a greased baking tray and, if you like, brush with milk or dust with flour. Bake for 15 minutes.

AGA method

Place the scones on to the prepared baking tray and brush with milk or dust with flour. Bake in the Roasting Oven, on the second set of runners, for 10–15 minutes, or until golden. Remove from the oven and cool on a wire rack.

Variation

Date and Walnut Scones: Omit the sultanas, and substitute 40g (1½oz) chopped dates and 25g (1oz) chopped walnuts.

Erddig Apple Scones

This recipe comes from Erddig, a National Trust house and estate in North Wales. At Erddig, apple scones are served with Welsh cheese. Each year the estate holds an Apple Day, when the Head Gardener puts on a display of the old apple species grown in the garden. There is a demonstration of cider-making by one of the Bulmer cider family, and cider is available to drink. You can buy apples direct from the growers and original pictures of apples direct from the artists.

Makes two scone rounds, each cut into 12 wedges, or 20 round scones

450g (1lb) self-raising flour
1 teaspoon salt
110g (4oz) butter
50g (2oz) caster sugar, plus
    extra for sprinkling
450g (1lb) dessert apples
Milk to mix

Preheat the oven to 200°C, 400°F, gas mark 6. Grease and flour a baking sheet. Sieve the flour and salt into a large bowl. Cut the butter into small pieces and rub into the flour until the mixture resembles coarse breadcrumbs. Stir in the caster sugar. Peel and core the apples, grate half and roughly chop the rest. Stir into the mixture. Add sufficient milk to make a soft dough. Turn it on to a floured board. Knead for a couple of minutes. You now have two choices. Either cut the dough into 2 large rounds and score each piece into 6 wedges, or use a round cutter to stamp out 12 x 7.5cm (3in) rounds. Knead together lightly the leftover dough and cut into rounds. This should give, approximately, 10 more scones. Brush the tops with milk, sprinkle with a little sugar and bake for approximately 20 minutes.

AGA method

Place the scones on to the prepared baking tray and brush with milk, then sprinkle over a little sugar. Bake them on the fourth set of runners in the Roasting Oven for 15–20 minutes, or until they are golden. Remove from the oven and cool on a wire rack.

Drop Scones

In Scotland, Wales and England, Drop Scones are small, thick pancakes, generally eaten with butter, jam or both, at tea or supper time. The Welsh name for these is *froes*. Traditionally, the griddle on which the scones were cooked was greased with suet. Nowadays lard is best, but olive oil will do. Children (well supervised – the griddle is very hot) love to help make these and quickly become adept at flipping them over. If you haven't got a griddle, a heavy-based frying pan will do the job equally well. If it is non-stick it will need very little greasing indeed.

Makes 15–20 scones

225g (8oz) self-raising flour
½ teaspoon salt
1 tablespoon caster sugar
1 egg, beaten
175ml (6fl oz) milk
Lard or olive or sunflower
 oil

Sieve the flour, salt and caster sugar together into a bowl. Make a well in the centre and add the egg and half the milk. Beat until the mixture is thick and smooth. Add the rest of the milk gradually, stirring all the time, until the mixture is the consistency of cream. Pour it into a jug. Leave to stand for 15–30 minutes.

Heat the griddle and rub a piece of lard over it, or grease a frying pan with sunflower oil. Pour tablespoons of the batter on to the griddle. Fry them until bubbles appear on the surface and the undersides are light brown. Flip them over with a palette knife and brown the other side. Add more lard to the griddle and start again. Keep the cooked scones in a folded napkin or tea towel. Serve warm with butter and jam.

AGA method

Prepare the batter as above. Lightly oil the Simmering Plate with a little oil on a piece of kitchen paper, then drop tablespoons of the mixture on to the surface. Cook one side until bubbles appear on the surface, then flip over and brown the other side. Cook the scones in batches, keeping them warm in a folded napkin or tea towel.

Old Hannah's Cheshire Potato Cakes

North-west England grows superlative potatoes, so it is appropriate that this recipe comes from Styal in Cheshire. I don't know who Old Hannah was, but immortality through a recipe is the dream of every good cook.

Makes approximately 12 cakes

225g (8oz) self-raising flour
½ teaspoon salt
50g (2oz) butter or
 margarine
225g (8oz) leftover or fresh
 mashed potatoes
1 egg, beaten
A little milk if required

Preheat the oven to 375°F, 190°C, gas mark 5. Grease a baking tray. Put the flour and salt in a bowl with the fat. Rub the fat into the flour using your fingertips, then fork in the mashed potatoes. Make a well in the centre of the mixture and drop in the beaten egg. Fork it into the mixture using a little milk, if necessary, to give a soft, pliable dough. Finish by kneading the dough with your hands until smooth. Roll it out to approximately 1.25cm (½in) thick and cut into rounds with a pastry cutter. Space them out on the prepared baking sheet and bake for 30 minutes. Take out of the oven and wrap in a clean tea towel to keep them warm and soft. Split, butter and spread them with jam or syrup and serve while hot. Leftover cakes can be reheated, but they will have a crispy surface.

AGA method

Prepare the potato cakes as above. Slide the grid shelf on to the floor of the Roasting Oven. Place the baking tray on the grid shelf and bake for 25–30 minutes. If they are browning too quickly, protect with the cold plain shelf.

Welsh Cakes

Pice ar Maen is Welsh for 'cakes on the stone'. It is traditional to cut them into either circles or triangles. Few small houses in rural Wales had an oven, but Welsh cakes could be cooked on a griddle on an open fire. Serve them hot dusted with sugar or cold with butter.

Makes approximately
12 cakes

225g (8oz) self-raising flour
Pinch of salt
Pinch of mixed spice
Pinch of cinnamon
110g (4oz) butter
75g (3oz) caster sugar
75g (3oz) currants
25g (1oz) chopped peel
1 egg
Milk to bind

Preheat and grease a griddle or heavy-based frying-pan. Sift together the flour, salt and spices and rub in the butter until the mixture resembles fine breadcrumbs. Stir in the sugar and the currants and peel. Mix with the egg and milk to a firm but not dry dough. Roll out to 6–12mm (¼–½in) thick and cut into rounds. Cook the Welsh Cakes on a moderately hot griddle till brown on both sides – about 10 minutes in all.

AGA method

Prepare the Welsh cakes as above. Place a piece of Bake-O-Glide silicone liner directly on to the Simmering Plate. Grease sparingly, put the cut rounds on top, and cook for about 2–2½ minutes per side, or until golden.

Chelsea Buns

Chelsea Buns were originally made in Chelsea, London.

Makes 9 buns

225g (8oz) plain flour
2 teaspoons caster sugar
10g (½oz) fresh yeast or
    2 teaspoons dried yeast
125ml (4fl oz) milk
½ teaspoon salt
15g (½oz) butter
75g (3oz) mixed dried fruit,
    candied peel, currants or
    raisins
½ teaspoon mixed spice
50g (2oz) light soft brown
    sugar
25g (1oz) melted butter
2 tablespoons honey

Sift 50g (2oz) of the flour into a small bowl and add the caster sugar. Crumble in the fresh yeast or spoon in the dried yeast and beat in the milk with a wooden spoon. Leave this mixture in a warm place for about 20 minutes, by which time it should be frothy. Sift together the remaining flour and the salt into a large bowl and rub in the butter with your fingers. Make a well in the centre and pour in the yeast mixture. Using one hand, gradually work in the flour until you have a dough. When it leaves the side of the bowl clean, turn the dough out on to a lightly floured surface and knead for 10 minutes until it is very smooth. Put it back in the bowl, cover with a cloth and leave to rise for 1½ hours. It should double in size. Knead the dough on a lightly floured surface for a minute, then roll it out to a rectangle 30 x 23cm (12 x 9in). Mix the fruit, brown sugar and spice together. Brush the dough with melted butter and spread the fruit mixture on top to within 2.5cm (1in) along the longer edges. Roll up the dough from the long sides and press the join to seal.

Preheat the oven to 220°C, 425°F, gas mark 7. Cut the roll into nine slices and pack them cut side upwards, in rows of three in a greased 18cm (7in) square cake tin. Leave to rise in a polythene bag in a warm place for about 30 minutes. Remove the bag. Warm the honey and pour over the buns. Bake for about 20–25 minutes until golden brown.

AGA method

Make the dough as above. Warm the honey on the Simmering Plate and pour over the buns. Slide the oven grid shelf on to the floor of the Roasting Oven. Place the tin on the grid shelf and bake for 25–30 minutes. Slide in the cold plain shelf above the buns if they are browning too quickly.

Singin' Hinnies

Traditionally, Singin' Hinnies are cooked on a griddle or in a heavy-based frying pan. You can also bake them in an oven. Allow about 15 minutes in all, turning and flattening them after 7–8 minutes. Serve warm, split and buttered. Singin' Hinnies are a Northumbrian delicacy. 'Hinnie' is a term of endearment, used especially for children. The fat in the hinnies makes them 'sing' when they are cooking; they are ready to eat when the singing stops. Originally, a Singin' Hinnie was one large scone, but the recipe I have been given is for individual small hinnies.

Makes approximately 8–10 hinnies

50g (2oz) butter
50g (2oz) lard
225g (8oz) plain flour
25g (1oz) currants
1 teaspoon baking powder
½ teaspoon salt
Milk and soured cream to
   mix

Preheat the oven to 180°C, 350°F, gas mark 4. In a mixing bowl large enough to take all the ingredients, rub the fats into the flour. Add the other dry ingredients. Mix to a soft dough with the milk and soured cream. Roll out and cut into rounds the size of a muffin, about 2.5cm (1in) thick. Cook for 7–8 minutes on each side on the griddle or in the oven.

AGA method

Prepare the dough as above. Place a piece of Bake-O-Glide silicone liner directly on to the Simmering Plate. Grease sparingly, put the cut rounds on top and cook for about 6–7 minutes per side, or until golden. Alternatively, cook low down in the Roasting Oven or in the centre of the Baking Oven (on three- and four-oven models).

Bara Brith

Bara Brith means 'spotted bread'. Recipes for it are traditional in all Celtic communities. This recipe comes from Wales. Use ordinary tea if you don't have any Earl Grey and note that ideally you should begin this recipe the day before you cook it.

Makes one loaf

225g (8oz) sultanas or
   mixed dried fruit
175ml (6fl oz) cold Earl
   Grey tea
225g (8oz) wholemeal flour
2 teaspoons baking powder
1 teaspoon mixed spice
175g (6oz) demerara sugar
Pinch of salt
2 eggs, well beaten

Preheat the oven to 180°C, 350°F, gas mark 4. Soak the fruit in the cold tea for at least 5 hours or overnight. Grease and line a 900g (2lb) loaf tin. Sift together wholemeal flour and the baking powder, and add the spice, sugar and fruit. Mix well. Stir in the eggs.
Spoon the mixture into the tin and bake for approximately 1 hour. Leave to cool in the tin. Keeps well; indeed it even improves.

AGA method

Prepare the Bara Brith as above. Owners of two-oven AGAs will get a better result by dividing the mixture between two 450g (1lb) loaf tins. Slide the grid shelf on to the floor of the Roasting Oven, then place the tin on the grid shelf, with the cold plain shelf directly above, and bake there for 30–40 minutes. For three- and four-oven models, use a 900g (2lb) loaf tin and cook in the Baking Oven, on the oven grid shelf placed on the oven floor for about 1 hour.

Orange and Raisin Teabread

Traditionally tea cakes and teabreads were yeast-based but over the years, many teabread recipes also use bicarbonate of soda and/or baking powder, as this one does. The recipe makes one large, rich teabread, and the orange zest and juice make it particularly interesting.

Makes 1 large teabread

350g (12oz) plain flour
1½ teaspoons baking powder
¾ teaspoon bicarbonate of soda
¼ teaspoon salt
175g (6oz) brown sugar
175g (6oz) seedless raisins
Grated zest of 1 orange
300ml (½ pint) orange juice
1 large egg, beaten
75g (3oz) melted butter

Preheat the oven to 180°C, 350°F, gas mark 4. Grease a 900g (2lb) loaf tin and line the base with baking paper. Sieve the flour, baking powder, bicarbonate of soda and salt into a bowl. Stir in the sugar, raisins and orange zest. Gradually beat in the orange juice with the egg and melted butter. Turn the mixture into the loaf tin and bake for 1 hour or until a knitting needle or skewer comes out clean. Cool in the tin.

AGA method

Prepare the teabread as above. Owners of two-oven AGAs will get a better result by dividing the mixture between two 450g (1lb) loaf tins. Slide the grid shelf on to the floor of the Roasting Oven. Place the tin on the grid shelf, with the cold plain shelf directly above, and bake there for 40–45 minutes. For three- and four-oven models, use a 900g (2lb) loaf tin and cook in the Baking Oven, on the oven grid shelf placed on the oven floor, for about 1 hour. Cool in the tin.

Date and Walnut Loaf

Dried and semi-dried dates have been part of British cuisine since they first arrived in this country with the Romans, while walnuts arrived later from France. Britain is at the northern extreme for growing walnut trees, but so many old recipes exist – both ones that use the nut as an ingredient and ones that give instructions for pickling the whole fruit – that walnut trees must once have abounded in southern Britain. This big loaf keeps well and is best eaten buttered.

Makes 1 large teabread

110g (4oz) butter
450g (1lb) chopped dates
110g (4oz) sugar
Pinch of salt
2 teaspoons bicarbonate
   of soda
300ml (½ pint) boiling water
110g (4oz) walnuts, cut in
   rough halves
2 eggs, beaten
450g (1lb) self-raising flour

Preheat the oven to 160°C, 325°F, gas mark 3. Grease a 900g (2lb) loaf tin and line the base with baking paper. Put the butter, dates, sugar, salt and bicarbonate of soda into a large mixing bowl. Pour over the boiling water and allow to cool. Add the walnuts, eggs and flour and mix until well combined. Spoon into the loaf tin and bake for 1–1¼ hours or until a skewer plunged into the middle of the loaf comes out clean.

AGA method

Prepare the loaf as above. Owners of two-oven AGAs will get a better result by dividing the mixture between two 450g (1lb) loaf tins. Slide the grid shelf on to the floor of the Roasting Oven. Place the loaf tin on the grid shelf, with the cold plain shelf directly above, and bake there for 40–45 minutes. For three- and four-oven models, use a 900g (2lb) loaf tin and cook in the Baking Oven, on the oven grid shelf placed on the oven floor for about 1–1¼ hours.

Cakes and Biscuits

Not that long ago, I walked into the dining room of a country house at around 3:30pm on a cold, wet, dark afternoon, feeling chilled and tired. The room was lit with warm lamps and the table, covered with a white damask cloth, was laid for tea, with plates piled high with succulent cucumber sandwiches, golden flapjacks and pale cream shortbread fingers. At one end of the table stood a plain sponge, dusted with icing sugar and filled with blackcurrant jam and cream – ready to be sliced. At the other end, a rich Dundee cake, packed with fruit and almonds. My spirits lifted immediately, even before I had taken my first sip of the steaming cup of tea that awaited me, or filled up my plate from all that abundance.

Cakes and biscuits, essential ingredients of such a sumptuous afternoon tea, share a long history with bread. The word 'cake' comes from the Ancient Norse *kaka*, originally a kind of fried dough. Every baked cake in this chapter evolved from bread, although cakes are now much sweeter and richer. Biscuits are also rich and sweet, but they have a crispness on the palate that makes them unique. While our traditional cakes are world-famous, and rightly so, biscuit-making is a field in which the British home baker can – and often does – excel.

The recipes in this chapter merely scratch the surface when it comes to the ingenuity and creativity of cake and biscuit makers over the centuries. Here are just a few of the traditional cakes and biscuits that are ideal to serve at afternoon or high tea. People have been drinking tea here since the middle of the 17th century, but the invention of afternoon tea, in the early 19th century, is attributed to Anna, Duchess of Bedford. Jane Pettigrew, in her book *Traditional Teatime Recipes* (National Trust), writes that the marriage of Charles II to a Portuguese princess, Catherine of Braganza, in 1662, established the practice of drinking tea when, as part of her dowry, Catherine brought with her a large chest of it. In imitation of the court (and encouraged by merchants bringing tea back from the Far East), tea-drinking became a fashionable activity. By the 19th century, breakfast was taken at nine or ten in the morning, and dinner was not until seven or eight in the evening. Tea took on a new role for the Duchess of Bedford who, by four o'clock, was getting hungry. She began to ask for a light meal to be served in her room at this time, a practice enjoyed by her friends. This idea of 'afternoon tea' became popular, and by the end of the 19th century, when women were also starting to eat out, tea rooms had become an established part of the social scene. Today I live in Kew, near the famous botanical gardens, where we are lucky enough to have Newens, established in 1870, one of the last traditional tea rooms in London. Mr Newen once told me that his father described how in the 1920s, on weekends and bank holidays, people would walk six deep over Kew Bridge from the nearest train station to eat at the many tea rooms that lined Kew Green. Today, only Newens remains, serving speciality cakes and biscuits, all baked on the premises.

Many of the biscuit recipes here are particularly regional specialities, associated with a particular town. The towns themselves are often very proud of their recipe – the football team in Grantham is even called the 'Gingerbreads', after the local Grantham Gingerbreads. Some of these regional biscuits were sold at the fairs that were held regularly throughout the year. Cornish Fairings, a crisp, golden biscuit with a characteristically crackled surface, share their name with the small china souvenirs, or 'fairings', that used to be sold, or won, at fairs – presumably because a bag of biscuits was also a souvenir of a kind. Ashby Statutes, also known as Langley Wakes Cakes, were made to eat during 'Wakes Week', an annual week's holiday originating in Lancashire. Some recipes would be lost today if it weren't for home bakers, perhaps because the locals tend to take them for granted. Laura Mason, collecting information about Shrewsbury Biscuits for her book *Traditional Foods of Britain: An Inventory*, found that 'little curiosity about them is expressed by the inhabitants themselves'. She comments 'it seems this once famous speciality has lost its identity and is ripe for a revival'. What better incentive to get baking?

In this chapter there are four recipes spiced with ginger, ranging from the aforementioned Grantham Gingerbreads to the sweet and sticky Yorkshire Parkin. These are a mere fraction of the many gingerbread recipes to be found in Britain, where ginger has been used as a spice since the Middle Ages. Medieval gingerbreads were in fact made from spiced breadcrumbs, mixed with honey, and many towns had their own particular gingerbread, sold as treats at fairs. Another familiar tradition is the making of gingerbread men and gingerbread pigs for November 5th, Bonfire Night.

Seed cakes were popular in the 18th century, when plain cakes were accompanied not by tea, but by a glass of fortified wine. They are represented here by a Caraway Cake and a superb Poppy-seed Cake. Lemon Madeira Cake tastes good, naturally, with a nice glass of Madeira. But if that's not to your taste, all these plain cakes are particularly good with a cup of coffee.

I was spoilt for choice when it came to apple cakes, eventually choosing two from the West Country which also use cider – one of our national drinks, it is much underrated in cooking but well represented in this book. Pear and Ginger Loaf couples two tasty ingredients in a marriage well made, while Devon Cider and Apple Cake is also nice and spicy.

And, of course, I had to include a Victoria Sponge. The recipe I chose – in which you first weigh the eggs, then use the same weights of flour, butter and sugar – may sound odd, but gives very good results. A couple of tips: do make sure all the ingredients are at room temperature (eggs straight from the fridge do not give as good a result), and weigh your ingredients carefully. While I'm a great believer in doing without the measuring scales, particularly if you have cooked the recipe before, I do make an exception for baking. Unless stipulated, all cakes and biscuits should be cooled on a wire rack.

Lemon Madeira Cake

The 'madeira' in the title actually refers to the perfect accompaniment to this plain, old-fashioned cake – a glass of Madeira. I would add that a medium sherry tastes good, too. In the 18th century, cake was often eaten with a glass of fortified wine rather than tea, and was correspondingly plain. This recipe was given to me as the favourite of an old lady who always took her cake in this traditional 18th-century fashion.

Makes a 15cm (6in) cake

100g (4oz) soft butter
125g (5oz) caster sugar
2 eggs
Zest and juice of 1 lemon
225g (8oz) self-raising flour

Preheat the oven to 150°C, 300°F, gas mark 2. Grease and line a 15cm (6in) round deep cake tin. Cream together the butter and sugar until light and fluffy. Beat in the eggs a little at a time; then add the rind and juice of a lemon. Gently fold in the flour using a large metal spoon and spoon the mixture into the lined cake tin. Place in the centre of the oven and bake for approximately 1 hour. Cool on a wire rack.

AGA method

Try to make this cake when the AGA has done a lot of cooking and therefore will be slightly lower in heat. If you have two cold plain shelves, you can change them over after 25 minutes to keep a more consistent lower temperature. You can also make this cake in the AGA Cake Baker if you have one.

Prepare the cake mix as above and pour into the cake tin. Slide the grid shelf on to the floor of the Roasting Oven. Place the cake tin on the grid shelf and bake for 10 minutes. Slide the cold plain shelf directly above the cake and continue baking for another 30–40 minutes, or until a skewer comes out clean. Remove the cake from the tin and cool on a rack. Alternatively, cook the cake on the oven grid shelf placed on the floor of the Baking Oven (for three- and four-oven models) for about 1 hour. If it is browning too quickly, slide the cold plain shelf directly above.

Centenary Celebration Fruit Cake

This plain fruit-cake recipe – the sort of cake that might be called a 'cut-and-come-again' cake – was developed to be served in all National Trust properties in East Anglia during their centenary year in 1995. It is a modern recipe but I chose it for this book partly because it is a National Trust book, but also because it illustrates my conviction that cooking is never static – plain fruit cakes (as opposed to rich fruit cakes) are traditional but new recipes are always being developed.

Makes a 20cm (8in) cake

300g (10oz) plain flour
1 level teaspoon
    baking powder
3 level teaspoons
    mixed spice
175g (6oz) caster sugar
50g (2oz) ground almonds
175ml (6fl oz) sunflower oil
175ml (6fl oz) milk
3 eggs
50g (2oz) sultanas
75g (3oz) mixed peel
125g (4oz) glacé cherries,
    chopped finely

Preheat the oven to 180°C, 350°F, gas mark 4. Either grease and flour or line with baking paper a 20cm (8in) cake tin. Sieve the flour, baking powder and spice into a large mixing bowl. Stir in the sugar and ground almonds. Beat together the oil, milk and eggs. Then pour the mixture into a well in the centre of the dry ingredients and blend together, mixing well. Fold in the fruit and pour into the prepared tin. Bake for approximately 1 hour, or until a skewer pushed into the centre of the cake comes out clean. Remove the cake from the tin and allow to cool.

AGA method

Try to make this cake when the AGA has done a lot of cooking and therefore will be slightly lower in temperature. If you have two cold plain shelves – always useful to the AGA owner – you can change them over after 25 minutes, to keep a more consistent lower temperature. You can also make this cake in the AGA Cake Baker if you have one. Prepare the cake mix as above and pour into the cake tin. Slide the grid shelf on to the floor of the Roasting Oven. Place the cake tin on the grid shelf and bake there for 10 minutes. Slide the cold plain shelf directly above the cake and continue baking for another 30–40 minutes, or until a skewer comes out clean. Alternatively, cook the cake on the oven grid shelf placed on the floor of the Baking Oven (on three- and four-oven models) for about 1 hour. Remove the cake from the tin and cool on a rack.

Rich Fruit Cake with Guinness

This cake makes a perfect Christmas cake. The use of Guinness is an inspired touch. Rich but not too sweet, the cake stays wonderfully moist.

Makes an 18cm (7in) cake

225g (8oz) butter
225g (8oz) soft brown sugar
4 eggs, lightly beaten
275g (10oz) plain flour
2 level teaspoons
    mixed spice
225g (8oz) seedless raisins
225g (8oz) sultanas
110g (4oz) mixed peel
110g (4oz) chopped walnuts
    (hazelnuts or dates could
    be substituted)
8–12 tablespoons Guinness

Preheat the oven to 160°C, 325°F, gas mark 3. Prepare an 18cm (7in) cake tin with baking paper. Cream together the butter and sugar. Add the lightly beaten eggs, a little at a time, mixing well between each addition. Using a large spoon, carefully fold in the flour. Add the mixed spice, fruit, nuts and 4 tablespoons of Guinness. Turn into the prepared cake tin and smooth out evenly. Bake in the centre of the oven for 1 hour, then reduce the heat to 150°C, 300°F, gas mark 2 for a further 1½ hours. Remove from the tin when cooled and prick with a skewer. Spoon over the remaining Guinness. Keep for at least one week before using. This cake will keep well for months wrapped in foil.

AGA method

Prepare the cake as above and pour into the prepared tin. Place the cold plain shelf on to the fourth set of runners in the Roasting Oven and place the cake tin on top. Bake for 15 minutes, then transfer the shelf, with the cake tin on top, to the Simmering Oven and continue to bake for another 2½–3½ hours, or until a skewer comes out clean from the centre of the cake. Cool in the tin and then prick with a skewer and spoon over the remaining Guinness as described above.

Lardy Cake

Although this is called a cake, it is really a fruity, spicy bread enriched with lard.

Makes a 20cm (8in) cake

15g (½oz) fresh yeast or
   1 teaspoon dried yeast
150ml (¼ pint) warm water
1 teaspoon sugar
225g (8oz) strong white
   bread flour
1 teaspoon salt
1 teaspoon oil
75g (3oz) lard
75g (3oz) currants or
   sultanas
75g (3oz) sugar
1 level teaspoon mixed spice
A little milk and sugar to
   glaze

To make the bread dough: mix the yeast in 2 or 3 teaspoons of lukewarm water and mix in the sugar. Leave until frothy (about 20 minutes) in a warm place. Sift the flour and salt into a large bowl, make a well in the centre, add the yeast mixture and the rest of the water and draw in the flour to form a dough ball. Knead the dough for about 10 minutes, then put it in a polythene bag which has a teaspoon of oil in it. Leave it in the bag to rise to double its size at room temperature. This should take approximately 2 hours. Knead again for about 10 minutes and put it back in the polythene bag for a further 30 minutes.

Preheat the oven to 220°C, 425°F, gas mark 7. Chop the lard into small pieces and mix with the fruit, sugar and spice. Divide the mixture into three. Roll out the dough to a rough oblong shape, spread one-third of the fruit mixture on to two-thirds of the dough, fold in 3 by folding over the empty third, then fold again. Repeat the process twice more, rolling out, spreading the fruit mix and folding. The last time, form the dough into a 20cm (8in) square and place in a 20cm (8in) square tin. Brush with milk and sprinkle with a little sugar. Bake for 35–40 minutes. Leave in the tin for a few minutes so that the cake absorbs any extra lard. Then turn out and cool on a rack.

AGA method

Make the dough for the Lardy Cake as above, ready to go into the oven. Slide the oven grid shelf on to the floor of the Roasting Oven. Place the tin on the grid shelf, and bake there for 25–35 minutes. Remove from the oven and leave in the tin for a few minutes so that the cake absorbs any extra lard.

Dundee Cake

The main difference between a Dundee and other fruit cakes? No spice, more butter, the inclusion of ground almonds and, of course, the almond decoration on the top.

Makes a 20cm (8in) cake

225g (8oz) plain flour
Pinch of salt
225g (8oz) butter
225g (8oz) caster sugar
4 large eggs
350g (12oz) sultanas
350g (12oz) currants
75g (6oz) chopped
   mixed peel
110 (4oz) glacé cherries
Grated zest of 1 lemon
25g (1oz) ground almonds
25g (1oz) whole almonds

Preheat the oven to 150°C, 300°F, gas mark 2. Line a 20cm (8in) round cake tin with baking parchment, cutting the parchment so that the top is about 5cm (2in) above the top of the tin.

Sift together the flour and salt. Beat the butter until soft, add the sugar and cream the two until they are light and creamy. Beat in the eggs, a little at a time. Fold in the flour and the sultanas, currants, peel, cherries, lemon zest and ground almonds, taking care that all is well combined. Spoon the mixture into the tin and level the top. Split the whole almonds in two and arrange them in a pattern of concentric circles on the top of the cake. Bake the cake for about 2 hours, then test with a skewer to see if it is cooked (the skewer should come out clean from the centre of the cake). If the top is getting too brown too quickly, cover it with a dampened piece of greaseproof paper. Cool in the tin for 30 minutes, then turn out and cool on a wire rack. To store the cake, wrap it in its lining paper in foil. The cake will taste even better if you keep it for two weeks or so before cutting.

AGA method

Prepare the cake as above, then pour the cake mix into the tin. Place the cold plain shelf on to the fourth set of runners in the Roasting Oven, put the cake tin on top and bake for about 15 minutes. Transfer the shelf, with the cake tin on top, to the Simmering Oven. Continue to bake for another 2–3 hours, or until a skewer comes out clean from the centre of the cake.

Mrs Middlemiss's Rich Fruit Cake

This is the rich fruit cake for you if you prefer one without any alcohol. Mrs Middlemiss baked cakes during the 1980s at Little Moreton Hall in Cheshire. She must have retired by now, but when she was baking the cakes, they were worth a detour as much as the house was!

Makes a 20cm (8in) cake

110g (4oz) caster sugar
110g (4oz) soft dark
   brown sugar
225g (8oz) butter
50g (2oz) treacle
4 eggs
75g (3oz) self-raising flour
200g (7oz) plain flour
1 teaspoon mixed spice
700g (1½lb) mixed dried
   fruit: try candied peel,
   currants, sultanas, glacé
   cherries, crystallised
   ginger, chopped dates and
   chopped prunes
1 tablespoon milk

Preheat the oven to 150°C, 300°F, gas mark 2. Grease and line a 20cm (8in) square cake tin. Cream together the sugars, butter and treacle and add the eggs one at a time, beating well between each addition until well combined. Sift the flours and mixed spice into a separate bowl, add the dried fruit and mix together. Gradually fold into the creamed mixture and finally add the milk. Spoon the mixture into the cake tin and bake in the centre of the oven for 2½–2¾ hours.

AGA method

Prepare the cake as above and pour the mixture into the tin. Place the cold plain shelf on to the fourth set of runners in the Roasting Oven and place the cake tin on top. Bake for about 15 minutes, then transfer the shelf, with the cake tin on top, to the Simmering Oven. Continue to bake for another 2–4 hours or until a skewer comes out clean from the centre of the cake.

Yorkshire Parkin

Parkin is a gingerbread that contains oats. It was originally cooked on a griddle and eaten especially at Celtic and Christian festivals from 31 October to 11 November, including Bonfire Night. Parkin comes thick or thin, but in Yorkshire they prefer it thick, as in the recipe below.

Makes a 20cm (8in) cake

225g (8oz) butter
225g (8oz) golden syrup
110g (4oz) self-raising flour
110g (4oz) wholemeal flour
110g (4oz) rolled oats
110g (4oz) oatmeal
225g (8oz) sugar
1 heaped teaspoon
    ground ginger
½ teaspoon baking powder
1 egg, beaten and made up
    to 180ml (6fl oz) with
    milk
½ teaspoon salt

Preheat the oven to 160°C, 325°F, gas mark 3. Thoroughly grease a 20cm (8in) square cake tin. Melt the butter and golden syrup together in a saucepan. Mix all the dry ingredients together in a mixing bowl and stir in the melted ingredients. Add the egg and milk and thoroughly combine using a wooden spoon. Pour into the well-greased tin and bake for approximately 45 minutes. Remove from the tin while still slightly warm to avoid sticking. The Parkin will keep very well in an airtight tin or will freeze. Parkin is traditionally kept in a tin with a sliced Cox's apple to keep it damp, and left to mature for at least a week.

AGA method

Assemble the Parkin as above. Bake in the Roasting Oven, on the fourth set of runners, for 2 minutes, then move to the Simmering Oven for an hour. Continue as above. Alternatively, cook the cake on the oven grid shelf placed on the floor of the Baking Oven (for three- and four-oven models) for about 45–50 minutes. Slide the cold plain shelf above the Parkin after 30 minutes for extra protection.

Caraway Cake or Seed Cake

Caraway cake was the original seed cake, and was very popular in the early 19th century, when the seeds would have been comfits – seeds dipped in sugar. This is in the English tradition of plain cakes – perfect at coffee time when you want something that is not too rich.

Makes a 23cm (9in) cake

175g (6oz) butter
175g (6oz) caster sugar
3 eggs
3 teaspoons caraway seeds
225g (8oz) plain flour
Pinch of salt
1 teaspoon baking powder
1 tablespoon ground
   almonds
1 tablespoon milk

Preheat the oven to 160°C, 325°F, gas mark 3. Grease and line a 23cm (9in) cake tin. Cream together the butter and sugar until fluffy and pale. Add the eggs one at a time, beating well after each addition; then mix in the caraway seeds. Sift the flour, salt and baking powder together and fold gently into the mixture. Then add the ground almonds and milk. Spoon into the prepared tin, level out, and bake for approximately 1 hour or until firm to touch.

AGA method

Prepare the cake as above and pour into the tin. Place the cold plain shelf on to the fourth set of runners in the Roasting Oven, place the cake tin on top, and bake for about 10 minutes. Transfer the shelf, with the cake tin on top, to the Simmering Oven and continue to bake for another 1–2 hours, or until firm to touch.

Alternatively, cook the cake on the oven grid shelf placed on the floor of the Baking Oven (for three- and four-oven models) for about 45 minutes to 1 hour. If it is browning too quickly, slide the cold plain shelf directly above.

Devon Cider and Apple Cake

I had trouble deciding which of the seven apple-cake recipes I have collected over the past years to include here. My final choice comes from Castle Drogo, designed by Sir Edwin Lutyens in the 1920s. It dominates the Teign Valley in Devon, high up on a spur of Dartmoor, one of the last wildernesses in the UK.

Makes a 20cm (8in) cake

1 large cooking apple,
  peeled and chopped
50g (2oz) sultanas
Scant 150ml (¼ pint)
  dry cider
110g (4oz) butter
110g (4oz) soft brown sugar
2 eggs, lightly beaten
225g (8oz) wholemeal or
  plain flour
1 teaspoon baking powder
1 teaspoon allspice
1 teaspoon cinnamon
Zest of 1 lemon, grated
1 tablespoon demerara
  sugar

Preheat the oven to 180°C, 350°F, gas mark 4. Grease or line with baking paper a 20cm (8in) cake tin. Soak the chopped apple and sultanas in the dry cider. In a separate bowl, cream together the butter and sugar until light and fluffy. Gradually beat in, little by little, the eggs. Sift together all the dry ingredients and fold into the mixture together with the lemon rind. Add the soaked fruit and cider and gently mix until it is well incorporated. Spoon into the prepared tin, scatter the demerara sugar over the top and bake for 45–60 minutes.

AGA method

Try to make this cake when the AGA has done a lot of cooking and therefore will be slightly lower in heat. If you have two cold plain shelves, you can change them over after 25 minutes to keep a more consistent lower temperature. You can also make this cake in the AGA Cake Baker if you have one. Prepare the cake mix as above and pour into the cake tin. Slide the grid shelf on to the floor of the Roasting Oven. Place the cake tin on the grid shelf and bake for 10 minutes. Slide the cold plain shelf directly above the cake and continue baking for another 30–40 minutes, or until a skewer come out clean. Remove the cake from the tin and cool on a rack. Alternatively, cook the cake on the oven grid shelf placed on the floor of the Baking Oven (for three- and four-oven models) for about 45 minutes to 1 hour. If it is browning too quickly, slide the cold plain shelf directly above. Remove the cake from the tin and cool on a rack.

Cornish Cider Cake

Did you know that there is a *Good Cider Guide* produced by CAMRA, the same organisation that promotes real ale? Cornish cider apples have wonderful names – Lord of the Isles, Tommy Knight and The Rattler are three varieties that are handpicked for using in Cornish cider. This cider cake recipe comes from Lanhydrock, a wonderful National Trust property set in a beautiful valley near Bodmin. It is a modern version of an old recipe associated with the house.

Makes an 18cm (7in) cake

- 110g (4oz) butter
- 110g (4oz) soft brown sugar
- 2 beaten eggs (room temperature)
- 225g (8oz) wholemeal flour
- 1 teaspoon bicarbonate of soda
- ½ teaspoon nutmeg
- 240ml (8fl oz) dry cider

Preheat the oven to 190°C, 375°F, gas mark 5. Grease an 18cm (7in) cake tin, and line the bottom with baking paper. Cream the butter and sugar together until light and fluffy. Beat in the eggs. Sift all the dry ingredients and fold into the mixture. Add the cider slowly and beat to a soft dropping consistency. Bake for 1–1¼ hours. When cooked the cake should be springy to touch and leave the sides of the tin. When cold, store in an airtight tin for at least 24 hours before serving.

AGA method

Try to make this cake when the AGA has done a lot of cooking and therefore will be slightly lower in heat. If you have two cold plain shelves, you can change them over after 25 minutes to keep a more consistent lower temperature. You can also make this cake in the AGA Cake Baker if you have one. Prepare the cake mix as above and pour into the cake tin. Slide the grid shelf on to the floor of the Roasting Oven. Place the cake tin on the grid shelf and bake for 10 minutes. Slide the cold plain shelf directly above the cake and continue baking for another 30–40 minutes, or until a skewer comes out clean. Remove the cake from the tin and cool on a rack. Alternatively, cook the cake on the oven grid shelf placed on the floor of the Baking Oven (for three- and four-oven models) for about 1–1¼ hours. If the cake is browning too quickly, slide the cold plain shelf directly above.

Almond Cake

This is in the 18th-century tradition of plain cakes. The almonds keep it moist. It's the perfect cake for coffee, when nothing too rich or elaborate is required.

Makes a 20cm (8in) cake

225g (8oz) butter
225g (8oz) caster sugar
4 eggs
1 teaspoon almond essence
225g (8oz) plain flour
1 teaspoon baking powder
50g (2oz) ground almonds
25g (1oz) flaked almonds

Preheat the oven to 160°C, 325°F, gas mark 3. Grease and line a 20cm (8in) cake tin. Cream together the butter and sugar until pale and fluffy. Beat in the eggs one at a time. Add the almond essence. Sift together the flour and the baking powder and lightly fold into the cake mixture. Finally stir in the ground almonds. Spoon into the prepared cake tin and sprinkle the flaked almonds on top. Bake in the oven for approximately 1½ hours. Cool on a wire tray.

AGA method

Prepare the cake as above and pour the cake mix into the tin. Place the cold plain shelf on to the fourth set of runners in the Roasting Oven, put the cake tin on top and bake for about 15 minutes. Transfer the shelf, with the cake tin on top, to the Simmering Oven, and continue to bake for another 2–2½ hours or until a skewer comes out clean from the centre of the cake.

Alternatively, cook the cake on the oven grid shelf placed on the floor of the Baking Oven (on three- and four-oven models) for about 1¼–1½ hours. If the cake is browning too quickly, slide in the cold plain shelf directly above.

Poppy-seed Cake

This delicious and unusual cake is in the British tradition of seed cakes (see page 341). It was given to me by a cook from Buckland Abbey in Devon, home of Sir Francis Drake, where it has been a great favourite.

Makes a 20cm (8in) cake

110g (4oz) blue poppy
  seeds
225ml (8fl oz) milk
225g (8oz) butter
225g (8oz) light raw cane
  sugar
3 eggs, separated
225g (8oz) self-raising
  wholemeal flour

Preheat the oven to 350°F, 180°C, gas mark 4. Grease and line a 20cm (8in) cake tin. Bring the poppy seeds to the boil in the milk, turn off the heat and leave them to soak for 25 minutes in the covered pan.

Cream the butter and sugar together until light and fluffy. Add the egg yolks, one at a time, and beat thoroughly. Fold the flour gently into the creamed mixture and stir in the seeds and milk. Whisk the egg whites until stiff and carefully incorporate into the mixture. Spoon it into the prepared tin and bake for 1–1¼ hours or until the centre is firm and the cake has stopped 'singing'. Let it stand for 10 minutes, then turn out to cool.

AGA method

Pour the cake mix into the tin. Place the cold plain shelf on to the fourth set of runners in the Roasting Oven and place the cake tin on top. Bake for about 10 minutes, then transfer the shelf, with the cake tin on top, to the Simmering Oven and continue to bake for another 1–2 hours or until firm to the touch. Stand for 10 minutes then turn out to cool.

Alternatively, cook the cake in the centre of the Baking Oven (on three- and four-oven models) for about 1–1¼ hours. If the cake is browning too quickly, slide the cold plain shelf directly above.

Victoria Sponge Cake

There are three important rules for making any sponge cake – firstly, all the ingredients must be at room temperature; secondly, the flour and sugar must be sifted very well; and finally, the longer you beat it, the lighter it is.

Makes a 23cm (9in) cake

4 large eggs
Equal weights to the eggs of
    butter, caster sugar and
    self-raising flour
Icing sugar, to dust

Flavourings
Either a few drops of vanilla
    essence or zest of
      1 lemon or zest of
      1 orange

For the filling
3–4 tablespoons raspberry
    jam
150ml (¼ pint) double
    cream, whipped stiff

Preheat the oven to 175°C, 350°F, gas mark 4. Line a 23cm (9in) springform tin with baking paper. Beat the butter with an electric beater, a wooden spoon or a balloon whisk until pale in colour and creamy. Gradually beat in the sugar, and beat vigorously at least another 5 minutes once the sugar is in. The mixture should almost double in volume and be very pale in colour. Beat in the eggs, one at a time, beating vigorously between additions. If the mixture curdles, beat in a small spoonful of the measured flour with the egg. Stir in the chosen flavouring at this point. Finally fold in the flour, very gently. Spoon the mixture into the prepared tin and bake for about 45 minutes in the preheated oven. The cake is cooked when a skewer inserted in the centre comes out clean.

Cool on a wire rack. When cold, cut the cake in half and spread the bottom half with raspberry jam and whipped cream. Put the top back on lightly and dust with icing sugar.

AGA method

Prepare the cake mix as above. Place in two 20cm (8in) cake tins. Place the grid shelf on to the floor of the Roasting Oven and put the cake tins on top. Slide the cold plain shelf on to the third set of runners and bake the cake for 20 minutes or until it is golden on top and springs back when lightly pressed.

Alternatively, cook in the centre of the Baking Oven (on three- and four-oven models) for about 20 minutes. If it is browning too quickly, slide the cold plain shelf directly above.

Pear and Ginger Loaf

Ginger has been used in British cookery for centuries. Medieval cooks in well-off households used dried ginger in every kind of dish, but from the 18th century it was in baking, specifically cakes and biscuits, that ginger was especially popular. The taste and texture of pear has a particular affinity with ginger.

Makes 1 small loaf

225g (8oz) self-raising flour
½ level teaspoon ground ginger
110g (4oz) soft brown sugar
110g (4oz) butter
1 ripe pear
1 egg, beaten
3 tablespoons milk

Preheat the oven to 180°C, 350°F, gas mark 4. Well grease or line with baking paper a small loaf tin. Sift the flour and ginger together and then stir in the soft brown sugar. Using your fingertips, rub in the butter. Peel, core and finely chop the pear and stir it into the flour mixture. Add the beaten egg and milk and mix to a stiff dough. Turn into the loaf tin and bake for approximately 55 minutes.

AGA method

Prepare the pear and ginger loaf as above. Slide the grid shelf on to the floor of the Roasting Oven. Place the tin on the grid shelf, with the cold plain shelf directly above, and bake there for 40–45 minutes or until a skewer comes out clean. Cool in the tin. Alternatively, cook the loaf in the centre of the Baking Oven (for three- and four-oven models) for about 45–55 minutes. If it is browning too quickly, slide the cold plain shelf directly above.

Coconut Bakewell Tart

In 1820, Mrs Greaves, landlady of the White Horse Inn in Bakewell, Derbyshire, was entertaining. She told her cook to make a pudding out of an egg mixture cooked and spread with strawberry jam. The inexperienced cook put the jam at the bottom of the pudding. Mrs Greaves's guests commented favourably and Bakewell puddings, now called tarts, have been made in Bakewell – and elsewhere – ever since.

Serves 6

350g (12oz) shortcrust
    pastry
110g (4oz) butter
110g (4oz) sugar
2 large eggs, beaten
50g (2oz) desiccated
    coconut
110g (4oz) ground rice
3–4 tablespoons jam or
    lemon curd

Icing

4–6oz (110–175g) sifted
    icing sugar
2–4 drops vanilla essence
    (optional)
1–2 tablespoons warm
    water

Preheat the oven to 180°C, 350°F, gas mark 4. Grease a 25cm (10in) flan dish and line with the shortcrust pastry. Keep the pastry trimmings. Cream together the butter and sugar until light and fluffy and gradually add the beaten egg. Mix in the desiccated coconut and ground rice. Spread the uncooked pastry case with jam or lemon curd, spoon in the mixture and spread evenly. Roll out the leftover pastry and make lattice strips for the top. Bake in the oven for about 1 hour or until firm. While allowing the tart to cool, make the icing as follows.

Put the sifted icing sugar and (if you wish) a few drops of vanilla essence in a basin and gradually add the warm water. The icing should be thick enough to coat the back of a spoon. If necessary, add more water or sugar to adjust the consistency. Spread the icing on the cooled tart.

AGA method

Make and assemble the tart as above. Bake the tart on the Roasting Oven floor, with the cold plain shelf directly above, for 25–35 minutes, or until set. If the tart is not browning enough, remove the plain shelf for the last 5–10 minutes.

Grantham Gingerbreads

Grantham Gingerbreads were first created in 1740 when a local baker in Grantham, Lincolnshire, while making a flat, hard biscuit for travellers called Grantham Whetstones, added a raising agent to the mixture by mistake. Since then, Grantham has taken its gingerbreads to its heart. It is known as 'the gingerbread town' and its local football team are known as 'The Gingerbreads'.

Makes approximately 30 gingerbreads

100g (4oz) butter
350g (12oz) sugar
1 egg, beaten
2–3 teaspoons ground
    ginger
250g (9oz) self-raising flour

Preheat the oven to 145°C, 280°F, gas mark 1. Grease a large baking tray. Beat the butter in a bowl with a wooden spoon to soften it, then work in the sugar followed by the beaten egg. Sift the ground ginger into the flour and add to the mixture, which will be quite dry and crumbly – a bit like shortbread. Using your hands, bring the mixture together into about thirty small balls the size of a walnut and place on the baking tray, leaving plenty of space between each one. Cook in the oven for 30 minutes. The gingerbreads should remain pale in colour and have a texture and appearance rather like a macaroon.

AGA method

Prepare the Gingerbreads as above. Bake them in the Roasting Oven, on the fourth set of runners, for 2 minutes, then move to the Simmering Oven for 1 hour. They should remain pale in colour and have a texture and appearance rather like a macaroon.

Fruity Gingerbread

This gingerbread recipe comes from Little Moreton Hall in Cheshire: a modern recipe for a medieval food from a medieval house. Early gingerbread recipes contained breadcrumbs and used honey as a sweetener. Black treacle or molasses has been popular since the trading ships started coming back from the West Indies in the 16th century.

Makes a 20cm (8in) gingerbread

110g (4oz) butter
110g (4oz) soft brown sugar
125ml (4fl oz) black treacle
1 egg, beaten
150ml (¼ pint) warm milk
110g (4oz) plain flour
110g (4oz) wholemeal flour
2 teaspoons ginger
2 teaspoons cinnamon
1 teaspoon bicarbonate of
   soda
50g (2oz) mixed dried fruit

Preheat the oven to 150°C, 300°F, gas mark 2. Grease and line a 20cm (8in) square cake tin. Melt the butter, sugar and treacle in a saucepan – cool and add the beaten egg and warm milk. Sift the flours, spices and bicarbonate of soda together in a mixing bowl and add the mixed dried fruit. Make a well in the centre of the dry ingredients, pour in the treacle mixture and beat very thoroughly. Pour into the tin and bake in the oven for approximately 1 hour. Cool for a couple of minutes in the tin, then on a rack.

AGA method

Use the AGA hotplates to make the cake mix as above. Slide the grid shelf on to the floor of the Roasting Oven. Place the cake tin on the grid shelf and bake for 10 minutes. Slide the cold plain shelf directly above the cake and continue baking for another 30–40 minutes, or until a skewer comes out clean. Cool for a few minutes in the tin then on a rack.

Corfe Castle Rock Cakes

These are called rock cakes because they look like nobbly rocks, and they are my favourite 'I'd forgotten they were coming and there's no time to get to the shops' recipe, partly because they taste delicious just out of the oven. Experiment with the fruit; you could try dried cranberries or chopped ginger as an alternative to the currants and sultanas.

Makes approximately 8–9 cakes

225g (8oz) self-raising flour
½ teaspoon nutmeg
110g (4oz) butter
110g (4oz) sugar
50g (2oz) currants
50g (2oz) sultanas
25g (1oz) mixed peel
2 eggs, beaten
Milk, if needed

Preheat the oven to 190°C, 375°F, gas mark 5. Put the flour and nutmeg into a bowl and rub in the butter. Stir in the sugar; then mix in the fruit and mixed peel. Add the beaten eggs and mix to a stiffish dough, adding milk, if necessary. Divide into 8 or 9 pieces and place on a greased baking sheet. Bake in the centre of the oven for about 25 minutes, until the cakes just start to brown at the edges. Cool on a wire rack.

AGA method

Prepare the Rock Cakes as above. Cook on the third set of runners in the Roasting Oven for 10–15 minutes, turning once, until the cakes just start to brown at the edges. Cool on a wire rack.

Eccles Cakes

Eccles is a small town on the outskirts of Manchester. Eccles cakes seem to have caused nearly as much controversy as trifle. Two 19th-century bakers, James Birch and William Bradburn, both claimed to be selling the 'authentic' version from rival shops across the road from each other in the early 19th century – who was right? Should they be round or square? Should they contain only currants, or other fruit as well? This recipe allows you to choose the fruit you put in. What is not in doubt is that they are rich in fruit and spices and very good served warm from the oven.

Makes approximately 4 cakes

450g (1lb) puff pastry
Caster sugar for decoration
Milk

For the filling
225g (8oz) stale cake crumbs, or use crushed trifle sponges if not available
225g (8oz) jam of your choice
225g (8oz) dried mixed fruit
½ teaspoon mixed spice
½ teaspoon cinnamon

Preheat the oven to 210°C, 425°F, gas mark 7. Grease a large baking sheet or line it with baking paper. Roll out the pastry and cut into circles approximately 10–13cm (4–5in) in diameter – this is probably easier to do if you use a saucer or something similar. Mix all the filling ingredients together until well combined and place a dessertspoon of filling on to each round. Brush the edge of each round with milk, bring up to the centre and pinch to seal well. Now turn your sealed pastry parcel over, so that the seam is underneath. Gently roll it flat to about 6mm (¼in) thick and pat it into a round shape. Place the cakes on to the greased baking sheet and cut three slits in the centre of each one. Brush them with milk, sprinkle with caster sugar and bake in the oven for about 15 minutes, or until the pastry is crisp and brown. Cool on a wire rack.

AGA method

Prepare the Eccles Cakes as above. Cook on the third set of runners in the Roasting Oven for about 15 minutes, until crisp and brown.

Macaroons

Macaroons were often served with wine in the 18th and 19th centuries, and macaroon recipes have appeared in cookery books since at least the late 17th century. The name comes from Italy – in the Neopolitan dialect, a *maccarone* is a dumpling or small cake. I collected this recipe from a Cornish cook at Trelissick, a beautiful garden near Falmouth, Cornwall, in the 1980s.

Makes approximately 9 macaroons

200g (7oz) caster sugar
25g (1oz) granulated sugar
110g (4oz) ground almonds
1 tablespoon rice flour
3 egg whites
2–3 drops of almond essence
Rice paper
Split almonds

Preheat the oven to 180°C, 350°F, gas mark 4. Mix the sugars, ground almonds and rice flour together in a bowl. Add the egg whites and essence and beat everything together with a wooden spoon for about 5 minutes. Scrape down the sides of the bowl and leave to stand for 5 minutes. Meanwhile, cut the rice paper into 7.5cm (3in) squares and place shiny side down on a baking sheet. Continue to beat the almond mixture for a further 5 minutes until thick and white. Using a bag and 12mm (½in) nozzle, pipe on to the rice paper – place a split almond in the centre of each macaroon and bake in the oven for 20–30 minutes.

AGA method

Prepare the Macaroons as above. Slide the grid shelf on to the floor of the Roasting Oven. Place the baking tray on the grid shelf and bake for 5 minutes. Slide the cold plain shelf directly above the Macaroons and continue baking for another 15–20 minutes. Remove from the tray and cool. Alternatively, cook the Macaroons in the centre of the Baking Oven (on three- and four-oven models) for about 20 minutes, turning once.

Oat Biscuits

These oat biscuits are nutty and sustaining.

Makes approximately 12–16 biscuits

110g (4oz) margarine or
   butter
2 teaspoons golden syrup
¼ teaspoon bicarbonate of
   soda dissolved in
   1 dessertspoon hot water
110g (4oz) granulated sugar
75g (3oz) plain flour
100g (4oz) rolled oats

Preheat the oven to 200°C, 400°F, gas mark 6. Grease or line with paper a large baking tray. Gently melt the margarine and syrup in a saucepan. Add the bicarbonate of soda dissolved in the hot water and all the remaining ingredients. Stir with a wooden spoon until well mixed together. Place small drops on the greased baking tray, with plenty of space between each one for spreading. Bake for approximately 10 minutes.

AGA method

Prepare the Oat Biscuits as above. Slide the oven grid shelf on to the floor of the Roasting Oven, place the baking tray on top and bake for 8–10 minutes. Remove from the tray and cool.

Shortbread

Shortbread is a biscuit with a long history. Tradition says Mary, Queen of Scots brought them to Scotland in 1550. The name harks back to the 'short cakes' baked in the 16th century. The classic proportions are always the same: 3 parts flour to 2 parts butter to 1 part sugar. I consulted the best shortbread cook I know for the perfect mix of flours; Kate has been cooking shortbread professionally for, among others, an acclaimed farm shop in the South West. She varies the flour by using one-third cornflour.

Makes approximately 12 biscuits

110g (4oz) plain flour
50g (2oz) cornflour
110g (4oz) butter
50g (2oz) caster sugar
Caster sugar to decorate

Preheat the oven to 160°C, 325°F, gas mark 3. Sieve the flour and cornflour together. Cream the butter until it is soft, then add the caster sugar and beat until the mixture is pale and creamy. Work the butter and sugar into the flour mixture a tablespoon at a time. Place the shortbread mixture on to a large baking tray and roll out to an 8in (20cm) circle. Pinch the edges and prick well with a fork. Cut through into 12 sections with the back of a knife, then sprinkle with a little caster sugar. Leave to chill in the fridge for 15 minutes, then bake in a moderate oven for 35 minutes or until pale and golden brown. Cool on the baking tray.

AGA method

Prepare the Shortbread mix and assemble on the baking tray as above. Bake in the Simmering Oven, on the third set of runners, for 40–45 minutes, or in the Roasting Oven, on the fourth set of runners with the cold plain shelf on the second set of runners, for 10–15 minutes, or until lightly coloured. Remove to a wire rack. Alternatively, cook the shortbread on the oven grid shelf placed on the floor of the Baking Oven (on three- and four-oven models) for about 20 minutes. Cool on the tray, then move to a wire rack.

Cornish Fairings

Fairings are thin, crisp, spicy biscuits, approximately 8–10cm (3–4in) in diameter with a characteristic cracked surface. They were sold at the Fairs that were held at certain times of year and each county or town had its particular type of biscuit (see also Ashby Statutes, opposite).

Makes approximately 24 biscuits

110g (4oz) butter or margarine
110g (4oz) caster sugar
100ml (3½fl oz) golden syrup
225g (8oz) plain flour
2 level teaspoons baking powder
2 level teaspoons bicarbonate of soda
2 level teaspoons ground ginger
1 level teaspoon mixed spice

Preheat the oven to 150°C, 300°F, gas mark 2. Cream the butter, sugar and syrup together until well mixed, light and fluffy. Sift the flour, baking powder, bicarbonate of soda and spices together and add to the butter mixture until you have a soft dough. Make the dough into balls about the size of a walnut and put on a tray either well greased and floured or lined with baking paper. Flatten each ball slightly and keep them well apart; the biscuits spread as they cook. Bake for approximately 15 minutes. Cool on a wire tray.

AGA method

Prepare the Cornish Fairings as above. Slide the grid shelf onto the floor of the Roasting Oven and place the baking tray on top. Slide the cold plain shelf directly above the tray and bake for 10–12 minutes. Alternatively, cook the biscuits on the oven grid shelf placed on the floor of the Baking Oven (on three- and four-oven models) for about 15 minutes. Cool on a wire rack.

Ashby Statutes

Ashby Statutes are also called Langley Wakes Cakes. Derbyshire villages marked their annual Wakes or Fairs week in July and August by baking their own versions.

Makes approximately 16 cakes

125g (4oz) butter or
margarine
75g (3oz) caster sugar, plus
extra for the top
225g (8oz) plain flour
½ teaspoon baking powder
1 egg, well beaten
110g (4oz) mixed dried fruit
and/or nuts

Preheat the oven to 180°C, 350°F, gas mark 4. Either use mixed dried fruit or make your own mixture – I find finely chopped cherries, crystallised ginger and walnut pieces are a good combination. Either grease a baking sheet well or line it with baking paper. Cream the butter or margarine with the sugar until pale and fluffy. Sift the flour and baking powder, mix with the fruit and nuts and add to the mixture alternately with the egg to form a stiff dough. Roll out on a floured surface approximately 1cm (⅜in) thick and cut into 7.5cm (3in) rounds. Bake for about 15–20 minutes, until nicely brown. Leave to cool on the baking sheet for a few minutes and sprinkle with caster sugar.

AGA method

Prepare the dough as above and put the rounds on to a baking tray. Slide the grid shelf on to the floor of the Roasting Oven. Place the tray on the grid shelf, with the cold plain shelf directly above, and bake there for 15–20 minutes or until brown. If the cakes are not brown enough, remove the plain shelf for the final 5 minutes of baking.

Alternatively, cook in the centre of the Baking Oven (on three- or four-oven models) for 15–20 minutes, until brown.

Flapjacks

The name 'flapjack' was originally used for a griddle cake that had to be turned during cooking. 'Pancake, fritter or flapjacke' wrote John Taylor in 1634. Now it is a thick, sweet biscuit made with rolled oats.

Makes approximately 10 flapjacks

110g (4oz) butter
110g (4oz) golden syrup
50g (2oz) demerara sugar
225g (8oz) rolled oats

Preheat the oven to 180°C, 350°F, gas mark 4. Grease a 20cm (8in) square cake tin. Melt the butter, syrup and sugar in a saucepan. Stir in the rolled oats, turn the mixture into the cake tin and spread evenly. Bake for 30–35 minutes. Take out of the oven and cut into pieces immediately. Leave in the tin until cold.

AGA method

Use the AGA hotplates to melt the butter, sugar and syrup, then continue as above. Slide the tin on to the grid shelf on the floor of the Roasting Oven, with the cold plain shelf slid on to the second set of runners, and bake for 15–20 minutes. Cool in the tin for a few minutes before turning out and cutting. Alternatively, cook the Flapjacks in the centre of the Baking Oven (on three- and four-oven models) for about 20–25 minutes.

Whittingham Buttons

Whittingham is a small village deep in the moors in Northumberland. This is a very local recipe, which was probably discovered by accident – who would have thought of putting custard powder in a biscuit? It works, though – they are crisp and sweet. In Northumberland you can buy them at the bakers, but anywhere else you will have to make them yourself.

Makes 12–16 biscuits

175g (6oz) butter or
    margarine
75g (3oz) icing sugar
175g (6oz) plain flour
50g (2oz) custard powder

Preheat the oven to 180°C, 350°F, gas mark 4. Cream the butter and sugar together very thoroughly until light and fluffy. Add the flour and custard powder and mix to form a firm dough. Break off small pieces, the size of a large walnut, and roll into a ball with your hands or place small spoonfuls on to a greased baking sheet and flatten slightly. Bake in a preheated oven for 10–15 minutes or until lightly golden. Cool on a wire rack.

AGA method

Prepare the biscuits as above. Slide the grid shelf on to the floor of the Roasting Oven and place the baking tray on top. Slide the cold plain shelf directly above the biscuits and bake for 8–10 minutes. Remove from the tray and cool.

Alternatively, cook the biscuits in the centre of the Baking Oven (on three- and four-oven models) for about 10–15 minutes, turning once, until lightly golden.

Shrewsbury Biscuits

This is a very old recipe. Shrewsbury Cakes, as they were then known, are mentioned in a document of 1561 but were probably made well before this date. The baker who made them famous is mentioned in *The Ingoldsby Legends*, published in the middle of the 19th century: 'Mr Palin, prince of cake pounders / The mouth liquefies at the very name.' Palin the baker ran a confectionery shop on the corner of Castle Street and School Lane in Shrewsbury during the late 18th and early 19th centuries.

Makes approximately 20 biscuits

50g (2oz) butter
50g (2oz) sugar
1 egg
50g (2oz) currants
175g (6oz) plain flour
½ teaspoon mixed spice
Caster sugar to decorate

Preheat the oven to 190°C, 375°F, gas mark 5. Either grease two large baking sheets or line them with baking paper. Cream the butter and sugar until pale and fluffy. Add the egg and beat in well. Fold in the currants, flour and mixed spice and knead lightly into a smooth ball. Roll out on a floured surface to about 5mm (¼in) thick. Cut into rounds with a 6cm (2½in) fluted cutter and put on the baking trays. Bake in the oven for 15 minutes – after 5 minutes take out and sprinkle with caster sugar; then continue to cook until firm and very light brown in colour.

AGA method

Prepare the biscuits as above. Slide the grid shelf on to the floor of the Roasting Oven and place the baking tray on top. Slide the cold plain shelf directly above the biscuits and bake for 5 minutes. Take out of the oven and sprinkle with caster sugar, then continue to bake for 10 minutes or until firm and very lightly brown in colour. Alternatively, cook the biscuits on the second set of runners in the Baking Oven (on three- and four-oven models) for about 15 minutes – after 5 minutes, take out and sprinkle with caster sugar, then continue to cook until firm and very light brown in colour. Remove from the tray and cool.

Honey Oatcakes

A cross between a flapjack and a biscuit, this recipe was given to me at Anglesey Abbey near Cambridge. There, the oatcakes are baked using flour which is stone-ground using ancient millstones at the local water mill situated on the river Lode.

**Makes approximately
15–20 oatcakes**

225g (8oz) butter
3 tablespoons clear honey
125g (5oz) light brown sugar
125g (5oz) coconut
50g (2oz) rolled oats
225g (8oz) wholemeal flour
1¼ teaspoons baking
    powder

Preheat the oven to 160°C, 325°F, gas mark 3. Grease a baking tin approximately 25 x 18cm (10 x 7in). Melt the butter and honey over a low heat. Mix all the dry ingredients together and add to the butter and honey. Spread in the tin and bake in the oven for 20 minutes. While still warm, cut into triangles and leave to cool in the tin.

AGA method

Prepare the Honey Oatcakes as above. Slide the grid shelf on to the floor of the Roasting Oven and place the baking tray on top. Slide the cold plain shelf directly above the tray and bake for 10–15 minutes. Leave to cool in the tray. Alternatively, cook the oatcakes on the oven grid shelf placed on the floor of the Baking Oven (on three- and four-oven models) for about 20 minutes.

Northumbrian Ginger and Cinnamon Biscuits

These are similar (except for the cinnamon) to the Cornish Fairings on page 358 – crisp biscuits are favourites everywhere. This spicy and delicious recipe comes from the other end of England.

Makes approximately 30 biscuits

170g (6oz) butter
170g (6oz) sugar
4 tablespoons golden syrup
300g (10oz) plain flour sifted with 2 teaspoons each of bicarbonate of soda, ginger and cinnamon

Preheat the oven to 160°C, 325°F; gas mark 3. Line a baking sheet with baking parchment. Melt the butter, sugar and golden syrup in a saucepan. Add the flour, bicarbonate of soda, ginger and cinnamon and mix well. Roll small amounts of the mixture in your hands to form balls, approximately the size of a large walnut. Place these well apart on the baking sheet and flatten the top slightly of each one. Bake for approximately 10–15 minutes until golden. Transfer to a wire rack to cool.

AGA method

Prepare the biscuits as above using the AGA hotplates. Slide the grid shelf on to the floor of the Roasting Oven and place the baking tray on top. Slide the cold plain shelf directly above the biscuits and bake for 10–12 minutes or until golden.

Alternatively, cook the biscuits on the oven grid shelf placed on the floor of the Baking Oven (on three- and four-oven models) for about 10–15 minutes, until golden. Remove from the tray and cool.

Jams and Preserves

'The rule is, jam tomorrow and jam yesterday – but never jam today.' It seems unlikely that the White Queen in Lewis Carroll's *Alice Through the Looking Glass*, a hopelessly disorganised woman, ever made her own jam. Maybe if she had, there would have been 'jam today'.

Preserving food is a preoccupation we can all understand, although today it is more a pleasure than a necessity, when there are preserves aplenty to buy in the shops. Even so, the most expensive jams and pickles are often packaged to look as though they are homemade – because there is definitely something special about homemade pickles and preserves. Jams and preserves are not difficult to make, although they do take time. Generally they cost less than the shop-bought version, and if you grow your own fruit and vegetables, they can cost virtually nothing. If you don't grow your own fruit you can visit a 'Pick Your Own' farm, adding to the enjoyment.

Come January or February, when I was a child, our family kitchen was always full of steam and smelt of oranges – my mother was making her annual batch of marmalade. We had no freezer, so she watched the greengrocer's shelves like a hawk from Christmas onwards, awaiting the arrival of the Seville oranges. Much less beautiful than sweet oranges, knobbly, odd shapes and sizes, and sometimes still with their stalks and leaves attached, Seville oranges have an all-too-short season of just a few weeks. Today it is easy; you can buy the oranges and freeze them for later, if you haven't the time to make the marmalade now. But back then, once you had bought the oranges, you had to make your marmalade as soon as possible.

Good marmalade used to be expensive and in short supply. In my childhood, five of us ate mountains of toast and marmalade every morning, so it made good economic sense for my mother to make her own. When I got married, she bought me a preserving pan and gave me her recipe. I made it then because

I loved the taste, but I make it now because, as well as the taste, I am hooked on the process. I love chopping the fruit, and the smell – I even like the time it takes. Because, although my mum's recipe takes three days, making marmalade is a well-loved ritual, not a chore.

Preserves make wonderful presents, if you can bear to give them away. And you never have to worry about having made too much of anything because once made, (with the exception of Lemon Curd), preserves keep for a long time. Jams are probably best eaten within a year, but chutneys, like fine wines, improve with age.

There are, of course, recipes for jam for most fruits, across the world, and there is no shortage of recipes for strawberry and raspberry jam. But the recipes included in this chapter were chosen either for their particular ingredients or for a combination of ingredients that is particularly traditional to British cooking. Marrow and Lemon Jam is an example of a good and tasty preserve, where ingenuity is part of the equation – marrow (or squash or courgettes) grows well in many parts of Britain, but the season is short and almost too bountiful. The recipe comes from Mrs Beddows, who was famous for her jams. Her Blackberry and Apple Jam solves the problem of blackberry pips by calling for both blackberry and apple purées, and then combining the two with sugar – the result is thick and aromatic. I love anything with quince as an ingredient, and the Quince Jam is a wonderful pale pink in colour, with a taste all of its own. Although cherries are available almost all year round, the season when the fruit is abundant and tastes best is short. Cherry Conserve extends the pleasure to be had from this gorgeous fruit, and can be used as a sauce with ice cream – or even one of the rice puddings.

Mincemeat and Mince Pies have a long history. With a filling of meat, preserved fruit, chopped nuts and apples, moistened with vinegar or lemon juice, they were called *chewettes* in the Middle Ages, but had become mince or shred pies by the 16th century. As Christmas pies, in the 17th century, they were banned by the Puritans, who tried to suppress the celebration of Christmas during Cromwell's time. No wonder Samuel Pepys comments – on Christmas Day, 1666 – that he left his wife in bed 'desirous to sleep, having sat up to 4 this morning seeing her maids make mince pies'. At that date the pies had only just come back on the menu, and would still have had meat in them. But in the 19th century the meat was replaced by suet (chopped fat of animal origin). Amy's Mincemeat, a 20th-century recipe, contains no fat at all. It just goes to show that traditional recipes are always changing.

Chutneys are Anglo-Indian. Malays, Indonesians and Indians traditionally serve *sambals* (uncooked relishes) and *chatnis* (cooked relishes) with meals. At the end of the 17th century the East India Company ships brought these strong, sweet pickles back to Britain, where they quickly became popular. A recipe for Piccalilli, a sweet mustard pickle of mixed vegetables, was recorded as early as 1694. I make Frances's Spicy Apple and Onion Chutney every year in September, using apples from a tree in our garden, species unknown. The apples don't keep well, and some years they don't even seem to ripen, but they make chutney that tastes good from the moment it is made. We like to eat it with cold meats and any kind of cheese.

I pickle shallots and onion using Sara Paston-Williams's recipe for Sweet Pickled Onions, from her book *Good Old-Fashioned Jams, Preserves and Chutneys*, and also use her recipe for that old favourite, Lemon Curd.

A preserving pan is useful but not essential for these recipes. A sugar thermometer and a jam funnel for pouring mixtures into jars are also useful but, again, are not essential. You must wash the jars you are going to use for your preserves, then sterilise them by boiling in a large pan for 10 minutes, and drying them in an oven at 110°C (225°F) for 15 minutes, after which they will be ready for use. I store jams and marmalade in the fridge because I do not have a cool larder, but chutneys and pickles are fine on a shelf, or in a cupboard.

Amy's Mincemeat

Mincemeat originally contained meat and commercial mincemeat still contains suet, a meat product. With no suet, this homemade version, originally from West Devon, is suitable for vegetarians. Homemade Mincemeat rewards the effort of making it; both the taste and the texture are quite different from the commercial product. Don't worry about the quantity; it keeps for a long time.

Makes about 2.6kg (6lb)

1.3kg (3lb) cooking and/or
    eating apples, peeled,
    cored and finely chopped
    or grated
Juice and finely grated zest
    of 1 orange
Juice and finely grated zest
    of 1 lemon
600ml (1 pint) medium
    sweet cider
450g (1lb) brown sugar
1 teaspoon ground
    cinnamon
1 teaspoon grated nutmeg
1 teaspoon ground cloves
450g (1lb) raisins
450g (1lb) currants
225g (8oz) glacé cherries,
    halved
100ml (3½fl oz) rum

Put the apples, juices, zest and cider in a large pan or preserving pan. Bring to the boil, reduce the heat and simmer for 10 minutes. Stir in the sugar, cinnamon, nutmeg, cloves, raisins and currants. When the sugar has dissolved, simmer the mixture for a further 15 minutes. Remove the pan from the heat and stir in the glacé cherries. Allow the mixture to cool completely and stir in the rum. Pack into sterilised glass jam jars and cover.

AGA method

Make the mincemeat using the AGA hotplates.

Mince Pies

Use Amy's Mincemeat to create these delicious mince pies – a great British Christmas tradition.

Makes approximately 16–20 mince pies

225g (8oz) shortcrust pastry
(see page 64)

For the sweet pastry
110g (4oz) plain flour
Pinch of salt
50g (2oz) butter
50g (2oz) icing sugar
1 egg yolk
2 teaspoons water

For the filling
Approximately 225g (½lb)
mincemeat

Sunflower oil
Milk, for brushing
Caster sugar, for sprinkling

Make up the sweet pastry as follows: combine the flour, salt, butter and sugar in a food processor and process until the mixture resembles coarse breadcrumbs. Add the egg yolk and water and process until the mixture forms a ball – stop the machine as soon as the ball has formed. Place the pastry in a plastic bag and chill for 30 minutes.

Preheat the oven to 170°C, 350°F, gas mark 5. Roll out both types of pastry. Using fluted cutters, cut round bases 6cm (2½in) in diameter from the shortcrust pastry and lids 4cm (2in) in diameter from the sweet pastry. Brush a patty tin with 6cm (2½in) bowls with oil and line each bowl with the bases. Prick them with a fork. Spoon a teaspoon of mincemeat into each one. Brush the edge of the pastry with milk and cover with the sweet pastry lids. Prick the tops with a fork. Brush the tops with milk, dust with caster sugar and bake for approximately 15 minutes until golden brown. Cool on a wire rack. Serve warm with Brandy Butter (see page 259). Mince Pies keep for a month in an airtight container.

AGA method

Prepare the pastry and assemble the pies as above. Slide the grid shelf onto the floor of the Roasting Oven and place the mince pies on top. Bake for 10–15 minutes, or until golden brown.

Apple and Sage Jelly

Ellen Jefferies is famous at Erddig, North Wales, for her spiced jelly preserves using fruits from the garden, orchard and hedgerow and either fresh herbs or spices from the store cupboard.

Makes about 8 small jars

900g (2lb) apples, chopped
but not cored or peeled
Large bunch of fresh sage
Pared zest and juice of
1 lemon
Sugar, granulated or
preserving

This recipe takes two days to make. Put the apples, sage, lemon zest and juice in a preserving pan. Add sufficient water to cover them. Cover the pan and simmer until the fruit is very soft. This should take around 30 minutes. Strain through a jelly bag overnight.

The next day, measure the juice into a clean preserving pan. Add 450g (1lb) sugar for each 600ml (1 pint) of juice. Heat gently until the sugar has dissolved, then boil rapidly until setting point is reached, stirring from time to time. Skim, pour the jelly into warm, sterilised jars and cover. Seal when still hot.

AGA method

Place the apples, sage and lemon zest and juice in a preserving pan, with barely enough water to cover them. Bring to the boil on the hotplates and place in the Simmering Oven for 30 minutes, until the fruit is soft. Use the AGA hotplates to make the jelly, and the Simmering Oven or Warming Oven to warm the jars.

Pear and Rosemary Jelly

This is another of Ellen Jefferies's wonderful jelly preserve recipes.

Makes about 8 small jars

900g (2lb) pears
Pared zest and juice of
    2 lemons
Large bunch of rosemary
Sugar, granulated or
    preserving
225ml (8fl oz) pectin, if
    necessary

Proceed as for Apple and Sage Jelly, adding the pectin at the end if it is difficult to get the jelly to set.

AGA method

Bring the fruit up to boiling point on the hotplates, then soften in the Simmering Oven. Use the hotplates to make the jelly, and the Simmering Oven or Warming Oven to warm the jars.

Cherry Conserve

'Take the best and fairest of cherries' begins the receipt from 1685, on which this recipe is based. Cherries will always be precious. Cherry conserve is very special, and the addition of alcohol (optional) turns it into a luxury. Cherries are low in pectin, so the availability of pectin sugar today takes the guesswork out of achieving a set. But even with pectin, don't expect a firm set. This is a runny treat.

Makes 1.4–1.8kg (3–4lb)

900g (2lb) dark red cherries
Juice and zest of 2 lemons
800g (1¾lb) sugar with
    pectin
2–3 tablespoons cherry
    brandy or Kirsch

Stone the cherries and place them with the zest and lemon juice in a large, heavy-based pan. Simmer very gently for about 15 minutes or until really soft, stirring from time to time to prevent them from sticking. Add the sugar and stir over a low heat until dissolved. Increase the heat and boil rapidly until setting point is reached (approximately another 5 minutes). Stir in the alcohol of your choice, if you wish, then ladle into the prepared jars and cover when cold with waxed discs and cellophane secured with rubber bands.

AGA method

Use the AGA hotplates to make the conserve, and the Simmering Oven or Warming Oven to warm the jars.

Blackberry and Apple Jam

Supermarket blackberries can be used for the recipe, but in a perfect world this recipe is made with blackberries gathered from the hedgerow and windfall apples. You don't need perfect fruit for it. I like a mixture of cooking and eating apples because then the ultimate purée has more texture to it. It's also worth trying the pick-your-own farms, if you can't find a suitable hedgerow.

Makes approximately 8 jars

900g (2lb) blackberries
300ml (½ pint) water
350g (12oz) cooking apples
   or eating apples
   (prepared weight)
1.3kg (3lb) sugar

Pick over and wash the blackberries, put them in a pan with 150ml (¼ pint) of water and simmer slowly until soft – sieve to remove the pips. Peel, core and slice the apples and add the remaining 150ml (¼ pint) of water. Simmer slowly until soft and make into a pulp with a spoon or a potato masher. Add the blackberry purée and sugar, bring to the boil and boil rapidly, stirring frequently, until setting point is reached. Test for a set by cooling a little of the mixture on a cold plate (put the plate in the fridge first) – if a skin forms, it is ready. Pot into warm, sterilised jars and cover.

AGA method

Use the AGA hotplates to make the jam, and the Simmering Oven or Warming Oven to warm the jars.

Marrow and Lemon Jam

This was a popular jam during World War II when we could import no food and had to improvise with what we had. Fruit was too precious to be made into jam but marrows were plentiful. Fruit is not in short supply now but the jam is still pretty good and it's a great way to use up any excess marrows from the garden. In wartime, lemons were not available − but they do help to bring out the flavour.

Makes approximately 6 jars

900g (2lb) marrow
   (prepared weight)
900g (2lb) sugar
Thinly peeled zest and juice
   of 2 lemons

You need to start this recipe the day before it is cooked. Peel the marrow, remove the seeds and cut into pieces about 12mm (½in) square. Place in a basin, sprinkle with the sugar and allow to stand overnight. Tie up the lemon zest in a piece of muslin and place in a large, heavy pan with the marrow, sugar and lemon juice. Simmer until the sugar has dissolved, then boil until setting point is reached (see Blackberry and Apple Jam, opposite) and the marrow looks transparent. Remove the muslin bag, pot into warm, sterilised jars and cover.

AGA method

Use the AGA hotplates to make the jam, and the Simmering Oven or Warming Oven to warm the jars.

Trelissick Lemon Curd

This recipe, originally from *Good Old-Fashioned Jams, Preserves and Chutneys* (National Trust), uses a slow cooker. I have also given instructions for those of you who don't have one. Lemon curd should be kept in the fridge and eaten within a month or so of making. If your curd curdles while you are making it, remove it quickly from the heat and stand it over a basin of cold water. Whisk hard until the curdling disappears, then continue as before.

Makes approximately 3 jars

Finely grated zest and juice of 2 large lemons, preferably unwaxed and organic
4 large eggs, lightly beaten
175g (6oz) caster sugar
110g (4oz) unsalted butter, melted

Place the lemon zest and juice in a basin or dish that will fit in the slow cooker. Add the beaten eggs, sugar and melted butter and stir well. Cover with a piece of foil and place in the slow cooker. Pour enough boiling water into the slow cooker to come halfway up the basin or dish, then cover with the lid of the slow cooker. Cook for about 1½–2 hours until thick. Stir well with a wooden or plastic spoon (metal implements spoil the flavour), then pot in warm, sterilised jars.

If you do not have a slow cooker, follow this method. Put the lemon zest and juice in a heatproof basin set over a pan of barely simmering water. Take care not to let the bottom of the bowl touch the water. Add the well-beaten eggs, sugar and melted butter. Stir the mixture frequently with a wooden or plastic spoon for about 20 minutes or until thick.

AGA method

Use the Simmering Plate to make the Lemon Curd, and the Simmering Oven or Warming Oven to warm the jars. The Simmering Oven can be used in place of a slow cooker.

Marmalade

You need to begin this recipe two days before you pot the marmalade.

Makes between 9 and 12 jars

About 1.6kg (3½lb) Seville oranges
2 lemons
Water
2.6kg (6lb) sugar
Knob of butter

On the first day, cut the fruits in half. Squeeze and retain the juice. Scrape out the shells and put the pips and pith into a piece of muslin in a pudding basin. Slice the shells into thin strips and put in a preserving pan. Measure the juice and make it up with water to 3.6 litres (6 pints). Tie up the muslin with the pips and pith into a bag and hang from the handle of the pan so that it dangles in the water. Cover with a cloth and leave overnight. On the second day, bring the fruit and water to the boil and simmer for about half an hour, until the peel is tender. Cover and leave overnight. On the third day, preheat the oven to 100°C, 200°F, gas mark 1. Measure the sugar into a baking tin and warm in the oven. Bring the fruit and water to the boil. Put a saucer into the freezer compartment of the fridge. When the fruit and water is boiling hard, tip in the warmed sugar and stir until dissolved. Put the jars in the oven to warm. Boil the marmalade rapidly, stirring, until setting point is reached. Test for the setting point by dropping a teaspoon of Marmalade on to the chilled saucer, putting it back into the fridge and waiting until it cools. If a skin is formed, it will set. Once you have reached this point, put a walnut-sized knob of butter into the Marmalade. Leave for 10 minutes to cool, then put into the hot jars. Cover and label when cold.

AGA method

Because the Simmering Oven gives a gentle heat, less evaporation occurs when you soften the peel, so reduce the water content by 300ml (½ pint). Bring to the boil on the Boiling Plate, then move to the Simmering Oven for 1–1½ hours. Use the hotplates to make the marmalade, and the Simmering Oven or Warming Oven to warm the jars.

Quince Jam

A recipe to preserve a precious fruit. The quince was the original golden apple that Paris gave to the goddess Aphrodite in the garden of the Hesperides. If you find the earthly version on sale, buy them immediately. Better still, if you have a garden, plant a quince tree. Quinces ripen in October, when the leaves start to fall, and are even better if used after a frost.

Makes approximately 3–4 jars

900g (2lb) quinces, peeled and grated
1.4kg (3lb) sugar
Juice of 1 lemon

Put the prepared quinces in a pan with enough water to cover and cook slowly until the fruit is really soft – this takes at least 30 minutes. Then add the sugar and lemon juice and stir until dissolved. Boil rapidly until setting point is reached. Pot and cover in the usual way. Makes about 2.2kg (5lb).

AGA method

Bring the quinces up to the boil on the Boiling Plate, and boil for 5 minutes. Cover and transfer to the Simmering Oven for 1–2 hours, or until the quinces are soft. Continue as above, using the AGA hotplates to finish the jam. Use the Simmering Oven or Warming Oven to warm the jars.

Quince Salami

This old and unusual recipe was once known as Quince Marmalade or Dried Suckets of Quince. Tudor marmalades were rather different from what we call marmalade today. Originally, they were made from quinces (imported from Portugal, where the name for quince is *marmelo***). In those days, the marmalade was boiled for much longer than today, until it was solid. It also looks like salami!**

Serves 6–8

1 generous kilo (2–2½lb)
   large quinces, thinly
   peeled
850g (1¾lb) caster sugar
Juice of 1 lemon
175g (6oz) mixed
   crystallised fruits, such as
   cherries, pineapple, pears,
   apricots and plums,
   chopped if large
225g (8oz) blanched
   almonds, roughly
   chopped

Put the quinces in a large saucepan, cover with water and bring to the boil. Boil, covered, until the quinces are soft (this may take quite a long time). Remove the saucepan from the heat and place the fruit in a colander to drain. Reserve the cooking liquid. While they are still hot, core the quinces and purée them in a food processor or blender.

Measure 225ml (8fl oz) of the cooking liquid into a saucepan. Reserve two tablespoons of sugar and dissolve the rest in the liquid over a very low heat. Stir continuously until the syrup is clear, then bring it to the boil without stirring and let it boil for a minute or two until it thickens. Add the quince purée and continue cooking and stirring until the mixture becomes very thick and leaves the side of the pan. Remove the saucepan from the heat, stir in the lemon juice, the crystallised fruits and almonds. Stir until they are well distributed throughout the quince paste.

Turn the mixture out on to a smooth surface, lined with clingfilm. Using the clingfilm as a container, work it into a sausage shape as soon as it is cool enough to handle. Then roll it in the remaining sugar and chill it well. Slice thinly.

AGA method

Bring the quinces to the boil on the Boiling Plate, then boil for 5 minutes. Cover and transfer to the Simmering Oven for 1–2 hours, or until the quinces are soft. Continue as above, using the AGA hotplates to finish the recipe.

Rhubarb Chutney

Rhubarb reached Europe in the 16th century and was originally grown in physic borders for medical use. It wasn't until the 19th century that it began to be appreciated as a fruit, an ingredient of pies, pastries and for eating as chutney.

Makes approximately 6–8 jars

900g (2lb) rhubarb
225g (8oz) onions
700g (1½lb) brown sugar
225g (8oz) raisins
1 teaspoon mustard seeds
1 teaspoon mixed spice
½ teaspoon ground pepper
1 teaspoon ground ginger
1 teaspoon salt
600ml (1 pint) wine or cider
    vinegar

Cut the rhubarb into 2.5cm (1in) lengths. Peel and chop the onions finely. Put all the ingredients into a large, heavy pan and simmer gently, stirring frequently until the mixture is of a thick consistency (like jam) with no excess liquid. This should take less than 45 minutes. Put into warm, sterilised pots and cover tightly.

AGA method

Use the AGA hotplates to start the chutney off, then move the pan to the Roasting Oven floor and continue to cook there for 30–45 minutes, checking and stirring every 15 minutes or so.

Frances's Spicy Apple and Onion Chutney

This recipe from Northumberland is simplicity itself. It tastes good with all cold meats and is superlative with cheese. Don't worry about what apples to use, as it's a very easy-going recipe. I prefer to use a mixture of eating and cooking apples, which I feel gives the best texture, but use what is best value and available to you. By the way, it will probably get eaten, but it does keep – and even improve – for at least a year.

Makes approximately 10 jars

1.3kg (3lb) apples, peeled, cored and chopped

900g (2lb) onion, finely sliced

110g (4oz) raisins

50g (2oz) yellow mustard seeds

1.2 litres (2 pints) wine or cider vinegar

225g (8oz) fresh tomatoes, chopped

4 teaspoons salt

225g (8oz) caster sugar

2 teaspoons cayenne pepper or 1 teaspoon of minced chilli

Put all the ingredients in a preserving pan and bring to the boil, stirring while the sugar dissolves. Boil all together for an hour. Pot in warm, sterilised jars and cover when cold.

AGA method

Use the AGA hotplates to start the chutney off, then move the pan to the Roasting Oven floor and continue to cook there for 45 minutes to an hour, checking and stirring every 15 minutes.

Sweet Pickled Onions

This is the best recipe I have ever used for pickling onions. The resulting onions are sweet and crisp. Do be careful not to cut away too much when you trim the tops and roots of the onions or they will disintegrate and become soggy. Do not worry if any small yellow spots appear on your pickled onions; they are perfectly harmless. This recipe originally appeared in *Good Old-Fashioned Jams, Preserves and Chutneys*. Please note that this recipe takes two days to make.

Makes approximately 4 jars

1.35kg (3lb) small pickling onions, trimmed
50g (2oz) cooking salt
2–3 fresh tarragon sprigs
1–2 green or red fresh chillies, halved (optional)
1 1.5 litres (1¾–2½ pints) white wine vinegar
350g–450g (12–16oz) sugar

Put the onions into a large bowl and cover with boiling water. Leave for about 20 seconds and then pour off the water. Cover with cold water, then peel the onions, keeping them under the water when peeling. Put them into a bowl, sprinkling each layer with salt. Cover with a clean cloth and leave overnight.

Rinse well and shake off as much water as possible. Pack into clean, dry jars, adding a washed tarragon sprig and half a chilli to each jar. Boil the vinegar and sugar together for 1 minute, adding 225g (8oz) sugar to each 850ml (1½ pints) vinegar. Pour the hot vinegar over the onions. Cover tightly and store for 2–3 weeks before eating. Use within 6 months.

AGA method

Use the AGA hotplates to heat the vinegar and sugar before pouring the hot mixture into each jar.

Piccalilli

'Take vinegar one gallon, garlic one pound, ginger one pound, turmeric, mustard seed, long pepper and salt of each 4 ounces'. These are some of the ingredients for an Indian pickle written down in 1765. By this time the East India Company had familiarised the well-off with *chatnis* from the East. In Piccalilli the mustard acts as a preservative as well as the vinegar. This recipe comes from Oxburgh Hall in Norfolk, where they pickle seasonal vegetables from their kitchen garden.

**Makes approximately
6 jars**

2.75kg (6lb) prepared
    vegetables (a mixture of
    diced cucumber, marrow,
    courgette, beans,
    cauliflower florets and
    small onions)
450g (1lb) cooking salt
25–40g (1–1½oz) mustard
    powder
25–40g (1–1½oz) ground
    ginger
175g (6oz) white sugar
1 litre (2 pints) distilled malt
    vinegar
20g (¾oz) cornflour
15g (½oz) ground turmeric

Layer the prepared vegetables on a large plate with the salt and leave overnight covered with a cloth. Next day, drain and rinse the vegetables under cold running water, then dry well. Stir the mustard, ginger and sugar into most of the vinegar in a large pan, retaining just enough to make a thin paste with the cornflour and turmeric. Add the vegetables and simmer until you have a texture you like; crisp or less crisp, your choice. Add the cornflour and turmeric paste to the pan. Bring to the boil, stirring carefully, and boil for 2–3 minutes. Pour into warm, sterilised jars and cover with a cloth. Leave until completely cold, then seal. Store for 2–3 months before using.

AGA method

Use the AGA hotplates to make the Piccalilli, as directed in the recipe above.

Drinks

'A delicate combination of ingredients, all of which contribute their share in building up a unique beverage, possessing an individualism of its own.' This general definition of a good mixed drink is from a small book of drinks recipes, published in 1958 by 'Bernard' – evidently so well-known as a barman that he didn't need a surname. I think his definition applies equally well to this chapter's select list of recipes for traditional alcoholic tipples, and some non-alcoholic coolers.

In the Middle Ages, everybody drank ale – from the moment they were weaned. Water wasn't safe and most milk was made into butter or cheese, with the whey and any spare milk generally given to the old and the sick. Broadly speaking, any drink brewed from malted grain and water was considered ale. The best ale came from the south of England, and was made from malted barley. But elsewhere oats – and even beans – were added to the mash. The drink wasn't as strong as today's version, and it didn't keep as well. Beer – made from hops – kept better than traditional ale, but it needed more specialist equipment and, if possible, a brewhouse. Hops for beer were brought to Britain by merchants from Flanders and Holland, in the 1400s, but it was only in the 16th century that a hop-based ale – or beer – became popular. Just as today, beers were brewed to different tastes and strengths. The malt would be used several times when brewing: its first use produced the strong beer, used again it would be weaker, and the third or subsequent brew would be weak or 'small' beer. Beer was often heated in winter – Lamb's Wool is so-called because of the froth on the top of this warmed drink. Spiced and sweetened, these are celebration drinks for any time of the year when it's cold.

Cider was only drunk in regions where there were cider orchards, and was generally for special occasions. In 1587, speaking of cider and perry (the latter made from pears, rather than apples), William Harrison remarked that 'Certes these two are very common in Sussex, Kent, Worcester and other steads where these sort of fruit do about, howbeit, they are not their only drink at all times'.

My recipe for a cooling Cider Punch comes from a book of cider recipes produced for H P Bulmer, a cider company in Herefordshire, a county famous for its cider apples.

Cider-drinking was bounded by place, but wine-drinking was restricted to those who could afford it. Although there had been vineyards in England, custom – and probably bad weather, too – dictated that wine was imported, from the 16th century onwards. All imported goods were expensive but wine had an additional import duty, and sweet wine – very popular, and stronger than ordinary claret – was subject to yet another, separate tax. Because of its cost, the drink became a status symbol for Elizabethans, and it was considered the mark of a gentleman to offer your guests some wine. Like beer and cider, wine was sugared and spiced, and heated up as a winter drink. The old Christmas tradition of 'wassailing' – drinking a toast to your fruit trees from a wassail cup of heated beer, cider or wine, ostensibly to encourage a good crop next year – was a much-loved seasonal pastime, enjoyed by gentry and commoners alike. The Mulled Wine recipe here is from Buckland Abbey, home of that Tudor buccaneer, Sir Francis Drake – it makes a good modern wassail cup.

Distilled wine, or *aqua vitae*, was introduced here in the 16th century. Originally consumed for reasons of health, it quickly became drunk for pleasure. By the 18th century, rum or brandy-based hot punches, ladled from a steaming bowl into glasses called 'rummers', were all the rage. In Scotland, *Usquebaugh*, or whisky – fermented barley and water – remains the country's national drink. Since toddies are supposed to originate from Scotland, the Hot Toddy recipe has a whisky base. Last but not least, there are three delicious recipes for non-alcoholic coolers. Orange Cordial and Lemonade are recipes that have been served daily to thirsty visitors at Sissinghurst, the beautiful National Trust garden in Kent, while Barley Water is a modern reworking of a 17th-century recipe.

Mulled Wine

This particular mull is rather like a hot sangria – rather appropriate as the recipe comes from Buckland Abbey, the home of Sir Francis Drake, commander of the English fleet that defeated the Spanish Armada in 1688.

Makes 6–8 glasses

1 orange
12–14 whole cloves
1 litre (1¾ pints) red wine
1 litre (1¾ pints) lemonade
50g (2oz) brown sugar
150ml (¼ pint) orange juice
1 cinnamon stick 15cm (6in)
    long

Stud the orange with the cloves and cut in half. Place all the ingredients in a large pan and bring very slowly almost to a simmer. Serve hot but do not allow to boil.

AGA method

Use the AGA hotplates to make the Mulled Wine, starting on the Boiling Plate and moving to the Simmering Plate. The Mulled Wine can be kept warm in the Simmering Oven or Warming Oven (on four-oven models).

Mulled Ale

Who better than Mrs Beeton to provide a recipe for Mulled Ale? She considers the amount below 'sufficient for 4 persons', and the cost − in my edition of 1881 − is given as one shilling.

Serves 4

1.25 litres (2 pints) good ale
1 tablespoon caster sugar
½ teaspoon whole cloves
½ standard wine glass rum
   or brandy
Freshly grated nutmeg, to
   taste

Heat the ale with the sugar and cloves. Don't allow it to boil. At the same time, warm a jug by rinsing it out with boiling water. Pour the hot ale into the jug, adding the brandy or rum and grated nutmeg to taste.

AGA method

Use the AGA Boiling Plate to make the Mulled Ale, but move it to the Simmering Plate before it boils.

Hot Toddy

Hot Toddy is the name used in the English-speaking world for a mixed drink with a spirit base that is served hot (it doesn't refer to a particular recipe). For me, it conjures up thoughts of steaming mugs of something slightly sweet and definitely alcoholic, and a hazy picture of people in oilskins or heavy outdoor clothes sitting round a roaring fire. They have just been out in very inclement weather and their fingers are clasped around the mugs; their faces are still very cold, but inside they are glowing.

Scotland is thought to be the original home of the Hot Toddy, so I am giving a whisky-based recipe for this deeply comforting drink. Other spirits, such as brandy or rum, can be used. Oh, another thing – Hot Toddy won't cure the flu or a bad cold, but it will help to make the symptoms bearable.

Makes 1 mug

1 tablespoon honey
Juice of ½ lemon
200ml (7fl oz) very hot (but
    not boiling) water
50ml (2fl oz) blended whisky

Mix the honey and lemon juice together with a little of the hot water until blended. Add the measure of whisky, then fill the mug with hot water. Drink while the mixture is still very hot.

AGA method

Use the AGA hotplates to make the toddy.

Cider Punch

'Good cider 'tis a drink divine
Better by far than all your wine
Good in grief, good in joy,
Good for maid, man and boy'
Anon, 19th century

Recipes for alcoholic punches abound. Everyone loves a celebration, and something fruity, alcoholic and fizzy adds to the occasion. I thought this recipe of Mary Berry's tasted particularly delicious. After all, cider is the wine of the West Country. You will need to start preparing this punch the day before you need it.

Makes 6–10 glasses

175g (6oz) strawberries
Zest and juice of 1 orange
3 tablespoons orange
    liqueur (I used Cointreau)
600ml (1 pint) medium cider
600ml (1 pint) sparkling
    water

To serve
Ice cubes
Mint leaves

Wash and hull the strawberries, then place in a small bowl. Shave the zest from the orange carefully so that the strips are really thin. Put them in the bowl with the strawberries and add the orange liqueur and squeezed orange juice. Cover the bowl and leave to stand overnight.

Next day, just before you are going to serve the punch, add the cider, sparkling water and ice cubes. A fresh mint leaf in each glass is the finishing touch.

Lamb's Wool

This comforting drink was originally devised for warming cold Oxfordshire herdsmen coming in from the fields. Oxfordshire has always been famous for its wool, so the name is particularly appropriate. Lamb's Wool got its name from the white, woolly-looking froth on the surface of this steaming drink.

Serves 4

600ml (1 pint) brown ale
1 glass white wine
A pinch of grated nutmeg
A pinch of ground ginger
1 tablespoon soft brown
    sugar
600ml (1 pint) milk

Place the ale and wine in a pan and heat gently until just below boiling. Stir in the spices and sugar. Heat the milk in another pan, then beat in the ale, a little at a time, so that it froths. Serve hot.

AGA method

Use the AGA hotplates to make the Lamb's Wool.

Lemonade

Sissinghurst Castle Garden in Kent on a very hot day – not only were the flowers wilting, but so was I. I was rescued with a glass of homemade lemonade, so I rang up Mark Britcher, head chef at Sissinghurst Restaurant a few years back, for the recipe. It is simple, but carefully thought out – and he should know what works best: on some hot days they make over 114 litres (25 gallons) of lemonade for their thirsty customers. Lemonade is best made the day before you intend to serve it.

Makes 6 glasses

3 unwaxed lemons
75g (3oz) granulated or
    lump sugar
750ml (1¼ pints) water

To serve
Ice cubes
Mint leaves or borage
    flowers and leaves

Chop the lemons and put them in a food processor with the granulated or lump sugar. Process until you have a fairly fine pulp: the processing 'pulls' the natural oils from the lemons. Put the mixture in a glass jug and stir in the water. Chill overnight before use. Serve with ice cubes and a sprig of mint or borage. This lemonade will keep for two to three days in the fridge.

Barley Water

The recipe is based on a drink from 1685 called A Dainty Cooling Drink for a Hot Fever: 'Take French barley one ounce, boil it first in a quart of fair water a good while, then shift it and boil it in another quarter of water. Shift it again and boil it in a bottle of fair spring water to a quart, then take 2 ounces of sweet almonds, lay them to soak all night then stamp and strain them in the last barley water. Put to it 4 spoonsful of damask rose water, the juice of one lemon and with sugar sweeten it to your taste. Drink of this often when you are dry or hot.'

Barley water was thought to be medicinal but there is no proof of this. But it is agreed that it is a great thirst quencher.

Serves 4

50g (2oz) pearl barley
1.25 litres (2 pints) water
Juice and zest of 2 lemons
Sugar to taste

To serve
Ice cubes
Mint leaves

Wash the barley and put it to boil with the water and the thinly peeled zests of the lemons. Boil very gently for 2 hours, then strain. Add sugar to taste, stir to dissolve it and leave to cool. Just before serving, add the juice from the 2 lemons. Serve poured over ice with a mint leaf to decorate.

AGA method

Bring the barley, water and lemon zest to boil on the Boiling Plate, then boil for 10 minutes. Move to the Simmering Oven for 2 hours. Continue as above.

Homemade Orange Cordial

Keep this cordial in the fridge. Serve poured over ice cubes with slices of fresh orange or lemon in the glass and use still or sparkling water to top up. It will keep for two to three weeks.

Makes approximately 1.5 litres (2½ pints)

1 lemon
3 oranges
675g (1½lb) granulated or
    caster sugar
25g (1oz) citric acid
300ml (2 pints) boiling
    water

Rub the zest from the lemon and oranges, cut the fruit in half and squeeze out the juice. Chop the shells into chunks. Put the sugar, citric acid, lemon and orange zest, juice and chunks of shell in a large bowl. Add the boiling water, stir to help the sugar dissolve and leave to cool and stand, preferably overnight. Strain to remove the lemon and orange pieces. Pour the cordial into a jug or clean bottles and store in a refrigerator. Use diluted as required. The cordial can be kept for two or three weeks.

AGA method

Use the AGA hotplates to boil the water.

Confectionery

Making sweets is hobby cooking – totally unnecessary but enjoyable. I have only included in this section recipes for sweets that can be achieved reasonably easily in a domestic kitchen, with nothing too technical or too dangerous, although you do need to take care making fudge. The fudge recipe is borrowed from an expert. Laura Mason has written a scholarly and fascinating history of sweets, delving into the ancestry of sherbet lemons, liquorice allsorts, toffee and love hearts.

Chocolate Fudge

Fudge, apparently, reached this country from the United States but since that was over a hundred years ago, I think a recipe can now be considered traditional. Laura Mason developed this recipe from one written down just after the First World War.

500g (18oz) sugar
250g (9oz) butter
250g (9oz) dark chocolate
  (minimum 60% cocoa
  solids – check the label)
600 ml (1 pint) milk
Vanilla essence to taste
110g (4oz) walnuts
  (optional)

Line a 20cm (8in) square tin with baking paper. Put the first four ingredients into a large pan over a low heat. Allow the butter and chocolate to melt and bring to a gentle boil, stirring constantly. Cook over a fairly moderate flame, still stirring constantly, and boil gently until a little of the mixture forms a soft ball when it is dropped into cold water. Add the vanilla and the walnuts if desired. Leave to cool in the pan for about 20 minutes, then stir until it stiffens. Pour or press into the lined tin and leave to set before cutting into squares.

Note: Laura says this is not the easiest recipe to handle: the mixture tends to separate while you are heating it, but keep beating – the end result is delicious.

AGA method

Use the AGA hotplates to make the fudge, following the instructions above.

Chocolate Truffles

Chocolate truffles probably acquired their name in the 1920s, according to Alan Davidson, because they look like the savoury truffle, which is a fungus, a highly rated delicacy which emerges from under the ground usually as a smallish lump, covered in earth, having been tracked down by either a pig or a dog trained for the purpose. These, however, are easy to make and wickedly indulgent: homemade chocolate truffles really are special.

75g (3oz) plain chocolate
2 tablespoons brandy or
   rum (optional)
50g (2oz) unsalted butter
50g (2oz) icing sugar
75g (3oz) ground almonds
Cocoa powder or vermicelli
   for decoration

Melt the chocolate and butter in a basin over hot water. Stir in the brandy or rum and add the icing sugar and ground almonds. Cover the bowl and chill until firm. Divide into small balls, roll in vermicelli or cocoa and store covered in the fridge. They keep well for several days. Grated orange rind or coffee essence can be substituted for the brandy or rum, if preferred.

Coconut Ice

This recipe comes from Sara Paston-Williams's *Jams, Preserves and Edible Gifts*. **Easy to make, good to eat and very pretty, coconut ice makes an excellent edible gift.**

Sunflower oil, for preparing
  the tin
450g (1lb) caster sugar
150ml (¼ pint) milk or
  single cream
150g (5oz) desiccated
  coconut
Cochineal or pink food
  colouring

Lightly oil a shallow 20 x 15cm (8 x 6in) tin with the vegetable oil and set aside. Place the sugar and milk in a heavy pan over a low heat and stir until the sugar dissolves. Increase the heat and bring to the boil, then allow the mixture to boil gently for about 10 minutes or until a little dropped into cold water forms a soft ball between finger and thumb (112–116°C or 235–240°F on a sugar thermometer).

Remove from the heat and beat in the coconut. Quickly pour half the mixture into the oiled tin and spread it evenly, using a wet knife. Stir a few drops of colouring into the remaining mixture so that it turns pale pink. Spread this evenly over the white coconut mixture and leave to cool. As soon as it begins to set, mark the mixture out into neat squares.

Leave until completely cold and set firm. Cut or break the coconut ice into pieces and eat it within a few days.

AGA method

Use the AGA hotplates, as directed above, to mix and boil the sugar and milk.

Peppermint Creams

Another perfect edible gift, these pretty-looking sweets have a delicate mint flavour.

450g (1lb) icing sugar
1 teaspoon lemon juice
1 egg white, lightly whisked
A few drops of oil of
    peppermint or
    peppermint essence

Sift the icing sugar into a bowl and mix with the lemon juice and enough egg white to make a pliable mixture. Flavour with the peppermint oil. Knead on a work surface lightly dusted with icing sugar, then roll out to a 6mm (¼in) thickness. Cut into small rounds with a 2.5cm (1in) pastry cutter. Leave the Peppermint Creams in a cool place for 24 hours to set and dry.

Appendices

The National Trust, Food and Farming

Our farmed landscapes in Britain bear the traces of change over thousands of years, the most recent revolution taking place after the Second World War. The drive to increase production was encouraged by subsidies and achieved by new industrial technologies, including machinery, agro-chemistry and animal feeds. Modern agriculture successfully provided cheap and plentiful food for consumers and greater profits for many in the food industry, but at a cost. High inputs of fuel, chemicals, fertiliser and feed were needed to increase production and these had a dramatic impact on soil and water quality. Vital wildlife habitats such as hedgerows were removed to accommodate machinery, and the farm workforce declined.

Today, food production is no longer regarded in isolation, and efforts are being made to manage its impact on the natural environment and rural communities. The National Trust's approach to farming has followed a similar pattern. Most of our land is managed by tenant farmers, who decide how they farm. Ten years ago, we took stock of the way that we value our land and recognised the role that farming plays in achieving our long-term conservation objectives. Since then, we have worked more closely in partnership with our tenant farmers to support their husbandry of the land. We're keen to encourage viable farms with high standards of food production, environmental management and animal welfare. To help achieve this, our specialist farm team has provided planning advice to hundreds of our farms. Over the last decade, we've made some real progress.

The majority of our farms are in environmental stewardship schemes and meet recognised farm-assurance standards. It is vital that farmers achieving these high standards are rewarded with better, fairer prices. We believe that traceability is key, so that buyers and consumers know the provenance of their food. We are working with several groups of farmers to market their produce to supermarkets or catering businesses. Lots of farmers now sell produce directly to consumers via box schemes, farm shops and markets. However, this is just the start. Our next steps are: to support quality food production at a bigger, mainstream scale; to prepare for a future with little oil and scarce water; and to ensure our land and farmers are able to grow what society needs for a sustainable and healthy diet.

Climate change is already having an impact on the world's major food-producing regions, particularly through reduced water availability. Food prices are fluctuating in response to a variety of factors. As pressures on land use rise further, there is a danger of making false choices between producing food and caring for the environment. Our long-term food security is entirely dependent on the health of our natural resources – the soil in which almost all food is grown and the water that is essential to all life.

A recipe for good food

In the past, the National Trust's focus on food mainly ensured that our farmland and catering business earned money to support our charitable work. Over the years, we have developed a clearer understanding of the links between our involvement with food and our work to promote and conserve the natural and historic environment for the benefit of the nation. We are changing the way we manage our land and our business to have a much more positive impact and to invest for the future. In addition to our farms, gardens and restaurants, our open spaces provide a feast of wild food; we produce meat and crops on our land. Whether we're producing, buying, selling, cooking or talking about food, there are some basic values that matter to us. Local and seasonal food is a priority for us, but only if it is also good quality and produced sustainably. We're encouraging our tenant farmers, suppliers and individuals to join us on this journey.

In the last 15 years, the amount of land used to grow fruit and vegetables in the UK has declined by a fifth. Orchards have been destroyed and we've lost many varieties of fruit and vegetables bred and adapted over centuries. We now import around 90% of our fruit and 40% of our vegetables into the UK.

The places in the care of the National Trust have a long history of horticulture, particularly grand estates with their kitchen gardens, glass-houses and orchards. Yet over the years, many of our walled gardens have been neglected or even turned into car parks – a clear demonstration of changing values! More recently, we've begun to realise how valuable these places are and how much we can learn from the past for the future. The National Trust has already restored many of our historic kitchen gardens and brought them back into production with the help of the local community – others will follow as part of allotment schemes and community projects. It helps to conserve the natural and cultural heritage of our gardens and orchards, and it brings them to life for our visitors. It is great for our chefs to serve the produce and to let their customers know that it was picked there that day. In future, we want to see more fruit and vegetables grown on National Trust land – not just in the kitchen gardens, and not just by our staff but by local people too. We want to garden in ways that improve the soil, let wildlife thrive and use a minimum of water and energy. We are responding to climate change, and the different growing conditions it is bringing, by adapting the kinds of plants that we grow and the way in which we grow them.

Food, Glorious Food

The whole food story, from plot to plate, is intimately represented in the places in our care and our practical experience in managing them. A wide variety of high-quality food is produced on National Trust land and from the coast and freshwater in our care, including:

- Beef and lamb from extensively grazed grasslands
- Milk and dairy products from rich pastures
- Fish and seafood from healthy stocks, caught sensitively
- Fruit and vegetables grown in fields on a large scale
- Vegetables and fruit from kitchen gardens, allotments and orchards
- Wild food from hedgerows and woodlands

Everyone benefits from consuming the food that the Trust and our tenant farmers produce and sell, which has a clear origin and rewards high standards of production. As part of this:

- People can buy food direct from Trust farmers or through local shops, pubs and markets
- Supermarket shoppers can buy food from the Trust's estate via farmers working together to supply the mass market
- Farmers and other producers receive a fair price for the food they sell
- Our chefs have the skills and knowledge to buy and cook seasonal food from local producers
- Food waste is minimised and composted
- People can visit the National Trust to learn about food and get involved in growing and cooking their own
- Local communities have the space and skills to grow their own food on Trust allotments
- Tea, coffee and other global foods are fairly traded and from a known origin

This food is produced in environmentally responsible ways, so that:

- Farming practices protect soil and water
- Wildlife habitats, landscapes and historic features are conserved
- Diverse animal breeds and plant varieties are chosen that suit the local environment
- Animals are looked after to high welfare standards
- Energy, water, fertilisers and chemicals are used efficiently
- Waste is minimised and managed effectively

Our 'Food, Glorious Food' campaign has encouraged members and visitors to 'grow their own', providing seeds, recipes and practical advice to those who want to learn to plant, harvest, cook and eat their own produce.

Local food

Since the late 1990s, the idea of encouraging local food economies has received much attention. Aims include reducing 'food miles', raising awareness of local production, and re-connecting farmers and consumers. Networks of farmers' markets have proved enormously popular, bringing produce directly to the public. Farm shops are also increasingly attractive to shoppers wanting to know more about the food they eat. Farm shops that rely on produce grown on the farm can also offer guarantees of quality, especially for home-produced meat.

Other methods of direct marketing have extended the reach of farm produce. The 'vegetable box', in which market gardeners or farmers deliver seasonal vegetables directly to the doorstep, is a growing industry; meat can also be ordered in a similar fashion. Many farms have developed websites with information about the farm and its produce and use post or courier to deliver items. The idea of the retailer is not completely ignored, however, and local food shops are an important element in local food economies; interest in this and the idea of 'food mapping' to understand local purchasing patterns is increasing.

A number of National Trust tenants have set up such schemes, including Coleshill Organics near Swindon. Sonia Oliver of Coleshill describes her experience of running a successful business: 'We love being right at the heart of the community, producing fresh, great-tasting fruit and vegetables for local people. We run a weekly box scheme, go to farmers' markets and supply produce to local shops, pubs and schools, all within 25 miles of the Coleshill Estate. We have a shop in the walled garden, and our open-door policy means that people can come and see the produce being grown. We had over 1,000 schoolchildren here last year, picking and eating their way around the garden! Equally important to us is growing organically – our customers really value knowing not only where their food is from but how it's been grown. We employ about 10 local people and we run apprenticeships to help new starters learn the tricks of the trade.'

At the Brockhampton Estate in Herefordshire, after the foot-and-mouth outbreak in 2001, property manager Les Rogers was looking for ways to support our tenant farmers: 'We wanted to help create farm businesses that were sustainable – not only for the environment, but for our tenants. They now supply cakes to our tea room, rear beef for local Trust restaurants and produce about 14 different jams and chutneys. The preserves have been incredibly popular in our tea room and shop, and other local shops are now selling them too. Thanks to this business, we've got our 100 acres of orchards back into full production after years of neglect.'

Details of producers, farmers markets and farm shops can be found on our website: www.nationaltrust.org.uk/food. The National Trust produces a range of cookery titles featuring traditional and historic British recipes. For more details, visit www.nationaltrust.org.uk/books.

Acknowledgements

First of all I would like to thank all the cooks at restaurants at National Trust properties whose recipes feature in this book.

Special thanks to Laura Mason whose advice and recipes I much appreciate; also Sara Paston-Williams, particularly for her historic recipes and her wonderful puddings; Kate Steggles, the shortbread supremo; and Mark Britcher at Sissinghurst for both the Lemonade and Orange Cordial recipes.

Alan Davidson's The Oxford Companion to Food has been my constant companion, as has Jane Grigson's English Food and Michael Smith's Fine English Cookery. Thank you to Tina Persaud for commissioning the book and Nicola Newman for encouraging and helping me all along the way.

Friends and family helped to test the recipes but a final thank you to the ever-supportive John, Fiona, Jules, Lucy, Dan and Rich.

All recipes are © Sarah Edington except the following:

Cheese and Anchovy Straws (p79), Cheese and Onion Pasties (p198), Cheese Soufflé (p196), Chicken Liver Paste (p96), Christmas Dinner with all the Trimmings (p101), Cornish Pasties (p140), Coronation Chicken (p98), Faggots (p157), Game Pie (p152), Glamorgan Sausages (p201), Green Sauce (p166), Jugged Peas (p179), Liver, Bacon and Onions (p156), Lobscouse (p135), Maids of Honour (p299), Mock Crab (p199), Omelette Arnold Bennett (p80), Pease Pudding and Ham (p116), Pork Pie (p114), Pot-roasted Shoulder of Venison (p146), Potted Trout (p55), Russian Salad (p177), Salad Dressing (p167), Salmon in Pastry (p62), Savoury Pudding (p213), Slow-roasted Belly Pork with Apples and Onions (p119), Welsh Rarebit (p203) all © Laura Mason, 2010.

An 18th-Century Trifle (p282), Apple Fritters in Ale Batter (p234), Apple Hat (p233), Baked Apples (p250), Boodles Orange Fool (p286), Brown Bread Ice Cream (p293), Casseroled Pigeon with Herbs and Spices (p94), Chicken or Rabbit Fricassee (p97), Claret Jelly (p289), College Pudding (p255), Custard Tart or Sweet Egg Pie (p224), Damson Snow (p292), Elderflower and Gooseberry Fool (p273), Fine Almond Blancmange (p279), Florence Nightingale's Kedgeree (p58), Lamb Casseroled in Ale with Prunes and Raisins (p128), Pears in Red Wine Syrup (p245), Pickled Herring and Fruit Pie (p70), Scotch Collops with Forcemeat Balls (p148), Spiced Bean Pottage (p182), Spicy Ground Rice Pudding (p248), Sussex Pond Pudding (p253), Sweet Pickled Onions (p389), Trelissick Lemon Curd (p381) all © National Trust, various dates.

Bibliography

Beeton, Isabella, *The Book of Household Management*, Ward Lock & Co, London, 1888

Campbell, Susan and Conran, Caroline, *Poor Cook*, Sphere Books, London, 1972

Dallas, E S, *Kettner's Book of the Table*, Centaur Press, London 1968

David, Elizabeth, *An Omelette and a Glass of Wine*, Penguin Books, Harmondsworth, Middlesex, 1986

Davidson, Alan, *The Oxford Companion to Food*, Oxford University Press, Oxford, 1999

Edington, Sarah, *National Trust Recipes*, National Trust, London, 1996

Edington, Sarah, *The Captain's Table*, National Maritime Museum Publishing, London, 2005

Edington, Sarah, *The National Trust Book of Healthy Eating*, National Trust, London, 1990

Edington, Sarah, *The National Trust Book of Recipes*, National Trust, London, 1988

Edington, Sarah, *Vegetarian Recipes*, National Trust, London 2002

Farmhouse Fare', The Farmers Weekly, London, 1950

Fitzgibbon, Theodora, *A Taste of Scotland*, Jarrold & Sons, Norwich, 1970

Grigson, Jane, *English Food*, Ebury Press, London, 2002

Grigson, Jane, *Jane Grigson's Fruit Book*, Michael Joseph, London, 1982

Grigson, Jane, *Jane Grigson's Fish Book*, Penguin Books, London, 1994

Hammond, Peter, *Food and Feast in Medieval England*, Sutton Publishing, Stroud, 1998

Humble, Nicola, *Culinary Pleasures*, Faber and Faber, London, 2005

Maher, Barbara, *Cakes*, Penguin Books, Harmondsworth, Middlesex, 1982

Making a Meal of It, English Heritage, Swindon, 2005

Mason, Laura, *The National Trust Farmhouse Cookbook*, National Trust, London, 2009

Mason, Laura, *Sugar-Plums and Sherbet*, Prospect Books, Totnes, Devon, 1998

Mason, Laura with Brown, Caroline, *Traditional Foods of Britain*, Prospect Books, Totnes, Devon, 2004

Paston-Williams, Sara, *A Book of Historical Recipes*, National Trust, London, 1995

Paston-Williams, Sara, *Good Old-Fashioned Jams, Preserves and Chutneys*, National Trust, London, 2008

Paston-Williams, Sara, *Good Old-Fashioned Puddings*, National Trust, London, 2007

Paston-Williams, Sara, *The Art of Dining*, National Trust London, 1993

Pepys, Samuel, *The Shorter Pepys*, Penguin, London, 1993

Pettigrew, Jane, *Traditional Teatime Recipes*, National Trust, London, 2007

Saberi, Helen and Davidson, Alan, *Trifle*, Prospect Books, Totnes, Devon, 2001

Sim, Alison, *Food and Feast in Tudor England*, Sutton Publishing, Stroud, Gloucestershire, 1997

Smith, Michael, *Fine English Cookery*, Faber Paperbacks, Whitstable, Kent, 1983

Spry, Constance, *The Constance Spry Cookery Book*, Pan Books, London, 1972

Stein, Rick, *Rick Stein's Seafood Odyssey*, BBC Worldwide, London, 1999

The Cookery Year, Readers Digest, London, 1974

Thompson, Flora, *Lark Rise to Candleford*, Penguin, Harmondsworth, Middlesex, 1977

Weir, Robin and Liddell, Caroline, *Recipes From The Dairy*, National Trust, London, 1998

WI, The and Smith, Michael, *A Cook's Tour of Britain*, WI Books, London, 1984

Willan, Anne, *Reader's Digest Complete Guide to Cookery*, Dorling Kindersley, London, 1989

Wright, Carol, *Country Cook Books: Cotswolds*, Cassell, London, 1975

US conversion chart

Dry measures

1 US cup	50g	2oz of breadcrumbs
1 US cup	75g	3½oz of rolled oats
1 US cup	90g	3½oz of desiccated coconut
1 US cup	100g	3½oz of walnut pieces, icing sugar
1 US cup	120g	4oz of white flour
1 US cup	150g	5½oz of wholemeal flour
1 US cup	175g	6oz of mixed peel, sultanas
1 US cup	200g	7oz Demerara sugar, rice
1 US cup	225g	½lb of cream cheese
1 US cup	300g	11oz mincemeat
1 US cup	350g	12oz of treacle, jam

Liquid measures

¼ US cup	60ml	2fl oz
1 US cup	240ml	8fl oz
1 US cups (1 US pint)	480ml	16fl oz

Butter and lard measures

¼ stick	25g	2 level tablespoons
1 stick (1 US cup)	100g	8 level tablespoons

Recipe Index